■ **A F T E R   T H E   L A W**

A book series edited by John Brigham and Christine B. Harrington

A THEORY OF LIBERTY

■ *AFTER THE LAW*
A book series edited by John Brigham and Christine B. Harrington

Also published in the series

Gigs: Jazz and the Cabaret Laws in New York City
by Paul Chevigny

Inside the State: The Bracero Program, Immigration, and the INS
by Kitty Calavita

A THEORY OF
LIBERTY

THE CONSTITUTION AND MINORITIES
■ H. N. HIRSCH

ROUTLEDGE NEW YORK LONDON

Published in 1992 by

Routledge
An imprint of Routledge, Chapman and Hall, Inc.
29 West 35th Street
New York, NY 10001

Published in Great Britain by

Routledge
11 New Fetter Lane
London EC4P 4EE

Library of Congress Cataloging-in-Publication Data

Hirsch, H. N.
    A theory of liberty : the Constitution and minorities / H.N. Hirsch.
        p.   cm.—(After the law)
    Includes bibliographical references and index.
    ISBN 0-415-90585-0   ISBN 0-415-90586-9
    1. Minorities—Legal status, laws, etc.—United States. 2. United States—Constitutional law. 3. Liberty. I. Title. II. Series.
KF4755.H57   1992
342.73′0873—dc20
[347.302873]   92-10561
                                                   CIP

British Library Cataloguing in Publication Data also available

In memory

Jack Armstrong
Duane Draper

CONTENTS

ACKNOWLEDGMENTS

Over the many years I have been working on this project I have accumulated a number of debts, and it is a pleasure to acknowledge them.

John Burke encouraged me to write this book, helped me at several stages to develop the argument, and read early drafts of several chapters as well as the final manuscript. At Harvard, where I began working, I also benefited greatly from many early conversations with Judith Shklar and Nancy Rosenblum; both continued to help by reading drafts of several chapters and then the whole manuscript. I also want to thank Sid Verba, Robert Putnam, and Arthur Maass for their advice and encouragement.

Various chapters were improved by the comments of George Kateb, Shannon Stimson, Rogers Smith, Michael Sandel, Robert Faulkner, Amy Bridges, Walter Murphy, Charles Beitz, Cheryl Welch, Mary Shanley, Steve Erie, Sam Beer, and Elizabeth Meehan. The editors of *Constitutional Commentary* accepted for publication and helped me improve an early version of the first part of chapter 3, as did the editors of *Political Theory* for a version of chapter 6. I am also grateful to the Fulbright Commission, to Sussex University, and to Shannon Stimson and Vivien Hart for an invitation to deliver a paper based upon a portion of chapter 4 at a conference in April, 1991.

I completed the manuscript after moving to the University of California, San Diego, where I have gained much from the advice and criticism of Tracy Strong, Peter Irons, and Alan Houston; all three helped me improve the final manuscript. Research assistance was provided by Keith Bybee, and secretarial assistance by Kelly Escobedo and Kathy Klingenberg.

The editors of this series, Christine Harrington and John Brigham, read the manuscript with great care at an early stage and have been helpful throughout. At Routledge, I want to thank Cecelia A. Cancellaro, Maura Burnett, and Michael J. Esposito for a smooth and enjoyable ride.

Financial assistance was provided by a summer fellowship from the National Endowment for the Humanities and by the University of California.

Finally, I want to thank Fred Greenstein, Ethel Klein, Ian Abramson, Priscilla Long, and Ann Craig for their moral support.

LaJolla, California
December 15, 1991

CHAPTER I

INTRODUCTION: LIBERAL JURISPRUDENCE, HISTORY, AND POLITICAL SCIENCE

I.

At any given time, American society and politics may be taken up with a significant constitutional question or questions. As this book is nearing completion in 1991, we have for some time been obsessed with at least two such questions: abortion and affirmative action. Each Supreme Court opinion on either of these subjects receives enormous amounts of publicity; such decisions become political fodder for legislative action and the platforms of political parties. The modern conservative movement, spectacularly successful in the election of Ronald Reagan to the presidency, owes at least some of its success to political opinion on both of these issues. The politics of abortion and the politics of affirmative action have been, and continue to be, at the center of national debate.

Yet as questions of law, rather than as questions of politics, abortion and affirmative action must be placed in the context of a particular intellectual framework: constitutional theory. This intellectual context is, and continues to be, contested terrain; there is no greater agreement here than in politics at large. Scholars debate the meaning of constitutional clauses, and the public debates the morality of a specific issue. Often the two debates take place in isolation, impoverishing both.

This book is an exercise in constitutional theory; it presents a series of essays organized around a central theme: the importance of the rights of minorities to American constitutionalism. In considering this topic, the first three chapters present an original theory of constitutional interpretation, a theory emphasizing the centrality of liberty to American ideology. Chapter 4 applies this theory to a number of recent cases and controversies, and chapter 5 considers some related issues in the jurisprudence of equal protection. The concluding chapter considers the implications of these constitutional questions for the current debate about the nature and importance of political "community." The intended audience of this book is thus both specialists—scholars and practitioners of constitutional theory—and members of the public hoping to place some contemporary political debates in their appropriate intellectual context.

This study begins with the premise that it is historically justified to treat liberty as the core constitutional value. It argues that liberty has been neglected in much current constitutional thinking, for some interesting and identifiable reasons. It presents an analysis of the meaning of liberty and its relation to due process, as well as a theoretical framework that allows the historical value "liberty" to be applied to contemporary problems. This framework understands liberty to require the absence of governmental arbitrariness, and, further, relates this question of arbitrariness to social "facts."[1]

By emphasizing the centrality of social facts to constitutional decision-making, the theory presented here argues for the inevitable "embeddedness" of constitutional doctrine in social and political reality. As we will see, when the law ignores social reality—social "facts"—it may be acting arbitrarily; when the law acts arbitrarily, it may thereby be abridging liberty and violating the Constitution. Different kinds of social facts relevant to arguments of this sort may include the existence—or lack—of an overwhelming societal consensus about a given moral issue,[2] or the existence of widespread prejudice against a given minority.[3] Or science or social science may provide evidence crucial to a constitutional case.[4] The existence of diversity—cultural, ethical, sexual—may be a fundamental social fact about the American polity highly relevant to a number of constitutional controversies.[5] Or, per-

---

[1] For a more narrow discussion of liberty and the relation between liberty and due process, see Sotirious A. Barber, *On What the Constitution Means* (Baltimore: Johns Hopkins University Press, 1984), chapter 5, esp. 123–27. Barber's narrow conception of liberty leads him to adopt a very weak notion of constitutional privacy; see esp. 144–45.

[2] See pp. 92–97.
[3] See pp. 134–46.
[4] See pp. 82–92.
[5] See pp. 97–104.

haps, looking closely at the facts of a given, specific case—at what actually happened between the parties in question—may be necessary to avoid arbitrariness.[6] In all of these ways, social reality may be linked to the question of arbitrariness and thereby to the Constitution.[7]

The theory of liberty that stands at the center of this project, providing the connection between social facts and the Constitution, differs from most current positions in constitutional debate. The theory is novel in considering questions concerning minorities in the context of liberty rather than solely in terms of equal protection. Moreover, the theory differs from most current "liberal" theories of the Constitution in that it does not eschew founders' intent, and in that it does not ground itself in contemporary moral theory; it differs from "conservative" theories in that it does not concentrate the search for intent at the level of constitutional clauses. Rather, like some liberal theories, it reformulates the level of generality upon which "intent" is understood. Moreover, unlike most current liberal theories, the theory as a whole, as well as its reformulation of the problem of intent, is squarely based upon history. The theoretical constructs of this book also cast new

---

[6] See pp. 116–23.

[7] By claiming that social facts exist and that they are "knowable," I am, of course, taking a position in a complex epistemological debate—a position I believe justified by the cases, and facts, here in question. For various perspectives on the broader philosophical questions at stake, see Richard W. Miller, *Fact and Method: Explanation, Confirmation and Reality in the Natural and the Social Sciences* (Princeton: Princeton University Press, 1987); Peter Winch, *The Idea of a Social Science* (London: Routledge and Kegan Paul, 1958), esp. chapter 1; and Tracy B. Strong, *The Idea of Political Theory: Reflections on the Self in Political Time and Place* (Notre Dame: University of Notre Dame Press, 1990), chapter 4. In its emphasis on social facts, my perspective bears some slight resemblance to the turn-of-the-century movement in American philosophy and law known as pragmatic instrumentalism; for a discussion, see Lief H. Carter, *Contemporary Constitutional Lawmaking: The Supreme Court and the Art of Politics* (New York: Pergamon Press, 1985), 107–09, 161–63. See also Robert Samuel Summers, *Instrumentalism and American Legal Theory* (Ithaca: Cornell University Press, 1982), esp. 54–56, 90; Edward A. Purcell, Jr., *The Crisis of Democratic Theory: Scientific Naturalism and the Problem of Value* (Lexington, Ky.: University Press of Kentucky, 1973), chapter 5; Gary J. Jacobsohn, *Pragmatism, Statesmanship, and the Supreme Court* (Ithaca: Cornell University Press, 1977), *passim*; and Martin Edelman, *Democratic Theories and the Constitution* (Albany: State University of New York Press, 1984), chapter 4. My theory differs from most pragmatic instrumentalist theories in that it does not take as its touchstone the advancement of progressive public policy, but grounds itself instead in a strong theory of rights and the value of liberty.

light on one of the central problems of contemporary jurisprudential analysis, the debate between interpretivists and non-interpretivists.[8] I argue that this distinction is itself irrelevant if the nature of the Constitution is properly understood.

The classification of an individual theorist as liberal or conservative is of course somewhat arbitrary, although, like obscenity, one tends to know them when one sees them. The basic ideological division between them concerns the desirability and legitimacy of modern judicial activism. In a very rough way, we can say that the Supreme Court, in the wake of the New Deal, redefined its role in American politics. No longer the protector of the economic system or the policeman of federalism, the Court defined itself, beginning in the 1940s, as the protector of the unprotected.[9] Cases such as Brown v. Board of Education were the result, and the activism of the Warren Court in the 1960s represented the full flowering of this new judicial role. Thus a rough litmus test of a given theorist's status as liberal or conservative is his reaction to the general ideological thrust of the Warren Court.

I cast myself as a liberal because I am, in general, in favor of the kind of modern judicial activism exemplified by the Warren Court, and I am in favor of such activism because I reject the basic conservative jurisprudential premise. That premise—which, up to a point, a number of liberals share, as will become clear in a moment—is that the Supreme Court's power to overturn the decisions of a democratically elected legislature is problematic; this "countermajoritarian difficulty"[10] leads conservatives, and some liberals, to emphasize a basic theoretical conflict between judicial review and democracy. This supposed conflict becomes the starting point for constitutional scholars as different as Robert Bork and Alexander Bickel, and for jurists as different as Felix Frankfurter and Antonin Scalia. "Conservative" theorists and jurists

---

[8] Interpretivism and non-interpretivism refer to theories that endorse judicial decisions made on the basis of values "in" the text of the Constitution (interpretivism) or decisions made on the basis of values "beyond" the text of the Constitution. See John Hart Ely, *Democracy and Distrust: A Theory of Judicial Review* (Cambridge, Mass.: Harvard University Press, 1980), chapter 2; see also Thomas C. Grey, "Do We Have an Unwritten Constitution," *Stanford Law Review* 27 (February 1975): 703–18; and Michael J. Perry, *The Constitution, the Courts, and Human Rights* (New Haven: Yale University Press, 1982), chapter 1.

[9] See pp. 194–98.

[10] The phrase is Alexander Bickel's; see *The Least Dangerous Branch: The Supreme Court at the Bar of Politics* (Indianapolis: Bobbs-Merrill, 1962), 16–18.

who start from this premise deduce from it a behavioral postulate (a postulate liberals usually reject)—judicial self-restraint. Both the premise and the behavioral postulate are wrong.

I reject the countermajoritarian premise, as must anyone who reads the *Federalist* carefully. Properly understood, American constitutionalism is *meant* to be countermajoritarian; the Constitution and the Supreme Court are meant to serve as a break upon the legislative process and to protect the rights of minorities.[11] *Federalist* 10 justifies the proposed Constitution by telling us that "complaints are everywhere heard" that "measures are too often decided, not according to the rules of justice and the rights of the minor party, but by the superior force of an interested and overbearing majority."[12] The Constitution is meant "to secure the public good and private rights against the danger" of self-interested factions.[13] Such arguments abound in the *Federalist*; the very idea of judicial independence is defended in #78 in terms of the Supreme Court's ability to defend the rights of minorities.[14] To argue that judicial review is problematic because it is undemocratic is to miss the point entirely.[15] The relationship between judicial review and democracy *is* an interesting problem, and this book will present some new ways of thinking about it.

"Countermajoritarian" conservatives are thus deficient in their basic premises; other conservative theories are deficient in other parts of their historical analysis. Thus, to take a prominent recent example, Rogers Smith[16] correctly identifies liberty as the central constitutional

[11] See pp. 45–71.

[12] Alexander Hamilton, James Madison, and John Jay, *The Federalist Papers* (New York: New American Library, 1961), 77.

[13] *Ibid.*, 80–81.

[14] David A. J. Richards, *Foundations of American Constitutionalism* (New York: Oxford University Press, 1989), 129.

[15] On the centrality of the problem of minorities to American constitutionalism, see Richards, *Foundations of American Constitutionalism*, 217, 218, 237, 238, 278, 279; Stephen Macedo, *Liberal Virtues: Citizenship, Virtue, and Community in Liberal Constitutionalism* (Oxford: Clarendon Press, 1990), 85, 168, 173; Morton White, *Philosophy, "The Federalist," and the Constitution* (New York: Oxford University Press, 1987), 131–148, 200–01, 212, 221.

[16] *Liberalism and American Constitutional Law* (Cambridge, Mass.: Harvard University Press, 1985). I call Smith a conservative because his theory leads him to endorse only rights that are relatively noncontroversial—such as some First Amendment rights—while ignoring many difficult questions concerning the rights of some minorities. Often, he endorses majoritarian sentiment (see, for example, 218, 243). Thus, for example, he endorses traditional "family" values (299, n.32), and is unconcerned with gay rights, which

value, but defines that liberty too restrictively, as limited to "rational" liberty; for Smith, "freedom" is completely identified with "reason."[17] The purpose of a liberal regime for Smith is, above all, to "promot[e] the capacities of all for reflective self-direction. . . ."[18] In developing this argument, Smith relies entirely on John Locke to the exclusion of other influences upon the framers; moreover, he ignores some crucial ways in which Locke was drawn upon in American constitutional discourse.[19] Liberty, as I will show, meant far more to the framers than "rational" liberty.

As for contemporary liberal jurisprudence, it presents a number of curious paradoxes, including the fact that liberals sometimes share the basic conservative concern with the "anti-democratic" nature of the Supreme Court. In a more general sense, liberals have simply not been able to work out an appropriate relationship to history. Liberal

---

are left to the legislature. This is because "many would still argue" that the "restraints" upon homosexual conduct "serve compelling state interests" (305, n.22). Note that he does not argue that such restraints *do*, in fact, serve compelling state interests, but only that "many" *claim* that they do. Moreover, even his exposition of the First Amendment contains some decidedly conservative arguments; for example, he argues for the restriction of obscenity, pornography, and other forms of "insulting" speech (see 243) and looks favorably upon the general proposition that there are "particular categories of worthless speech" (104; see also 108).

Smith is also conservative in a philosophic sense; he argues against a "standardless ascription of worth to all" (198) and that moral worth must be tied to the capacity to deliberate rationally. This view is both politically naive (rational deliberation is a luxury to many) and psychologically obtuse (the capacity for rational deliberation is but one human capacity, and may be a subordinate one at that). This simplistic view of rationality and its centrality Smith derives from Locke and attributes to the American Constitution, but, once again, a cursory reading of the *Federalist* makes this attribution questionable. In *Federalist* 10 man's "reason" is tied to his "self-love," and thus man's "opinions and his passions . . . have a reciprocal influence on each other. . . ." Hamilton, Madison, and Jay, *Federalist Papers*, 78. Because political opinions are tied to man's "passions" and "self-love," political factions result, necessitating a constitutional system that neutralizes factions and protects the rights of minorities. If man's reason were paramount, such a system might not be necessary. Thus even the most basic *Federalist* paper presents a psychological vision more sophisticated than Smith's.

[17] Smith, *Liberalism and American Constitutional Law*, 30.

[18] *Ibid.*, 5.

[19] In particular, Smith ignores the fact that the framers drew from Locke general arguments about limited government and arbitrary legislative action that went beyond the issue of "rationality." See below, pp. 36–38; 41–51.

jurisprudential writers are either nearly totally ahistorical (the most prominent example here is Ronald Dworkin) or are notoriously bad historians (for example, John Ely) or find it necessary to circumvent history entirely (for example, Michael Perry).[20] For the most part, liberals have surrendered the terrain of legal and constitutional history to the conservatives, such as Raoul Berger and Walter Berns, who put forward their jurisprudence of "original intent" at the level of individual constitutional clauses.[21]

One of the reasons conservatives cling to the original intent of constitutional clauses is because this commits them to a notion of the Constitution as binding law. In one sense, they are right—the Constitution *is* the nation's highest law, and, as such, should be binding upon us in some way.[22] But there are good reasons for rejecting this low-level, clause-bound originalism of contemporary conservatives, reasons that will become clear as we proceed. To anticipate, There are both valid philosophical reasons *and* historical evidence to support the contention that the framers themselves did not mean future generations to be bound by their very specific applications of general constitutional principles.[23] Moreover, the entire philosophy of "fundamental" rights—essential to American ideology, and constitutionalized by the Ninth and Fourteenth Amendments (among other clauses)—depends on subjective, and changeable, notions about the nature of society.[24]

But, this book will argue, our philosophy of fundamental rights is not without content; it contains some propositions—historical propositions—that do bind us in certain ways. Thus "history" and "intent" are not the same thing. If we eschew a jurisprudence based on clause-bound intent, we need not run headlong into a jurisprudence based on contemporary moral philosophy (as do Dworkin, and many others) nor into a kind of constitutional nihilism (as do other liberal theorists,

---

[20] Ronald Dworkin, *Taking Rights Seriously* (Cambridge, Mass.: Harvard University Press, 1977), *A Matter of Principle* (Cambridge, Mass.: Harvard University Press, 1985), and *Law's Empire* (Cambridge, Mass.: Belknap Press of Harvard University Press, 1986); Ely, *Democracy and Distrust*; Perry, *The Constitution, the Courts, and Human Rights*.

[21] Raoul Berger, *Government by Judiciary* (Cambridge, Mass.: Harvard University Press, 1977); Walter Berns, *The First Amendment and the Future of American Democracy* (New York: Basic Books, 1976).

[22] For a discussion of the constitution as "law," see Marbury v. Madison, 5 U.S. 137 (1803).

[23] See pp. 31–51.

[24] See pp. 51–71.

such as Laurence Tribe).[25] We must ask whether there is any space in between these poles (conservative original intent on the one hand; the contemporary moral philosophy or nihilism of the liberals on the other) in which we can maneuver, avoiding the obvious intellectual shortcomings of both extremes.

This book attempts to explore that space. This leads us back to a reconsideration of the idea of liberty in American constitutionalism, and the contemporary queasiness with the idea of liberty among liberal legal theorists. This queasiness, I will argue, is perhaps the greatest mistake of contemporary jurisprudence, for it is based on a series of intellectual errors and has enormous, and unfortunate, consequences, even when judged from the point of view of the liberal's own constitutional agenda.

Liberals still place great value on particular liberties, of course—freedom of speech and press, the protection of privacy, the safeguarding of the rights of criminals. What I mean when I say that liberals are queasy with the idea of liberty is not that they do not value these particular rights, but that they fail to appreciate or use liberty in the grand sense—as an organizing jurisprudential idea. As Lief Carter has remarked, "at virtually every point in constitutional history some inchoate theory, some enveloping vision of national need . . . seem[s] to drive constitutional decisions."[26] To the extent that liberals *have* such a theory in the contemporary debate, it is the kind of neo-Kantian vision of moral equality put forward most coherently by Dworkin and David Richards.[27] But the intellectual sleight of hand involved in reading Kant (or Rawls) into the American Constitution makes such an approach unacceptable as a theory *of the Constitution*, however compelling it may be in its own right.

Liberals lack a totally persuasive constitutional theory, and will continue to lack such a theory so long as they remain uncomfortable with historical analysis and with the idea of liberty. Together with their inability to defend adequately the existence of a right to privacy (and the right to an abortion), the liberal discomfort with liberty is responsible for the failure of liberal jurisprudence to attain any real intellectual coherence or widespread acceptance. But privacy as a constitutional right can only

---

[25] I call Tribe a "nihilist" because he denies that the text or history of the Constitution can tell us much worth knowing when we must decide hard cases; see below, pp. 17–18.

[26] Carter, *Contemporary Constitutional Lawmaking*, 28.

[27] David A.J. Richards, "Interpretation and Historiography," *Southern California Law Review* 58 (January 1985): 490–549.

be justified within a theoretical framework that straightforwardly organizes itself around the idea of liberty. And liberty can only be a value of
importance in a theory that is self-consciously historical.

II.

To document the difficulties liberals have with history, I will here
briefly discuss the work of Ronald Dworkin, John Ely, and Michael
Perry, three of the major jurisprudential theorists of the past twenty
years.[28]

Dworkin, working within a philosophical neo-Kantianism, presents
a strong theory of individual rights in which the most basic right is
"equal concern and respect."[29] From this fundamental philosophical
position, Dworkin proceeds by employing a series of definitions and
analogies to elaborate his constitutional positions. The central definitions for Dworkin, the ones most important to the debate about constitutional intent, is the distinction he makes between a constitutional
"concept" and a "conception." Here is what he says in the original
statement of his theory:

> Suppose I tell my children simply that I expect them not to
> treat others unfairly. I no doubt have in mind examples of the
> conduct I mean to discourage, but I would not accept that my
> "meaning" was limited to these examples, for two reasons.
> First I would expect my children to apply my instructions to
> situations I had not and could not have thought about. Second,
> I stand ready to admit that some particular act I had thought
> was fair when I spoke was in fact unfair, or vice versa, if one
> of my children is able to convince me of that later; in that case
> I should want to say that my instructions covered the case he
> cited, not that I had changed my instructions.[30]

---

[28] Although I am critical of their use (or lack of use) of history, I do not
mean to imply that I reject all of the substantive conclusions of these three
theorists. Indeed, as will become clear, I accept a number of Dworkin's theoretical conclusions (such as his distinction between constitutional "concepts" and
constitutional "conceptions"); my theory also resembles Ely's in that I am, in
a sense, seeking an "ultimate" form of interpretivism: that is, I am seeking to
remain faithful to the constitutional text and the intentions of the framers, but
not to their most specific applications of general ideas (Dworkin would say
their conceptions) in individual constitutional clauses; see text above and
Chapter 3. However, I disagree with Ely about the scope and content of our
"ultimate" interpretivism.

[29] Dworkin, *Taking Rights Seriously*, 272–73.

[30] *Ibid.*, 134.

Thus, Dworkin concludes, "I might say that I meant the family to be guided by the *concept* of fairness, not by any specific *conception* of fairness I might have in mind."[31]

The point of this elaborate analogy is that constitutional clauses, according to Dworkin, employ *concepts* rather than *conceptions*; this releases the modern Supreme Court from the burden of determining, or following, the specific conceptions of the framers. Thus, for example:

> The Supreme Court may soon decide . . . [Dworkin is writing in 1977] whether capital punishment is "cruel" within the meaning of the constitutional clause that prohibits "cruel and unusual punishment." It would be a mistake for the Court to be much influenced by the fact that when the clause was adopted capital punishment was standard and unquestioned. That would be decisive if the framers of the clause had meant to lay down a particular conception of cruelty . . . [b]ut it is not decisive of the different question the Court now faces, which is this: Can the Court, responding to the framers' appeal to the concept [as opposed to conception] of cruelty, now defend a conception that does not make death cruel?[32]

What is remarkable about these passages for present purposes is not the question of whether Dworkin is "correct," but the manner in which the argument is presented—with astounding brevity, and, more importantly, without any historical support, despite the fact that this is an argument about what the constitutional framers were actually doing by writing a constitution. No messy historical evidence to ponder; no footnotes to James Madison—nothing but bold and naked assertion.[33]

Similarly, Dworkin uses an analogy to explain his understanding of the fundamental methodology of legal analysis, and what he regards as the blurred line between judicial interpretation and judicial "creation." Once again, he begins by asking us to use our imaginations: "Suppose that a group of novelists is engaged for a particular project," he writes, "and that they draw lots to determine the order of play."[34] Each one, in turn, writes a chapter of the novel and sends it on to the next author. In this scenario, Dworkin says:

[31] *Ibid.*, emphasis in original.
[32] *Ibid.*, 135–36.
[33] Recent scholarship has, in fact, offered historical evidence for Dworkin's contentions. See p. 35.
[34] Dworkin, *A Matter of Principle*, 158.

every novelist but the first has the dual responsibilities of interpreting and creating because each must read all that has gone before in order to establish . . . what the novel so far created is. He or she must decide what the characters are "really" like; what motives guide them; what the point or theme of the developing novel is; how far some literary device or figure, consciously or unconsciously used, contributes to these, and whether it should be extended or refined or trimmed or dropped in order to send the novel further in one direction rather than another.[35]

In conclusion, Dworkin tells us that "deciding hard cases . . . is rather like this strange literary exercise," and that "the similarity is most evident when judges consider and decide common law cases."[36] Once again, the analysis is left uncluttered by history; no histories of the common law are cited; no judges who have written about their enterprise (of whom there are any number) are quoted; no examples are given. Jurisprudence is constructed through acts of imagination.

John Ely, by contrast, does attempt to ground his jurisprudence in historical understanding. His problem is that he simply gets his history wrong.

Ely's goal is to present a theory of jurisprudence that recognizes "the impossibility of a clause-bound interpretivism" (the title of one of his chapters) and yet still allows for a form of "ultimate" interpretivism. Quite persuasively, he argues that it is impossible for judges to limit themselves to the values embedded in constitutional clauses—which is the interpretivist aim—because there are clauses which *themselves* present an "invitation to look beyond their four corners."[37] That is, there are clauses which by their explicit terms point to values beyond the document—particularly, the Ninth Amendment[38] and the privileges and immunities clause of the Fourteenth Amendment.[39] Given these

---

[35] *Ibid.*, 158–59.

[36] *Ibid.*, 159. Although this is somewhat irrelevant to the current discussion, Dworkin's analogy is faulty. In law, judges can overrule previous decisions, unlike the chain novelist, who is stuck with the chapters written by previous authors. We might say a judge is like a chain novelist who can tear up any chapter but the first—the text and history of the Constitution itself.

[37] Ely, *Democracy and Distrust*, 13.

[38] "The enumeration in the Constitution, of certain rights, shall not be construed to deny or disparage others retained by the people."

[39] "No State shall make or enforce any law which shall abridge the privileges or immunities of citizens of the United States."

clauses, even the most circumspect judge must accept that the text of the Constitution itself endorses vague "rights."

But what rights? Ely's argument is that these clauses do not allow judges to find additional *substantive* rights in the Constitution, because, he says, such judicial intervention denies the essentially democratic nature of the American polity. Only to protect the democratic process itself, Ely says, should judges intervene—either by protecting the channels of political communication (by, for example, strongly enforcing First Amendment rights) or by acting to protect minority groups that are systematically excluded from effective participation because of prejudice and hostility against them.

Ely's argument thus contains a clever twist that allows him to argue, at the same time, for both judicial activism (keeping the channels of political communication open; protecting unrepresented groups) and judicial restraint (judges should avoid enforcing any other substantive values). But upon what is this latter prohibition based? Upon Ely's understanding of the nature of American democracy—his reading of American history. Ely, although essentially a liberal, thus shares the countermajoritarian premise of the conservatives.[40] "Majoritarian democracy," he tells us, "is . . . the core of our entire system. . . ."[41] There is a basic "incompatibility" between judicial review of any kind and democracy.[42] There has never been, he says, any American theorist who has posed "any serious challenge to the general notion of majority control" nor has there been any such challenge "among Americans generally."[43] When he discusses American political theory, it is the strain of "egalitarianism" and "popular control" he finds paramount.[44] "The consent of a majority of those governed is the core of the American governmental system," he says.[45]

Ely's claim that there has never been an American theorist challenging the general notion of majority control is, of course, simply false, and

---

[40] Classifying Ely as either a liberal or a conservative is thus a bit tricky, as his theory pulls in two directions at once. I have classified him as a liberal, however, because he endorses the activism of the Warren Court; see *Democracy and Distrust*, esp. 73–75. Although I believe he mischaracterizes the ideological thrust of that court (viewing it as concerned with "process" values and not "substantive" values; see esp. 74), his defense of many decisions of that period, and of many forms of judicial activism, is clear.

[41] *Ibid.*, 7.
[42] *Ibid.*, 11–12.
[43] *Ibid.*, 7.
[44] *Ibid.*, 76.
[45] *Ibid.*, 7.

the breadth and simplicity of his generalizations about majoritarianism ignore much of what is most essential about American government. Has he never heard of the American Senate, or of the electoral college? How would Ely account for the American theory of sovereignty, in which "the people" are sovereign because they adopted the Constitution itself, not because they are the source of day-to-day decision making?[46] Ely's understanding of consent is rudimentary, and his notion that democratic consent requires majoritarian approval of specific policies is simply wrong. Again, as any careful reader of the *Federalist* knows, the framers understood the new constitutional system to be one in which the people's long-term interests—protected by the Constitution—would be separated from their short-run preferences for specific policies. And those long-run interests included, contrary to Ely's description, not merely democratic *procedures*, but substantive *limitations* on the range of governmental action.[47] Moreover, the entire movement to write a federal constitution gained its most important source of support from the notion that simple democracy had gotten out of control in the states during the period governed by the Articles of Confederation.[48] Although deriving its authority from the people, the Constitution was not intended to set up a simple majoritarian democracy—this is an historical truth so fundamental that one wonders how a lawyer of Ely's obvious intelligence could build a jurisprudential edifice around its denial.

Like Ely, Michael Perry's starting point in what he perceives to be the problem of judicial "legitimacy"—the fact that judges are unelected and that therefore their decisions are "countermajoritarian." He begins his first chapter with the assertion that "we in the United States are philosophically committed to the political principle that governmental policymaking . . . ought to be subject to control by persons accountable to the electorate."[49] This, of course, is a half truth; "we in the United States" are also committed to other things, including the primacy of fundamental rights. Thus we can fault Perry, in much the same way we fault Ely, for a theoretically inadequate understanding of American constitutionalism, rooted in poor intellectual history.

Perry's "bad" history, however, is both deeper, and more complex,

---

[46] See Gordon S. Wood, *The Creation of the American Republic, 1776–1787* (New York: W. W. Norton, 1972), 530–32, 544–47.

[47] Timothy P. Terrell, "Liberty: The Concept and its Constitutional Context," *Notre Dame Journal of Law, Ethics and Public Policy* 1 (Summer 1985): 588.

[48] See Wood, *Creation of the American Republic*, Part 2; see below, pp. 45–50.

[49] Perry, *The Constitution, the Courts, and Human Rights*, 9.

than Ely's, for Perry concedes what Ely denies—that, in general, we *can* know what the framers intended by particular constitutional clauses:

> Ascertaining the *precise* contours of the original understanding of any given provision may be difficult, sometimes even impossible. . . . Still, it is usually possible to ascertain the rough contours of that understanding. And once the rough contours have been ascertained, it is frequently possible to say: Although we do not know exactly what the framers thought this provision *would* accomplish, there is strong evidence they thought it would *not* accomplish X; or strong evidence they did not think it would accomplish X; or no evidence, or wholly inadequate evidence, they thought it would accomplish X.[50]

Thus, according to Perry, much of the constitutional doctrine of the modern era has been promulgated in the face of strong evidence that the clauses in question were never intended to achieve the results in question. He includes in this category a breathtaking array of cases: Brown v. Board of Education, most First Amendment law, and the entire doctrine of "incorporation" (by which the provisions of the Bill of Rights have been made applicable to state, as well as federal, action).

But Perry does not wish to throw away the entire corpus of the modern Supreme Court, and thus sets for himself the task of developing a constitutional theory that allows us to accept the work of the modern Court *in spite of* this history. This he does by saying that the questions the Constitution poses are not legal questions at all, but rather *moral* questions. And furthermore, he tells us, the American people have a moral self-understanding as a *religious* people; this self-understanding, he says, is "basic" and "irreducible."[51] By the use of the term *religious*, Perry means that Americans "have understood themselves to be 'chosen' in the biblical sense of that word; that is, they have understood themselves to be charged with a special responsibility, *an obligation*, . . . to realize, as best they can . . . a 'higher law.' "[52]

An "integral" part of this religious self-understanding, according to Perry, is the notion of prophecy. "Invariably a people, even a chosen people, fail in their responsibility and need to be called to judgment—provisional judgment—in the here and now."[53] Thus, when the Supreme Court acts contrary to the (more or less) clear evidence of the

---

[50] *Ibid.*, 1, n.*; emphasis in original.
[51] Perry, *The Constitution, the Courts, and Human Rights*, 97.
[52] *Ibid.*; emphasis in original.
[53] *Ibid.*, 98.

intent of the framers of a particular constitutional provision, they are acting to represent "the institutionalization of prophecy."[54] We as a people are committed to the notion of moral evolution, and the Supreme Court alone among our governmental institutions can devote itself to such moral change.

The problems with this argument are so enormous[55] that the question must be posed: Why does Perry tie himself into such contortions to arrive at it? Conceding that history does give us relatively clear answers to questions of constitutional intent, he goes to nearly unbelievable lengths to say that it is nevertheless unproblematic for the Supreme Court to ignore such intent. Why? Broadening the question to include Dworkin and Ely, why do jurisprudential scholars with liberal instincts have such enormous difficulty with history—why must they ignore it, bend it, engage in it poorly, or find a way around it?

III.

The answer to this question is complex and multifaceted, but at the core of the failure of liberals to adequately deal with history are their preoccupation with constitutional intent and, more particularly, the fact that they understand intent (*a*) to be defined only at the level of constitutional clauses, and (*b*) at a very low level of abstraction. This, combined with the nature of their political and philosophical agenda,[56]

---

[54] *Ibid.*

[55] For example: What is the relation between this sense of "religious" and "real" religion? What is the source of this religious higher law? Is it a Supreme Being? And if a Supreme Being, does this not raise "establishment" difficulties under the First Amendment? Which denomination's Supreme Being (allowing that the religion in question is undoubtedly Protestant, which itself raises difficulties)? And how are we to know the answers to any of these questions?

[56] By "political" agenda, I mean, for example, the devotion of some liberal theorists to economic redistribution, and the attempt by some scholars to derive substantive welfare rights from the equal protection clause; this can only be accomplished by wholesale disregard of the history of the Fourteenth Amendment, even when that history is interpreted at the highest possible level of abstraction. On this issue see Frank Michelman, "Foreward: On Protecting the Poor Through the Fourteenth Amendment," *Harvard Law Review* 83 (November 1969): 7–59, and "Property as a Constitutional Right," *Washington & Lee Law Review* 38 (Fall 1981): 1097–1114; see also "Tutelary Jurisprudence and Constitutional Property," in Ellen Frankel Paul and Howard Dickman (eds.), *Liberty, Property and the Future of Constitutional Government* (Albany: State University of New York Press, 1990), 127–71. The philosophical agenda of many liberals is, once again, a sometimes vague Kantianism, emphasizing equal individual dignity. For a discussion, see Carter, *Contemporary Constitutional Lawmaking*, 143–44.

makes it impossible for liberals to be good, honest historians.[57]

One of the earliest items on the liberal agenda for the modern Court was, of course, the issue of racial equality, and the *Brown* decision is instructive in the way that it dodges historical questions. In *Brown* the Court was faced with fairly strong evidence that the framers of the Fourteenth Amendment had "intended" it to apply to a limited and specific list of fundamental civil rights, and that using the amendment to desegregate public schools went far beyond that list.[58]

In response to this evidence, the Court could have squarely stated that it was not governed by such specific intentions, that its job was to delineate the contours of "equal protection" for contemporary society—that is, that the search for clause-bound intent was simply beside the point. The Court did say that it needed to consider the needs of contemporary society, but only *after* fudging on the question of history—by saying that the available evidence was "inconclusive."[59] Then, as if to cover a fib, and almost as an afterthought, the Court added that it could not "turn the clock back to 1868 when the Amendment was adopted" but rather "must consider public education in the light of its full development and its present place in American life throughout the Nation."[60]

The question, of course, is why the Court used both of these arguments when they seem to cut against each other logically. If the evidence of intent is inconclusive, then why even mention "turning the clock back" to 1868 as a possibility? Simply, because no Supreme Court has ever been ready to say forthrightly that clause-bound intent is irrelevant.

Liberal jurisprudential theorists have not fared much better than the Court in attempting to grapple with clause-bound intent. Liberals have two basic responses to intent. One is to claim that intent can't be known; the other is to claim that clause-bound intent doesn't matter. Taken together, these liberal responses to arguments in favor of original intent are a bit like the neighbor who borrows and breaks your tool, only to respond, "I never borrowed it from you. And it was broken

---

[57] For a discussion of some basic questions concerning constitutional intent, see Walter F. Murphy, "Constitutional Interpretation: The Art of the Historian, Magician, or Statesman?," *Yale Law Journal* 87 (July 1978): 1752–71.

[58] See Richard Kluger, *Simple Justice* (New York: Alfred A. Knopf, 1976), 626–38; see also the sources cited in Paul Brest and Sanford Levinson, *Processes of Constitutional Decisionmaking*, 2nd ed. (Boston: Little, Brown, 1983), 404–20.

[59] 347 U.S. 483, 489 (1954).

[60] *Ibid.* at 492–93.

when I got it." The first response, as a generalization, is incorrect; the second, however, is more on the mark.

Laurence Tribe presents perhaps the best example of the "can't know" response. In his book *Constitutional Choices*, in a chapter entitled "The Futile Search for Legitimacy," he writes of "the ultimate futility of the quest for an Archimedean point outside ourselves from which the legitimacy of some form of judicial review or constitutional exegesis may be affirmed."[61] In the first few pages of the first chapter he states flatly that the "categories of constitutional discourse" are not "determinate," and that those who seek to ground decision making in "criteria of fidelity to constitutional text" are "destined to leave us, and themselves, unsatisfied."[62] "Anyone who insists . . . that 'fidelity to text' must be the core commitment of a constitutionalist" he tells us, "must confront the indeterminacy of text. . . ."[63] No constitutional "premises" exist in any "privileged place external to the disputants themselves and insulated from who they are and what groups they belong to."[64] As examples of the indeterminateness of the constitutional text Tribe then cites two issues—pornography and sexual intimacy:

> Compare, for example, the claim that the First Amendment protects pornography with the claim that the First, Ninth and Fourteenth Amendments protect sexual intimacy. Advocates of the pornography claim may say that even a portrayal of sex that degrades and subjugates women is surely "speech" and is thus entitled to the First Amendment's protection in terms of norms fairly inferable "from the Constitution itself." Advocates of the sexual intimacy claim may say that physically expressing sexual feeling to another is no less a form of communication—and may indeed be less coercive, and thus more purely "speech"-like—than depicting sex to a distant audience may be. Which group is advancing notions more remote from, say, the Constitution's text and thus bears the heavier burden of justifying judicial imposition of its "values"?[65]

Tribe's basic point here is familiar. That we simply can't know what the framers of a particular constitutional clause intended has long been

---

[61] Laurence H. Tribe, *Constitutional Choices* (Cambridge, Mass.: Harvard University Press, 1985), 5.
[62] *Ibid.*, 4.
[63] *Ibid.*, 5.
[64] *Ibid.*
[65] *Ibid.*, 6.

the claim of liberal jurisprudence. Other commentators have pointed to different problems: The paucity of some of the historical record; evidence of conflicting purposes on the part of legislators who support the same provision; difficulty identifying the key architects or supporters of any given provision.[66]

But let's take a closer look at Tribe's specific examples. He mentions two modern "rights": the claim that the First Amendment protects pornography, and the claim that there is a right of "privacy" or sexual intimacy. The truth is that both of these rights can be justified—and "derived" from the Constitution—in a principled manner that is neither capricious nor arbitrary. The right of privacy is elaborated in a series of Supreme Court decisions beginning with Griswold v. Connecticut,[67] and a number of scholars have found convincing historical evidence for at least the Court's most basic arguments.[68] And the proposition that the First Amendment protects pornography depends on valid First Amendment principles: the idea that the Constitution does not allow content-based discriminations, and the idea that it does not allow the prohibition of speech that merely "insults" but does not cause immediate, concrete harm.[69] Neither of these principles comes out of the clear blue sky; both have impressive pedigrees. Both can be tied to reasoned arguments about the purposes of the First Amendment. Thus neither of these two rights is as divorced from the Constitution as Tribe implies.

In a more general way, we can answer the line of criticism that claims that "intent can't ever be known" by posing a question: Is it possible for historians to write political history, including the history of individual legislative actions? If the answer is yes, then the line of criticism claiming "intent is always unknowable" is simply wrong. We can (at least potentially) know intent as well as we can know anything about the past. This is not to say that there won't be conflicting interpretations of intent, or gaps in the record. But to claim that intent is completely unknowable is to deny the possibility of writing intellectual and political history.

[66] See Carter, *Contemporary Constitutional Lawmaking*, esp. 54; Walter F. Murphy, "Who Shall Interpret? The Quest for the Ultimate Constitutional Interpreter," *Review of Politics* 48 (Summer 1986): 401–23; Brest and Levinson, *Processes of Constitutional Decisionmaking*, chapter 6, esp. 420–23; Walter F. Murphy, James E. Fleming, and William F. Harris II, *American Constitutional Interpretation* (Mineola, N.Y.: Foundation Press, 1986), 303–06.
[67] 381 U.S. 479 (1965); see below, pp. 72–73.
[68] See pp. 91–97.
[69] See pp. 97–100.

The alternative to the "can't know" response to the issue of constitutional intent for liberals is to say that intent doesn't matter; this comes in some form similar to Dworkin's theory of constitutional "concepts," outlined above. In essence, Dworkin sidesteps the whole question of whether intent can be known by saying that the specific intentions of the framers—their "conceptions"—are simply irrelevant to contemporary decision making. This is so because the Constitution enshrines broad "concepts"—ideals of equality and fairness that the founders intended the Supreme Court to apply to specific factual situations.

Dworkin's insight here is surely correct, and he makes a more elaborate and convincing case of his point in a later statement of his theory.[70] In the context of a discussion of racial segregation and the Fourteenth Amendment, he says that a "historicist" would inevitably discover that the legislators who framed and adopted the equal protection clause "had a variety of political opinions pertinent to racial segregation."[71] But, Dworkin says, their *dominant* conviction was *abstract*: that the Constitution should require the law to treat all citizens as equals." This dominant conviction is what "they actually described in the language" of the amendment. Many of these legislators, Dworkin says, "had the further concrete conviction that racial segregation did not violate" the requirements of equal protection, but the historicist, Dworkin says,

> who is committed to keeping faith with their convictions as a whole, must ask whether that concrete conviction was in fact consistent with the dominant one, or was rather a misapprehension, understandable in the circumstances, of what the dominant one really required. If the historicist himself believes that racial segregation is inconsistent with the conception of equality the framers accepted at a more abstract level, he will think that fidelity to their convictions as a whole requires holding segregation unconstitutional.[72]

Here, the language of "concrete" and "dominant" convictions has replaced the language of "conceptions" and "concepts," but the point is the same; it is the same point Chief Justice Marshall made in his

[70] Dworkin, *Law's Empire*, chapter 10.
[71] *Ibid.*, 361–62.
[72] *Ibid.*, 362, emphasis added. Dworkin continues: "He may hold a different view: that circumstances have changed so that although segregation was consistent with that conception in the late 19th century, it is not consistent now. Then, he will also think fidelity requires declaring segregation unconstitutional." *Ibid.*

oft-quoted contrast between a constitution and a legal code, and his comment that the Constitution is a political document "intended to endure for ages to come."[73] As Stephen Macedo has recently written, "the Constitution is law, but it is not a tax code; it contains not only rules but reasons and values to explore, aspire to, and progressively realize."[74] Whatever specific intentions concerning contemporary issues legislators may have had when voting for a particular constitutional provision, they expressed themselves in general and abstract language—"due process of law," "the equal protection of the laws," "cruel and unusual punishment"—knowing full well that such language would be applied to specific cases by future generations in case-by-case analysis.

The question is how we proceed from this basic insight concerning the nature of a Constitution. For Dworkin, the insight concerning the nature of constitutional concepts becomes the occasion for importing a heavy dose of contemporary moral philosophy into constitutional decision making:

> Constitutional law can make no genuine advance until it isolates the problem of rights against the state and makes that problem part of its own agenda. That argues for a fusion of constitutional law and moral theory. . . . It is perfectly understandable that lawyers dread contamination with moral philosophy . . . [b]ut better philosophy is now available than the lawyers may remember. Professor Rawls of Harvard, for example, has published an abstract and complex book about justice which no constitutional lawyer will be able to ignore.[75]

[73] McCulloch v. Maryland, 17 U.S. 316, 415 (1819).

[74] Macedo, *Liberal Virtues*, 166. On constitutional "aspirations," see Barber, *On What the Constitution Means*, and Gary J. Jacobsohn, *The Supreme Court and the Decline of Constitutional Aspiration* (Totowa, N.J.: Rowman & Littlefield, 1986).

[75] *Taking Rights Seriously*, 149. To be fair to Dworkin, a more recent statement of his theory in *Law's Empire* does mention, albeit briefly, the importance of history in constitutional decision making. For example, he says that "fairness in the constitutional context requires that an interpretation of some clause be heavily penalized if it relies on principles of justice that have no purchase in American history and culture, that have played no part in the rhetoric of national self-examination and debate." *Ibid.*, 377. He makes little of this, however; the enterprise of the great judge is still, as in earlier renderings of his theory, essentially a philosophic one. History constrains for Dworkin only at the far margins of decision making. At one point he gives two examples: "Any plausible working theory [of the Constitution] would disqualify an interpretation of our own law that (1) denied legislative competence or suprem-

From modern philosophical premises Dworkin proceeds to construct his constitutional theory, in which equality is the fundamental value and there is "no right to liberty"[76]; "the central concept of my argument," he says forthrightly, "will be the concept not of liberty but of equality." The core value of the Constitution, Dworkin tells us, is "equal concern and respect."[77]

But the conscientious reader has to pause for a moment at this point. Why this rush to embrace contemporary moral philosophy—no matter how intellectually compelling—and to import it into an eighteenth-century Constitution? The reason may well be that contemporary liberals like Dworkin fear that an eighteenth-century Constitution, by itself, cannot produce the results they seek. But if the Constitution is meant to govern—to bind—must there not be some way of reading *it* to reveal fundamental "concepts"? Why choose John Rawls as our touchstone—why not Robert Nozick? Indeed, why not Karl Marx?

Instead of looking to contemporary moral philosophy for the content of the Constitution's "concepts," why not look to history—both political history and the intellectual history of the American Constitution itself? What might such a constitutional theory based upon history look like? Might not the Constitution *itself* be committed to certain basic concepts—such as liberty? Might these concepts not have *some* content useful to us? In delineating such concepts, are we not, in some important sense, remaining faithful to the "intentions" of the framers? What follows will answer these questions.

(2)

IV.

Like any good saga, this one has enemies who appear on the horizon and must be disposed of before our main story can proceed and our heroic author can triumph. On this particular horizon stand a gaggle of political scientists and a few loose literary deconstructionists. They hang out together, they're tough, and they've won quite a few battles recently. An easy gang to fight it's not.

Political Scientist #1 says, "You blankety-blank liberals. When it

---

acy outright or that (2) claimed a general principle of private law requiring the rich to share their wealth with the poor." *Ibid.*, 255. Thus for Dworkin, history tells the great judge that legislatures can often pass laws competently, and that our economic system is based on the legality of private property—hardly startling propositions.

[76] *Taking Rights Seriously*, 265.
[77] *Ibid.*, 272–73.

comes down to current cases, you all say the same thing—so what's the point? And you all start with the result you want in some major cases and work backwards—you think we don't see what you do?"

Political Scientist #2 says, "Yeah. That's right. And another thing: you liberal guys think you're so smart. You're all messing around with policy questions—abortion, school desegregation, affirmative action— you don't know anything about, and the Constitution doesn't have a blankety-blank thing to say about either[Policy questions are for experts, or for politics, not for lawyers and courts.]

Political Scientist #3 says, "Yeah. And even when you do come up with an answer—you can't prove it's the single right answer everyone can agree with. So you haven't *proven* a blankety-blank thing."

Finally, the Literary Deconstructionist pipes up, with the blow meant to finish off our hero for good. "The Constitution can mean anything anybody wants it to," he says smugly. "Arguments about what the Constitution means are a waste of time. The Constitution is a text, like a play or a story. Interpretations are all a matter of taste."

I am, of course, caricaturing—a bit. But what can our hapless liberal hero even begin to say to these charges?

First, to deflect the easiest blow—the "policy" charge.[78] It's obvious our opposing gang is composed of white boys, and straight white boys at that.[79] If you're an unhappily pregnant woman, abortion is not a "policy" question. If you're a minority applicant to a university—or a white applicant who thinks he was kept out because of an affirmative action plan; if you're an alien who gets beaten up and whose kids are barred from public schools; if you're a gay man or lesbian in a state with restrictive sodomy laws; if you're the parent of a retarded child who is mistreated in a state-run institution—then none of these questions are "policy" questions. The American Constitution assumes that rights exist; nothing could be clearer. Whether a coherent theory can *define* those rights, and *connect* those constitutional rights to these

---

[78] See, e.g., Martin Shapiro, "Political Jurisprudence, Public Law, and Post-Consequentialist Ethics: Comment on Professors Barber and Smith," in Karen Orren and Stephen Skowronek (eds.), *Studies in American Political Development*, vol. 3 (New Haven: Yale University Press, 1989), 88–102, esp. 92, 95; Perry, *The Constitution, the Courts, and Human Rights*, 2. More generally, see Donald L. Horwitz, *The Courts and Social Policy* (Washington: Brookings, 1977), Richard E. Morgan, *Disabling America: The "Rights" Industry in Our Time* (New York: Basic Books, 1984), and John Agresto, *The Supreme Court and Constitutional Democracy* (Ithaca, N.Y.: Cornell University Press, 1984).
[79] "Straight" as opposed to gay, not as opposed to "honest."

contemporary issues, are interesting questions—questions this book (like others) is meant to address. But to call these questions "policy" questions is to speak from a position of deep skepticism about the existence of constitutional rights—a skepticism the framers did not share.[80] It is also to accept, in another form, the countermajoritarian premise: that "policy" questions should be left to the democratic legislature.

But that won't wash. We really only have three alternatives to settle *3 options* questions such as affirmative action, abortion, and the constitutionality of sodomy laws: guns, the ballot box, and the constitutional argument. Guns kill people.[81] The ballot box returns us to "go": emphatically, the Constitution does not leave questions concerning rights to the legislature. That leaves only constitutional argument.

It is no accident that the "policy" punch is leveled by political scientists, for modern political science is enamored of the idea that *all* politics is policy, that aggregating preferences is the essence of any political process. But the simple aggregation of preferences is not what the American Constitution is about. The *Federalist* talks repeatedly about justice, not about opinion polls. The wisdom of the people, for the framers, did not lie in their opinion on any given political question, but rather in their ability to see that their long-run interests required the adoption of the Constitution, which included restraints on their own power.

What *is* true is that policy questions are *implicated* by any number of constitutional issues. The challenge, then, is to develop a theory of constitutional interpretation that finds an important place for information about the real world. Hence the emphasis here on social and scientific "facts," and their relation to constitutional argument.

As for the argument that we liberals (or, for that matter, any contemporary jurisprudential theorist) work "backward," starting with our result[82]: the only appropriate response is a shrug, and a nonchalant, "why, of course. That's what the law is, you idiot." The law always proceeds inductively, from concrete results in specific controversies, out of which, over time, coherent theory is constructed. And a common

---

[80] See pp. 45–51.

[81] Anyone who thinks violence is not a possibility in contemporary America should consider the dramatic rise in "hate" crimes in recent years; see the articles in the *Chronicle of Higher Education*, 13 Feb. 1991, A2, and in the *Los Angeles Times*, 7 Feb. 1991, 3.

[82] See Shapiro, "Political Jurisprudence," 91; Carter, *Contemporary Constitutional Lawmaking*, 48.

law system is _supposed_ to begin with concrete results in real cases.[83] American jurisprudence has always been constructed, in large part, in response to contemporary events and specific Supreme Court doctrines. Every treatise, every theory of the Constitution, has had standing in the background—if not the foreground—some particular constitutional agenda. This is as true today—when most jurisprudential theories (including mine) can be read as a defense, or a critique, of modern judicial activism—as it was during the 1930s (when the issue was the judicial invalidation of the New Deal) or the 1870s and 1880s (when the debate centered on state regulation of private property in the emerging industrial economy). The issue isn't whether a theorist begins with a result and then justifies it; the issue that matters is whether the offered _justification works_—whether it fits together more or less coherently, and whether it fits more or less of the historical record as best we can reconstruct it.[84]

Legal reasoning is, of course, in some important sense, an ideal, and a worthy one. As Duncan Kennedy (usually no wild idealist[85]) has written, judges are "carriers of the notion that the ideal of justice is accessible to the reason of people acting in the real situations of political and economic life."[86] What matters is the quality of a jurisprudential theorist's legal reasoning, not the source of his impulses.[87]

As for the charge that we liberals all say the same thing, so why bother?[88]—there are a couple of responses that we can make. The first

---

[83] See Harvey Wheeler, "Constitutionalism," in Fred I. Greenstein and Nelson W. Polsby (eds.), _Handbook of Political Science_, vol. 5 (Reading, Mass.: Addison-Wesley, 1975), 1–91; see also pp. 33–35 below.

[84] For different discussion of "fit," see Dworkin, _Law's Empire_, 130–35, 227–28, 314–15, 342–45; Stephen Macedo, "The Constitutional Right to Privacy: A Defense" (unpublished paper delivered at American Political Science Association Meeting, Atlanta, Ga., 1989); Barber, _On What the Constitution Means_, 11, 155–59.

[85] Kennedy is a prominent member of the critical legal studies movement, dedicated to debunking myths and embracing legal reality.

[86] Duncan Kennedy, "Toward an Historical Understanding of Legal Consciousness: The Case of Classical Legal Thought in America, 1850–1940," in Steven Spitzer (ed.), _Research in Law and Sociology_, vol. 3 (Greenwich, Conn.: JJAI Press, 1980), 6.

[87] On the nature and importance of legal reasoning and the central place of "public justification" in liberalism, see Macedo, _Liberal Virtues_, esp. chapters 2 and 3. Although I agree with many of Macedo's conclusions, I believe that he, like many liberals, rushes too quickly away from history and into a philosophy he finds congenial. See, e.g., 92.

[88] See Shapiro, "Political Jurisprudence," 91; see also Carter, _Contemporary Constitutional Lawmaking_, 143.

is that we don't always agree on everything. For example, some liberals wholeheartedly endorse the Supreme Court's abdication of review over economic legislation during the New Deal, while some of us—including our current hero—are more uneasy with it, and believe contemporary liberal jurisprudence ought to face more squarely the importance of private property in the Constitution.[89] Some liberals think that "liberty of contract" in Lochner v. New York was a complete fabrication, while others of us (again, including the current author) think that there is a liberty of contract in the Constitution, that the problem with *Lochner* lies elsewhere.[90] A number of liberals are deeply troubled by Roe v. Wade.[91] Some liberals find a right to subsistence in the Fourteenth Amendment; most of us don't.[92] (I wish there were.) And so on.

Of course, we liberals do agree about the results in any number of cases, including cases such as Brown v. Board of Education. But *how* we reach our similar results is as important as those results themselves. Do we reach liberal results by imposing hearty doses of contemporary moral theory into the Constitution—which, as I've already indicated, is fraught with problems? Or do we proceed differently?

As for the charge that we don't "prove" anything definitively, that our results are not subject to standards of proof anyone can accept[93]— again, the appropriate response is a shrug. Such a blow could only be leveled by a social scientist, one enamored of the idea of falsifiability. But law isn't social science (although it should *use* social science where appropriate, as will become clear); arguments in law are good or bad, better or worse, firmer or weaker, but never "provable" and final. The law, as Dworkin tells us, is composed of *principles* as well as rules, and principles are messy things.[94] A principle that animates many First Amendment cases, for example—that "under the First Amendment, there is no such thing as a false idea"[95]—may well incline a decision in a specific case one way or another; such a principle lends strong support

---

[89] See pp. 105–13.

[90] See pp. 82–85.

[91] See, e.g., Michael J. Perry, *Morality, Politics, and the Law* (New York: Oxford University Press, 1988), 172–78; John Hart Ely, "Wages of Crying Wolf," *Yale Law Journal* 82 (April 1983): 920–49.

[92] See note 56 above.

[93] See Shapiro, "Political Jurisprudence," 91–92; see also the excellent discussion in Carter, *Contemporary Constitutional Lawmaking, passim.*

[94] *Taking Rights Seriously*, 22–28, 71–80. See also Laurence H. Tribe and Michael C. Dorf, "Levels of Generality in the Definition of Rights," *University of Chicago Law Review* 57 (Fall 1990): 1069, 1098–1100.

[95] Gertz v. Robert Welch, Inc., 418 U.S. 323, 339 (1974).

to the idea that the First Amendment protects obscene or racist speech.[96] But such a principle cannot *prove* that a given holding is "correct." Principles have "weight"; they don't prove things.[97] Legal arguments can't be "falsifiable." And, to quote Clifford Geertz, "better to paint the sea like Turner than attempt to make of it a Constable cow."[98]

Finally, for the blow from the deconstructionist: that the Constitution can mean "anything."[99] That claim is based on a false analogy. A literary text can (potentially) mean anything because the situations and people it describes exist only in the imagination; a literary text doesn't have anything to do with any political "act" in the real world. One actor's Hamlet can't be compared to some original Hamlet clause; thus one actor's Hamlet is (arguably) as "valid" as any other.

But the equal protection clause is not Hamlet. Can we really say that the Fourteenth Amendment can mean *anything*? Does the fact that it came in response to a civil war and that it was passed by the Reconstruction Congress have *no* signification for us? Could we really read "equal protection" to mandate state-imposed wife swapping? Certainly not with the same freedom that an actor could choose to play Hamlet in drag.

Of course, it *is* notoriously difficult for the Supreme Court (or for legal commentators) to reach agreement about some aspects of equal protection—although we should not lose sight of the fact that there is also some widespread agreement; Brown v. Board of Education was,

[96] Such a principle can also demonstrate why clause-bound intent is inappropriate, and can be tied to the Constitution's basic concept of liberty. That basic concept of liberty is that liberty can be restricted only for *agreed*, limited purposes (see chapter 2, pp. 50–51), and agreements about restrictions of speech change over time; see pp. 97–104.

[97] Dworkin, *Taking Rights Seriously*, 22–28.

[98] Clifford Geertz, *Local Knowledge: Further Essays in Interpretive Anthropology* (New York: Basic Books, 1983), 215.

[99] The scholarly literature on "law and literature" has become vast. A good place to start is the symposium in *Texas Law Review* 60 (March 1982). For an argument skeptical of our ability to find any true "meaning" in the Constitution, see esp. the article by Sanford Levinson, "Law as Literature," and the sources cited therein. See also Levinson, "Clashes of Taste in Constitutional Interpretation," *Dissent* (Summer 1988), 301–12.

Levinson correctly points out that although "many contemporary [legal] articles are replete with references to Wittgenstein, Nietzsche, or Derrida, not to mention homegrown writers like Stanley Fish and Richard Rorty," it is nevertheless "worth noting that there is nothing substantially new in skepticism about the clarity of language." "Clashes," 303. For a discussion of constitutional language, see chapter 3 below, pp. 88–91.

after all, unanimous. Literary theory does have a great deal to say to constitutional interpretation, including the general warning that we must be on guard against finding only what we want to find.[100] But to accept uncertainty and a range of interpretive possibilities we needn't accept the far more radical proposition that the Constitution can mean *anything*. There may be room for a more or less liberal or conservative "reading" of the Constitution, but there isn't room for finding either Karl Marx or St. Thomas Aquinas as the fountainhead of constitutional thought.

More importantly, these liberal and conservative readings of the Constitution must be *justified* by means of legal reasoning and historical analysis, the canons of which we might well be able to agree to. Initial premises can be identified and evaluated; the quality of historical scholarship can be judged. We can challenge the conservative tenet that judicial review is problematic because it is undemocratic, and the theoretical arguments based on this (supposed) fact. We can evaluate the quality of historical scholarship in various analyses of the Fourteenth Amendment.[101] And so forth.

It has been said that debates between constitutional scholars are like debates about religion; no one really expects to convince anyone else; people argue from faith.[102] But again, the analogy is faulty. An argument over the Pope is not like an argument over the constitutionality of abortion, or an argument over separate but equal. Did the framers of the Fourteenth Amendment "intend" to have equality extend to public schools? Does it matter whether they did or not? The first question is a relatively straightforward historical question, that may well have a reasonably satisfactory answer. The second question requires a coherent constitutional theory. Accepting or rejecting such a theory is, in some very limited sense, equivalent to accepting or rejecting a religious premise—but only in the sense that neither sort of theory is ultimately "provable." Legal reasoning has limits and standards in a way that religious conversations do not. We can ask of any example of legal reasoning, "what's your evidence?" and "does this evidence accurately reflect everything relevant to deciding this question?" Those are questions we usually cannot ask in religious conversations.

---

[100] On this danger see Rogers Smith, "Constitutional Interpretation and Political Theory: American Legal Realism's Continuing Search for Standards," *Polity* 15 (Summer 1983): 492–514.

[101] See pp. 55–66.

[102] See Sanford Levinson, "The Constitution in American Civil Religion," *Supreme Court Review* (1979): 123–51.

V.

A word about my choice of subject matter. I have chosen to focus on the rights of certain minority groups, such as the mentally ill, children, homosexuals, and the physically disabled—for several reasons. First, because, in general, a concern for minorities is central to American constitutional thought, and because contemporary theorists often forget that, or neglect to talk in detail about very many specific cases. Second, because such issues are often put forward by skeptics or critics of liberal jurisprudence as prime examples of "policy" questions judges ought not to consider; decisions protecting such groups are often pegged as prime examples of judicial "legislating."[103] Thus if a constitutional theory can adequately deal with these groups, it will have accomplished a great deal. Moreover, these issues are "pending" in a broad political sense and are thus timely.

Finally, a number of these groups are intriguing because they challenge, in some fundamental way, the liberal definition of citizenship. For example, children and lunatics, in standard liberal theory, have no rights at all.[104] I develop this theme and some of its implications in my final chapter, where I turn from constitutional argument to a consideration of the implications of these issues for the contemporary debate in political theory about the nature and desirability of political "community."

A word about style. In chapters 4 and 5 I quote extensively from case material because I think this is essential to any jurisprudential argument; all too often, theorists don't adequately discuss concrete cases. The endless quotation may be somewhat tedious, but is necessary to the development of my argument. Constitutional theory should be, above all, about real cases. Similarly, in the next chapter, I quote extensively from historical and interpretive works. My goal here is to put together a coherent analysis of the fundamental ideology of the Constitution, which I construct largely based on the scholarship of others.

---

[103] See, e.g., Horowitz, *Courts and Social Policy*, esp. chapter 1, and Agresto, *Supreme Court and Constitutional Democracy*, 11.

[104] See Martha Minnow, *Making All the Difference: Inclusion, Exclusion, and American Law* (Ithaca, N.Y.: Cornell University Press, 1990), 287, 299–300, and *passim*.

CHAPTER 2

LIBERTY:
THE BLACK BOX

I.

Constitutional commentary has always organized itself as a series
of debates about pivotal cases, and modern commentary is no exception. In this light, it is useful to begin any constitutional discussion
with Roe v. Wade, without question the single most controversial case
of the last two decades and perhaps of the last fifty years.[1]

At issue in *Roe* was the constitutionality of the Texas criminal
abortion laws. An unmarried pregnant woman and others brought a
class action suit challenging the law, which made it a crime to procure
or attempt an abortion except for the purpose of saving the mother's
life.

facts

The "Jane Roe" of the case was in fact one Norma McCorvey, who
reported in August 1969 that she had been gang-raped by three men
and a woman.[2] She was, at the time, "a twenty-one-year-old carnival
worker nicknamed Pixie,"[3] raped on the way back to her motel in a
small town in Georgia.

> The carnival and Pixie moved on to Texas. There, several
> weeks later, Pixie found herself pregnant. A high school drop-
> out, who was divorced and had a five-year-old daughter and
> little money, Norma McCorvey unsuccessfully sought an abor-
> tion. . . . "No legitimate doctor in Texas would touch me,"
> she ha[d] remembered. "I found one doctor who offered to
> abort me for $500. Only he didn't have a license, and I was

---

[1] Roe v. Wade, 410 U.S. 113 (1973).
[2] David M. O'Brien, *Storm Center: The Supreme Court in American Politics*
(New York: W. W. Norton, 1986), 23. McCorvey later admitted that she had
not been raped.
[3] *Ibid.*

29

scared to turn my body over to him. So there I was—pregnant, unmarried, unemployed, alone and stuck."[4]

The Supreme Court eventually found that the Texas abortion statute violated McCorvey/Roe's right to "privacy."

The Constitution nowhere mentions "privacy," and there begins the intellectual and political struggle the case has generated, for two crucial arguments must be accepted before the Court's decision can be regarded as legitimate: First, that the Constitution, in protecting liberty against deprivation "without due process of law," acts in a substantive manner to protect sexual and bodily privacy; second, that this privacy is "broad enough" (in Justice Blackmun's phrase) "to encompass a woman's decision whether or not to terminate her pregnancy."[5]

Like a Greek chorus, or a bad dream, the abortion dilemma returns repeatedly to any serious jurisprudential discussion, for the case raises fundamental questions of morality and politics as well as questions of jurisprudence, questions that have great resonance with a large portion of the American public. Is the fetus a "person"? Is the Supreme Court, by overturning statutes such as the Texas law, illegitimately "legislating"? Is a state, by establishing the restriction in the first place, legalizing one particular religious point of view?

All of these questions are important, but before the abortion dilemma can be addressed directly, this chapter must attack a more fundamental interpretive problem: What status does the Constitution give to "liberty," and of what does this liberty consist? For it is through the "liberty" of the Constitution that privacy—and the right to an abortion—is protected. (We will return to Roe v. Wade in the next chapter.)

The text of the Constitution mentions liberty in just three places: the preamble, which lists securing "the Blessings of Liberty to ourselves and our Posterity" as one of the purposes of the Constitution; and the Fifth and Fourteenth amendments, which prohibit the deprivation of "life, liberty, or property without due process of law." (The Fifth Amendment is a prohibition on the action of the federal government, while the Fourteenth acts upon the states.)

From this meager mention one cannot conclude very much, although it is clear from even these brief phrases that liberty is a fundamental constitutional commitment; whatever "liberty" is, it is as important as "life" or "property." But to give any real content to "liberty," we must

---

[4] *Ibid.*, 23, quoting Lloyd Shearer, "Intelligence Report," *Parade*, 23 January 1983.

[5] Roe. v. Wade, 410 U.S. at 153.

enter the domain of historians and political theorists. It is, in fact, from the general ideological background of the constitutional period that we can conclude that "liberty" is perhaps the single most important constitutional value. By examining the meaning of liberty in Montesquieu, Locke, Blackstone, and the common law, we will see a strong, recurrent theme that relates liberty to its opposite: arbitrary government action.

II.

We can begin an inquiry into the ideology of the Constitution by posing a question at the highest level of abstraction: Can we say that the constitutional system as a whole has an overriding purpose?

Indeed it does, and that is to embody the rule of law. This is not quite the platitude it may, at first blush, seem, for, as Judith Shklar has argued, the rule of law as an ideal is not ideologically neutral, but rather has always had particular political objectives, a fact neglected by many contemporary commentators.[6]

As described by Shklar, Western political theory contains "two quite distinct archetypes" of the rule of law, which have "become blurred by now and reduced to incoherence because the political purposes and settings that gave them their significance have become forgotten." Contemporary theories of the rule of law fail, according to Shklar, "because they have lost a sense of what the political objectives of the ideal of the rule of law originally were. . . ."[7]

The first of the two archetypes is Aristotle's, in which the rule of law is equivalent to the rule of reason. The most important condition for the rule of law "is the character one must impute to those who make legal judgments. Justice is the constant disposition to act fairly and lawfully";[8] this includes both the syllogistic reasoning typical of the law and the quality of empathy, "the psychological ability to recognize the claims of others as if these were [one's] own."[9] This version of the rule of law is completely compatible with a "dual" state, in which a large portion of the population is simply excluded from the protections of the legal order and relegated to second-class status—for example, as slaves.[10]

[6] Judith M. Shklar, "Political Theory and the Rule of Law," unpublished paper (1985).
[7] *Ibid.*, 1.
[8] *Ibid.*, 3.
[9] *Ibid.*, 4.
[10] *Ibid.*, 2.

In contrast to Aristotle's version of the rule of law stands Montesquieu, who was, of course, one of the major influences upon the American founding fathers.[11] For Montesquieu, the rule of law depends not upon the character of those who make legal judgments but upon the "institutional restraints that prevent governmental agents from oppressing the rest of society." For Montesquieu, familiar with the tradition of the dual state in the West (in which large portions of the population were subjugated) as well as with "oriental" despotism, "the greatest of human evils [is] constant fear[,] created by the threat of violence as well as the actual cruelties of the holders of military power in society."[12]

To avoid this psychology of fear, the individual must be made secure; liberty, Montesquieu says, "consists in security or in one's opinion of one's security."[13] This concern with security leads Montesquieu to examine carefully the criminal law, and to argue that the arbitrariness of the criminal law is destructive of security and therefore of liberty. And for Montesquieu, there is a crucial link between security and privacy; men can be truly secure only if the law takes certain types of conduct and places them (in Shklar's words) "entirely out of public control, because they cannot be regulated or prevented without physical cruelty [and] arbitrariness. . . ." By taking certain specified types of conduct out of the public realm and putting them behind a "fence" of privacy, arbitrary government action is avoided and the citizen can enjoy the security of liberty.[14] In this connection, Montesquieu discusses religious belief,[15] "crimes against nature,"[16] and speech.[17] The

[11] Judith M. Shklar, *Montesquieu* (New York: Oxford University Press, 1987), 111; Anne M. Cohler, *Montesquieu's Comparative Politics and the Spirit of American Constitutionalism* (Lawrence, Kans.: University Press of Kansas, 1988), *passim*; Laurence H. Tribe, *American Constitutional Law*, 2nd ed. (Mineola, N.Y.: Foundation Press, 1988), 560, n.3; A. E. Dick Howard, *The Road from Runnymede: Magna Carta and Constitutionalism in America* (Charlottesville: University of Virginia Press, 1968), 219; David A. J. Richards, *Foundations of American Constitutionalism* (New York: Oxford University Press, 1989), 35, n.110; Donald S. Lutz, *The Origins of American Constitutionalism* (Baton Rouge, La.: Louisiana State University Press, 1988), 140–42.

[12] Shklar, "Political Theory and the Rule of Law," 2, 6.

[13] Baron de Montesquieu, *The Spirit of the Laws*, eds. and trans. Anne M. Cohler, Basia Carolyn Miller, and Harold Samuel Stone (Cambridge: Cambridge University Press, 1989), Book XII, chapter 1; see also Book XII, chapter 2.

[14] Shklar, "Political Theory and the Rule of Law," 2–3.

[15] *Spirit of the Laws*, Book XII, chapter 4.

[16] *Ibid.*, chapter 6.

[17] *Ibid.*, chapter 12. In Shklar's words:

regulation of such essentially private activities through the criminal law brings a great danger of arbitrary government action; the citizen is no longer secure and liberty is destroyed. "Political liberty in a citizen," Montesquieu writes, "is that tranquility of spirit which comes from the opinion each one has of his security."[18] In other words, liberty is a state of mind; this state of mind results when the citizen is secure; the citizen is secure when the criminal law does not arbitrarily invade essentially private activities.

Here, in Montesquieu, we find many of the themes that stand behind the American Constitution's understanding of liberty. Government cannot regulate certain forms of private behavior without arbitrariness and hence the creation of insecurity and fear in the population. To avoid these psychological states, certain categories of behavior must be assigned to a private realm. The enjoyment of the security of this private realm is liberty.

III.

In his description of political liberty Montesquieu was drawing upon his knowledge of the British constitution. "There is . . . one nation in the world whose constitution has political liberty for its direct purpose," he writes.[19] It is the understanding of the British constitution that lay at the heart of the dispute between the American colonists and their British rulers, and hence that stood at the center of the American Revolution.

An essential part of the British constitution, of course, was the common law. In the history of the common law, three characteristics are especially noteworthy for our purposes.

The first is the extent to which the common law, as slowly accumulating judge-made law, was able to attain the status of "higher" law without great specificity as to the exact *content* of that higher law. As

---

Coercive government must resort to an excess of violence when it attempts to effectively control religious belief and practice, consensual sex and expressions of public opinion. The rule of law is meant to put a fence around the innocent citizen so that she may feel secure in these and all other legal activities. That implies that public officials will be hampered by judicial agents from interfering in these volatile and intensely personal forms of conduct. "Political Theory and the Rule of Law," 3.

[18] *The Spirit of the Laws*, Book XI, chapter 6; cf. Book XII, chapters 1, 2.
[19] *Ibid.*, Book XI, chapter 5.

judge-made law, relying on the interpretation of precedent, the maxims of British common law possessed a kind of magisterial subjective vagueness. The common law was "accretive" law,[20] in which general rules were never laid out precisely but could only be extracted—deduced—from a long line of concrete cases. Moreover, the process of deducing and proclaiming the content of such rules always took place in the context of yet another concrete legal controversy, and thus was often tied to a highly idiosyncratic set of facts.

The second characteristic of the common law flows from the first— the extent to which it became the special province of lawyers and commentators. Because the common law was not codified anywhere, it "belonged" to those who engaged in the process of interpretation.[21] This characteristic of the common law was a source of dissatisfaction among theorists influential with the Americans,[22] although this did not prevent the common law from being adopted and retained in the American states after the Revolution. The process through which the common law was "received" in the states was anything but systematic, and the American version of the common law remained highly dependent on lawyers and commentators.[23]

A final characteristic we should note is the extent to which the

[20] Lee Cameron McDonald, *Western Political Theory*, Part II (New York: Harcourt, Brace, Jovanovich, 1968), 279.

[21] To quote Edward S. Corwin:

> Certain it is that the contribution of medieval England to the American theory of Liberty versus Government [sic] exhibits some striking similarities to the strictly American phase of the subject. There is to begin with a fundamental document, Magna Carta, to symbolize the subordination of political authority to law. Then ensues the slow absorption of this document into judge-made law, a process which is attended by the projection of a portion of the latter into the status of a higher law of liberty. Lastly, this higher law of liberty becomes an avowed professional mystery—the arcana of the Bench and Bar. *Liberty Against Government* (Baton Rouge, La.: Louisiana State University Press, 1948), 22–23.

[22] Shannon C. Stimson, *The American Revolution in the Law: Anglo-American Jurisprudence Before John Marshall* (Princeton, N.J.: Princeton University Press, 1990), 15–22.

[23] See Howard, *Road from Runnymede*, 101–105 and 301f. Howard writes: "It is fair to say that there was never an articulate colonial theory of what it meant to say that the colonists were entitled to the laws of England. . . . It is doubtful if the colonists had any precise idea what was meant by the 'common law' or similar phrases. . . ." *Ibid.*, 101–02. For a discussion of the highly "selective" manner in which the common law was received in the American colonies, see also Lutz, *Origins of American Constitutionalism*, 59–63, and Stimson, *American Revolution in the Law*, 56, 129.

common law regarded "intent" as flowing from an interpretive process, and not "something locked into [a] text by its author."[24] Case-by-case adjudication, over time, meant that "intent" was something that emerged, not something definitively given at a single moment in time. "The late eighteenth century common lawyer conceived an instrument's 'intent'—and therefore its meaning—not as what the drafters meant by their words but rather as what judges, employing 'the artificial reason and judgment of law,' understood 'the reasonable and legal meaning' of those words to be."[25]

The American understanding of the British common law was tied to an idealized view of British history; it held that there had been a period of "gothic liberty" before the Norman conquest; that the conquest had imposed "the most abject vassallage upon the country,"[26] and that gradually, legal safeguards, most prominently Magna Carta, were built up, reestablishing political and civil liberty.[27] These safeguards, according to American popular understanding, remained effective until the cataclysmic seventeenth century, when the Stuart kings once again sought to impose arbitrary and tyrannical rule at the expense of liberty. In the Glorious Revolution, liberty was reestablished in England, but "it had been a close victory which would require the utmost vigilance to maintain."[28] Thus in their interpretation of their British past, American revolutionaries interpreted history as alternating between periods of liberty and periods of arbitrary rule.[29]

[24] H. Jefferson Powell, "The Original Understanding of Original Intent," *Harvard Law Review* 98 (March 1985): 899.

[25] *Ibid.*, 895–96. Powell's work has enormous implications for contemporary debates about constitutional interpretation in the light of framers' "intent." Powell concludes that "the [American] framers were aware that unforeseen situations would arise, and they accepted the inevitability and propriety of construction." *Ibid.*, 904.

[26] Bernard Bailyn, *The Ideological Origins of the American Revolution* (Cambridge, Mass.: Belknap Press of Harvard University Press, 1967), 81.

[27] *Ibid.*

[28] *Ibid.*

[29] As Leonard Levy points out, this American understanding of the British past was "highly selective and romanticized." *Original Intent and the Framers' Constitution* (New York: Macmillan, 1988), 139–40.

IV.

This same dichotomy—between liberty and arbitrariness—is a central feature in the political theory of Locke.[30] The argument against

[30] The extent of Locke's influence on America has been a subject of enormous scholarly controversy for many years. We can understand this controversy as having proceeded in three stages. The first stage, in which Locke is viewed as widely influential in America, is labeled by Isaac Kramnick as the "orthodox" interpretation: "Until the mid-1970s the orthodox view[,] shaped on the right by Leo Strauss, on the left by Harold Laski and C.B. MacPherson, and in the center by two hundred years of Whig history, personified in America by Carl Becker and Louis Hartz, had John Locke's liberalism, for better or for worse, as the dominant ideology from the seventeenth century through the nineteenth century in the English-speaking world." *Republicanism and Bourgeois Radicalism: Political Ideology in Late Eighteenth-Century England and America* (Ithaca: Cornell University Press, 1990), 35.

The second stage—republican revisionism—dethroned Locke and replaced his liberalism with civic republicanism as the defining American ideology. The key figure here is Pocock; see esp. J.G.A. Pocock, *The Machiavellian Moment: Florentine Political Thought and the Atlantic Republican Tradition* (Princeton: Princeton University Press, 1975). Also central here are Bailyn, *Ideological Origins of the American Revolution*, and Gordon S. Wood, *The Creation of the American Republic: 1776–1787* (New York: W.W. Norton, 1972). According to this school of thought, it is not Lockean liberalism but rather "civic humanism" and the "country" Whig tradition in England that is most relevant to America. For these revisionists, the basic political categories do not revolve around property or class but around "virtue."

The third, and most recent stage might be called neo-Lockeanism, exemplified by the work of Kramnick himself as well as the work of Diggins, Appleby, Pangle, Smith, and others. See John P. Diggins, *The Lost Soul of American Politics: Virtue, Self-Interest, and the Foundations of Liberalism* (New York: Basic Books, 1984); Joyce Appleby, "The Social Origins of American Revolutionary Ideology," *Journal of American History* 64 (1977–78): 935–58; Thomas Pangle, *The Spirit of Modern Republicanism: The Moral Vision of the American Founders and the Philosophy of Locke* (Chicago: University of Chicago Press, 1988); and Rogers M. Smith, *Liberalism and American Constitutional Law* (Cambridge, Mass.: Harvard University Press, 1985). See also the discussion of revisionism in Richard Sinopoli, "Liberalism, Republicanism and the Constitution," *Polity* 19 (Spring 1987): 331–52; and in Steven M. Dworetz, *The Unvarnished Doctrine: Locke, Liberalism, and the American Revolution* (Durham, N.C.: Duke University Press, 1990).

Kramnick provides an illuminating discussion of the various ideological agendas fueling the "anti-Lockean" movement, including a conservative fear of viewing class as central to American political ideology; see *Republicanism and Bourgeois Radicalism*, 36–37. Kramnick also makes a convincing case for viewing Lockean ideology as resurgent in the 1760s and as highly influential in America; see *ibid.*, 163–199. Other scholars have similarly made a convincing argument for once again viewing Locke as central; see Smith, *Liberalism and*

arbitrary government begins for Locke in theology, and in the definition of natural rights. God gives man life for certain purposes, and thus man has an absolute, God-given right, and obligation, of self-preservation. Man does not "own" himself, and thus he cannot do with himself anything arbitrary, anything contrary to the natural law. A man cannot enslave himself to another, for to do so he would be subject to the arbitrary will of his master and might lose his life: "This *Freedom* from Absolute, Arbitrary Power is so necessary to, and closely joyned with a Man's Preservation, that he cannot part with it, but by what forfeits his Preservation and Life together. For a Man, not having the Power of his own Life, *cannot*, by Compact, or his own Consent, *enslave himself* to any one."[31] The argument from slavery is generalized by Locke into an argument about arbitrary government; man cannot subject himself to *any* form of arbitrary will. Hence liberty—the right to be free from arbitrary government action—follows directly from man's natural right of self-preservation. As Rogers Smith puts it, for Locke men "cannot give up their liberty because it is essential to the life God gave them and commanded them to preserve, and they cannot be sure of that life's preservation if it is in the absolute, arbitrary power of another."[32]

Similarly, property originates in nature and, since men enter society "to make their property more secure, they can never be understood to have given the magistrate carte blanche. . . ."[33] In fact, legislatures can only pursue ends or goals that individuals, in a state of nature, agree

---

American Constitutional Law, 1–35 and *passim*; Pangle, *Spirit of Modern Republicanism, passim*; Stimson, *American Revolution in the Law*, 7, 8, 40–48, 96, 166, 168, n.42. Pangle argues that republican revisionists ignore and misunderstand the original texts to which they refer; "above all, the scholars of our day tend to misunderstand the thought, and hence the nature of the influence, of Machiavelli." *Spirit of Modern Republicanism*, 29–30; see below, note 90.

Although I think the "neo-Lockean" arguments of Kramnick, Pangle and others are quite convincing, there is yet another reason for regarding Locke as crucial to America: his influence on Blackstone. See below, pp. 38–41.

[31] John Locke, *Two Treatises of Government*, ed. Peter Laslett (New York: Mentor, 1965), par. 23, 325; emphasis in original.

[32] Smith, *Liberalism and American Constitutional Law*, 27. Smith continues by quoting Locke further: "Those who think men's lives can be protected only at the cost of liberty, by setting up an absolute ruler, must ask themselves, 'What Security, what *Fence* is . . . in such a State, *against the Violence and Oppression of this Absolute Ruler*? The very Question can scarce be born. . . .'" *Ibid.*, quoting Locke, *Two Treatises*, par. 93, 371; emphasis in original. See also Dworetz, *Unvarnished Doctrine*, 131.

[33] Smith, *Liberalism and American Constitutional Law*, 23.

they ought to pursue. This agreement, this "compact," fundamentally limits governmental power.[34] Locke writes that a legislature

> is *not* nor can possibly be absolutely *Arbitrary* over the Lives and Fortunes of the People. For it being but the Joynt power of every Member of the Society given up to that Person, or Assembly, which is Legislator, it can be no more than those persons had in a State of Nature before they enter'd into Society, and gave up to the Community. For no Body can transfer to another more power than he has in himself; and no Body has an absolute Arbitrary Power over himself, or over any other to destroy his own Life, or to take away the Life or Property of another.[35]

Thus in Locke, legislative power should never be arbitrary power, and, as Corwin long ago pointed out, there is a direct link between this theoretical formulation in Locke and the American due process clause:

> Not even the majority which determines the form of the government can vest its agent with arbitrary power, for the reason that the majority right itself originates in a delegation by free sovereign individuals who had "in the state of nature no arbitrary power over the life, liberty, or possessions" of others, or even over their own. In this caveat against "arbitrary power," Locke definitely anticipates the modern . . . concept of "due process of law" as *reasonable law*.[36]

V.

This Lockean ideology is central to Blackstone, whose *Commentaries* on the common law were the greatest single influence on the legal

---

[34] As Smith recounts,

In Locke's state of nature each man is sovereign over himself, and so legitimate civil societies and laws can result only from a compact among these individuals, who form themselves into a sovereign people. All valid laws must accordingly be traceable to popular consent. The people may assign the lawmaking function to a legislature or other governmental agency, but that body can legislate only on behalf of its authorized ends, or else the people can rightfully alter or abolish it. *Ibid.*, 68.

[35] *Two Treatises,* par. 135, 402.

[36] Corwin, *Liberty Against Government,* 46; emphasis in original.

thinking of the generation of the American constitutional founders.[37] In the words of Robert Ferguson, Blackstone "supplied . . . a precise delineation of laws that minimized controversy and ensured national cohesion."[38] In Blackstone we can see also a reflection of the generality, abstractness, and subjectivity of the common law.

Blackstone undertook, in his four volumes, published between 1765 and 1769, a systematic analysis of the principles of the common law. Blackstone writes that the common law—the basis of the English constitution—is designed with one overriding purpose: the protection of the absolute rights of individuals.[39] There are, for Blackstone, three such absolute rights: personal security, liberty, and property.[40] Of the three, liberty is central, the concept that organizes the entire theoretical structure. The laws of England, Blackstone says, are "peculiarly adapted to the preservation of this inestimable blessing. . . ."[41] There is in Blackstone, as in Locke, a distinction between "natural" liberty and "civil" liberty. "The absolute rights of man, considered as a free agent," Blackstone writes,

> endowed with discernment to know good from evil, and with power of choosing those measures which appear to him to be most desirable, are usually summed up in one general appellation and denominated the natural liberty of mankind. This natural liberty consists properly in a power of acting as one thinks fit, without any restraint or control, unless by the law of nature. . . .[42]

Every man, entering into society, gives up part of his natural liberty and agrees to obey society's laws. "Political . . . or civil, liberty, which

---

[37] See Daniel Boorstin, *The Mysterious Science of the Law* (Boston: Beacon Press, 1941), *passim*; Robert Ferguson, *Law and Letters in American Culture* (Cambridge, Mass.: Harvard University Press, 1984), 11, 14–16, 30–33, 290; and Gareth Jones, "Introduction," in Gareth Jones (ed.), *The Sovereignty of the Law: Selections from Blackstone's Commentaries on the Laws of England* (Toronto: University of Toronto Press, 1973). See also Dennis R. Nolan, "Sir William Blackstone and the New American Republic: A Study of Intellectual Impact," *New York University Law Review* 51 (November 1976): 731–68, and Richard Epstein, *Takings* (Cambridge, Mass.: Harvard University Press, 1985), chapter 2.

[38] Ferguson, *Law and Letters*, 32.

[39] Jones, "Introduction," *xlii*.

[40] *Ibid.*; Boorstin, *Mysterious Science of the Law*, 163. See William Blackstone, *Commentaries on the Laws of England*, vol. I (London: Dawsons of Pall Mall, 1966), Book I, 117–42.

[41] Jones, *Selections*, 60.

[42] *Ibid.*, 59.

is that of a member of society, is no other than natural liberty so far restrained by human laws (and no farther) as is necessary and expedient for the general advantage of the publick."[43] In Blackstone, as in Locke, men agree to give up as much natural liberty as is necessary to protect the public good, and the limits of legislative power are set by this agreement among sovereign individuals to so limit their liberty.

Thus we see here in Blackstone a manner of defining and construing liberty that will be central to the American constitution. Liberty is the general rule, and restrictions on liberty the exception. Such restrictions are only legitimate to protect the rights of others or the common good. "[T]he law," Blackstone says, "restrains a man from doing mischief to his fellow citizens," and thus "diminishes the natural" but "increases the civil liberty of mankind." If restrictions on liberty *have* no valid purpose, if they are mere "wanton and causeless restraint[s] of the will of the subject, whether practiced by a monarch, a nobility, or a popular assembly," then such laws are "tyranny." Laws should not "regulate and constrain our conduct in matters of mere indifference, without any good end in view. . . ."[44]

What *are* the matters of "mere indifference" the law ought not regulate? Blackstone gives an example:

> [T]he statute of king Edward IV which forbad the fine gentle-men of those times . . . to wear pikes upon their shoes or boots of more than two inches in length, was a law that favoured of oppresion; because, however ridiculous the fashion then in use might appear, the restraining it by pecuniary penalties could serve no purpose of common utility.[45]

Quaint as his example may seem to us, in these and similar passages Blackstone poses for us a central dilemma of American constitution-alism: Deciding what restrictions on liberty are matters of "mere indif-ference"; deciding "what would be pernicious either to ourselves or our fellow citizens."[46] Blackstone's discussion of liberty contains the seed, or, we might say, the prototype, for the central proposition of this study, what can be called the liberty theorem. The liberty theorem

[43] *Ibid.*

[44] *Ibid.*, 59–60.

[45] *Ibid.*, 60. Blackstone continues with another example: "But the statute of King Charles II, which prescribes a thing seemingly as indifferent; *viz.* a dress for the dead, who are all ordered to be buried in woollen; is a law consistent with public liberty, for it encourages the staple trade, on which in great measure depends the universal good of the nation." *Ibid.*

[46] *Ibid.*, 63.

is this: That liberty is the rule, and its restriction, the exception; further, that liberty can be restricted only for agreed, limited purposes.[47] We have seen these ideas expressed directly in Blackstone and Locke in roughly similar terms.

VI.

It was an understanding of liberty, derived in part from Blackstone and Locke, that lay at the heart of the American Revolution. In an important study, John Phillip Reid has pointed out that "liberty" had many facets for the generation of the founders:

> Liberty was the most cherished right possessed by English-speaking people in the eighteenth century. It was both an ideal for the guidance of governors and a standard with which to measure the constitutionality of government; both a cause of the American Revolution and a purpose for drafting the United States Constitution; both an inheritance from Great Britain and a reason republican common lawyers continued to study the law of England.[48]

Above all, "liberty in the eighteenth century was a concept of constitutional law. . . ."[49] It was a concept of law because Americans understood liberty to provide security. "Liberty and security were so interconnected in eighteenth century political thought that today it is almost impossible to untangle them."[50]

Liberty provided security because it protected property, and property make people independent of government. "Property" was "not limited to the physical,"[51] but was understood broadly to include basic constitutional rights, as it had been in Locke and in British common law.[52] A man's reputation, for example, was as much a part of his property as a piece of land; for James Madison, men had "property"

---

[47] This wording is borrowed from Louis Henkin, "Privacy and Autonomy," *Columbia Law Review* 74 (December 1974): 1415.

[48] John Phillip Reid, *The Concept of Liberty in the Age of the American Revolution* (Chicago: University of Chicago Press, 1988), 1.

[49] *Ibid.,* 3.

[50] *Ibid.,* 70.

[51] *Ibid.,* 72.

[52] See Walter F. Murphy, James E. Fleming, and William F. Harris II, *American Constitutional Interpretation* (Mineola, N.Y.: Foundation Press, 1986), 938.

in their opinions and the free communication of them.[53] "[L]iberty itself was property possessed."[54] Property and liberty were equivalent "because property secured independence. Material goods were valued less for their market worth, as a means of economic development, or as a capital resource, then as a guarantee of individual autonomy."[55] Liberty was thus "both a right possessed by individuals and a standard for defining other rights—rights that restrained the legitimacy of governmental power."[56]

The great evil was arbitrary governmental power. "There was no concept more dynamic, more exegetic, or more useful for eighteenth-century politics and law than the concept of arbitrary power," Reid writes. "For both constitutional law and nonconstitutional public law it was the most hermeneutic conception, serving more than any other to define law and set theoretical limits to governmental actions."[57] Those living under arbitrary rule were slaves; arbitrary power was the antithesis of liberty.

The Revolution gained its momentum from the doctrine that "arbitrariness lawfully could be resisted."[58] When the British Parliament enacted arbitrary measures, the Americans argued against them with their understanding of the British constitution—the British law. And, as we have seen, this "law" was a highly abstract phenomenon. "The law that the friends of liberty trusted to protect liberty was not a code of substantive rules or guiding principles. It was, rather, restraint upon arbitrary power—the old law, the folk law, the good law, the customary law of the community. . . . Generalities, not particularities, provided the norms for argument."[59]

This interpretation of the role of law, and liberty, in the American Revolution is confirmed by Bailyn. When faced with legislation from the British Parliament that looked increasingly arbitrary, the American colonists drew upon their understanding of the British constitution; the goal of that constitution "was the attainment of liberty."[60] Liberty,

---

[53] *Ibid.*

[54] Reid, *Concept of Liberty*, 72.

[55] *Ibid.* On the centrality of property to American constitutionalism, see Jennifer Nedelsky, *Private Property and the Limits of American Constitutionalism* (Chicago: University of Chicago Press, 1990), esp. chapter 1.

[56] Reid, *Concept of Liberty*, 117.

[57] *Ibid.*, 55.

[58] *Ibid.*, 143, n.7.

[59] *Ibid.*, 63–64.

[60] Bailyn, *Ideological Origins*, 69.

Bailyn writes, "was the capacity to exercise 'natural rights' within limits set not by the mere will or desire of men in power but by non-arbitrary law—law enacted by legislatures containing within them the proper balance of forces."[61]

What *were* these "natural rights"? When asking this question, Bailyn, like other scholars, finds them "defined in a significantly ambiguous way."[62] They were rights that were both "natural"—"God-given, natural, inalienable"—and *expressed* in the common law—"distilled from reason and justice through the social and governmental compacts . . . expressed in the common law of England. . . ."[63] Such man-made laws, however, "marked out the minimum not the maximum boundaries of right,"[64] producing further ambiguity. Liberty was conceived of "as the exercise, within the boundaries of the law, of natural rights whose essences were *minimally* stated in English law and custom. . . ."[65]

An excellent primary source for the understanding of liberty prevalent at this time (upon which Bailyn draws extensively) are the newspaper essays of Trenchard and Gordon, British political writers who produced a series of articles known as "The Independent Whig" and then a much longer series called "Cato's Letters."[66] "By Liberty," Cato says,

> I understand the Power which every Man has over his own Actions, and his Right to enjoy the Fruit of his Labour, Art, and Industry, as far as by it he hurts not the Society, or any Members of it, by taking from any Member, or by hindering him from enjoying what he himself enjoys. . . . True and impartial Liberty is therefore the Right of every Man to pursue the natural, reasonable, and religious Dictates of his own Mind; to think what he will, and act as he thinks, provided he acts not to the Prejudice of another.[67]

[61] *Ibid.*, 77.

[62] *Ibid.* See also Suzanna Sherry, "The Founders' Unwritten Constitution," *University of Chicago Law Review* 54 (Fall 1987): 1130.

[63] Bailyn, *Ideological Origins*, 77.

[64] *Ibid.*, 78.

[65] *Ibid.*, 79; emphasis added.

[66] These articles were enormously influential; see *ibid.*, 43–45. See also Michael Kammen, *Spheres of Liberty: Changing Perceptions of Liberty in American Culture* (Madison: University of Wisconsin Press, 1986), 30.

[67] Jacobson (ed.), *English Libertarian Heritage* (Indianapolis: Bobbs-Merrill, 1965), 127–28, 130, quoted in Kammen, *Spheres of Liberty*, 31.

In a passage that goes significantly beyond the more traditional, Lockean definition of liberty and its relation to property and civil government, Cato says that

> Civil Government is only a partial Restraint put by the Laws
> of Agreement and Society upon natural and absolute Liberty.
> . . . Where Liberty is lost, Life grows precarious, always miserable, often intolerable. Liberty is, to live upon one's own
> Terms. . . . Liberty is the divine Source of all human Happiness. To possess, in Security, the Effects of our Industry, is the
> most powerful and reasonable Incitement to be industrious.
> . . . All Civil Happiness and Prosperity is inseparable from
> Liberty.[68]

In another essay, Cato goes even further: "By the Establishment of Liberty, a due Distribution of Property and an equal Distribution of Justice is established and secured."[69]

Cato here is groping for a definition of a new kind of "political" or positive liberty,[70] different from the "civil" liberty of Locke and Blackstone. The relation between the two was barely discussed in the colonies, although the distinction was made more systematically in England.[71] By the time of the American constitutional convention, however, such inclinations toward positive liberty were submerged in other concerns, as we will see shortly.

Together with the first stirrings of this more radical vision of "politi-

---

[68] Jacobson, *English Libertarian Heritage*, 130, 131, 133, 135, quoted in Kammen, *Spheres of Liberty*, 31.

[69] *Ibid.*, 32.

[70] The distinction between positive and negative liberty is made by Isaiah Berlin; see "Two Concepts of Liberty" in *Four Essays on Liberty* (New York: Oxford University Press, 1969), 118–172. Negative liberty, according to Berlin, answers the question, "how much am I governed," while positive liberty answers the question, "by whom am I governed."

[71] The distinction was made in England by Joseph Priestly and Richard Price. To quote Kammen, Priestly and Price

> distinguished between civil liberty and an extension of it that they
> designated political liberty. By the former they meant the legally
> protected rights of individuals, especially protection of person and
> property. By the latter they meant the right of each man to participate fully in political life, and to give his consent to those decisions
> that would affect him. Radicals insisted that the maintenance of
> cherished freedoms depended upon broad popular involvement in
> public affairs. Without such widespread participation, no form of
> liberty would be safe. *Spheres of Liberty*, 33–34.

cal" liberty, Cato's writings contain a clear statement of what can be called the harm principle, which had also been present in the writings of Blackstone. Liberty means that a man is free "as far as . . . he hurts not the Society, or any Members of it. . . ."; a man should be free "to think what he will, and act as he thinks, provided he acts not to the Prejudice of another. . . ." In other words, a man cannot use his liberty to do harm; if he does no harm, he should be free and unrestrained.

VII.

Such, then, was the highly abstract notion of liberty dominating American thought at the time of the Revolution. Did this understanding carry over into the debates of the Philadelphia convention in 1787?

The simple answer is yes. The debate between Federalists and Anti-Federalists was, fundamentally, a debate about what constitutional mechanisms would best function to preserve the liberty that was the new nation's fundamental goal. To be sure, a subtle but important shift took place in the American understanding of liberty between the Revolution and the calling of the Philadelphia convention. Liberty was now understood more in terms of the rights of minorities; this shift was fueled by rapidly developing political events.

As Gordon Wood has demonstrated, the economic instability created by the War for Independence led to inflation and debt; this occurred at the same time as state legislatures were given increased power and the suffrage was expanded slightly.[72] The inevitable result was the election to state legislatures of a new class of men, together with a burst of populist legislation, such as the printing of paper money and the passage of debtor relief laws.[73] In the eyes of more established classes, this state legislative action was unjust, and dangerously treading upon the natural right to property. The call for a federal constitutional convention resulted from a desire to curb this excess of democracy in the states, and, increasingly, the protection of the rights of a minority—property holders, creditors—became a central concern. John Diggins has gone so far as to argue that the meaning of the term *liberty* underwent a "profound transformation" between the Revolution and the Constitution, "signifying at first freedom from tyranny and later protection from democracy."[74]

[72] Wood, *Creation of the American Republic*, Part 4.
[73] Nedelsky, *Limits of American Constitutionalism*, 4.
[74] Diggins, *Lost Soul of American Politics*, 363.

At the same time, we should remember the religious background of America's concern for liberty. America was settled by dissenting Protestant sects, and, however entrenched they may have been within particular states,[75] each sect—a minority in national terms—regarded its liberty as paramount. As Diggins has commented, "it is not surprising that Madison and Hamilton saw political factions behaving as religious sects and drew political lessons from the religious experience of sectarianism and denominationalism."[76] Thus for reasons stemming from economics, politics, and religion, the American ideology of liberty, by 1787, contained a strong focus on protecting the rights of minorities. And this ideology was shared by both supporters and opponents of the new constitution; "however much the Federalists and Anti-Federalists disagreed about *how* to keep majorities from oppressing minorities" William Nelson writes, ". . . they did agree that preventing such oppression and thereby preserving liberty was the main task of constitutional government."[77]

For the Federalists, liberty was, unquestionably, paramount. As Thomas Pangle has noted, "the word 'liberty' as Publius uses it [in the *Federalist*] often seems to serve as an encompassing term for the ultimate political good."[78] Throughout the *Federalist*, there is a close link between liberty, property, and personal rights. *Federalist* 44 tells us that the "first principles" of the "social compact" are "personal security and private rights."[79] In *Federalist* 10, Madison states forthrightly that "the

[75] See Leonard Levy, *The Establishment Clause: Religion and the First Amendment* (New York: Macmillan, 1986), chapter 2.

[76] Diggins, *Lost Soul of American Politics*, 78. Moreover, we should not overlook the extent to which the American understanding of religious freedom views religion as necessarily a private matter, thus lending support to the notion that "privacy" is a central element of American constitutionalism. For men like Jefferson and Madison, the protection of the privacy of religion was necessary *so that* public business could go forward; following Hume, they believed that allowing religion onto the public agenda could only lead to fanatical behavior and persecution. Where religion was not private, men could not agree with each other about much else. See *ibid.*, 79; see also Henry J. Abraham, *Freedom and the Court: Civil Rights and Liberties in the United States*, 5th ed. (New York: Oxford University Press, 1988), 325–28.

[77] William Nelson, *The Fourteenth Amendment: From Political Principle to Judicial Doctrine* (Cambridge, Mass.: Harvard University Press, 1988), 31; emphasis added.

[78] Pangle, *Spirit of Modern Republicanism*, 117.

[79] Alexander Hamilton, James Madison, and John Jay, *The Federalist Papers* (New York: New American Library, 1961), 282; Pangle, *Spirit of Modern Republicanism*, 118.

first object of government" is the protection of the "faculties of men, from which the rights of property originate."[80]

The importance of protecting property from the threat of democratically elected legislatures lent Federalist ideology a distinctively elitist cast. "Positive" liberty—the right to participate in politics—was to be subordinate; the "popular sovereignty" of the Revolution was replaced by a fear of popular majorities. As Nedelsky has most recently argued, "[b]y the 1780s, the confidence of the revolutionary era had waned, and the emphasis on consent had shifted. . . . The revolutionary claim that a man is a slave if his property can be taken away without his consent gave way to the grim realization that consent alone was not adequate protection; property was now threatened by duly elected . . . legislatures."[81] Liberty was largely negative liberty—the protection of civil rights, "which included both the rights of persons and of property." Such civil rights "were to be distinguished from political rights," which "were conceived of as mere means to the true end of government, the protection of civil rights."[82]

Active political participation would be undertaken by an elite. *Federalist* 35 argues that "the idea of an actual representation of all classes of people, by persons of each class, is altogether visionary." Some classes will naturally defer; "mechanics and manufactures will always be inclined, with few exceptions, to give their votes to merchants. . . . They know that the merchant is their natural patron and friend." They realize "that their [own] habits in life have not been such as to give them those acquired endowments, without which, in a deliberative assembly, the greatest natural abilities are for the most part useless. . . ."; they recognize "that the influence and weight, and superior acquirements of the merchants render them more equal" to political deliberation.[83] Instead of the direct political participation of all classes, the new constitution would protect the security—the liberty—of all.[84]

---

[80] Hamilton, Madison, and Jay, *Federalist Papers*, 78; Pangle, *Spirit of Modern Republicanism*, 118. Because of the unequal distribution of the faculties of men, *Federalist* 10 tells us, the distribution of property will be unequal, and this will be "an insuperable obstacle to a uniformity of [political] interests . . ." *Federalist Papers*, 78.

[81] Nedelsky, *Limits of American Constitutionalism*, 4.

[82] *Ibid.*, 5.

[83] Hamilton, Madison, and Jay, *Federalist Papers*, 214.

[84] By so doing, the founders believed that the Constitution would promote a sentiment of affection for the new government, which would lead men to undertake necessary civic duties. It is thus completely within a liberal framework of protecting rights that the founders considered the problems of citizen-

In addition, the Constitution would, when amended, protect a specific list of fundamental civil rights.

Initially, Federalists were cool to the idea of a Bill of Rights. As Leonard Levy has argued, many provisions of the Constitution as originally written had a libertarian character in the minds of the Federalist framers, including "the election of public officials, the representative system, the separation of powers, . . . and the requirement that revenue and appropriation measures originate in the House," which was "a protection of the natural right to property and a bar against taxation without representation."[85] The Constitution itself, many Federalists argued, *was* a Bill of Rights; Hamilton made this argument in *Federalist* 84.[86] Federalists tended to believe that civil liberties were in danger from repressive *state* action, which should be guarded against by state bills of rights.[87] "They also argued, inconsistently, that some states had no bills of rights but were as free as those with bills of rights."[88] Liberty, to Federalists, "did not depend on 'parchment provisions,'" which Hamilton called inadequate in 'a struggle with public necessity'; it depended, rather, on public opinion, an extended republic, a pluralistic society of competing interests, and a free and limited government structured to prevent any interest from becoming an overbearing majority."[89]

Pressure to add a Bill of Rights came from the Anti-Federalists. Although they spoke a language harking back to classical sources more often than the Federalists, the Anti-Federalists were, as recent scholarship has demonstrated, certainly not less and perhaps even more "Lockean" than were the Federalists. Anti-Federalists were attached, "above all," in Pangle's words, to "the primacy of individual liberty. This liberty they [saw] as exemplified in the individual's natural right to property, conceived as entailing the protection and encouragement of commerce, acquisition, and economic growth."[90] Most Anti-Feder-

---

ship. See Sinopoli, "Liberalism, Republicanism, and the Constitution," 334, 341–51.

[85] Levy, *Original Intent*, 150.

[86] Ibid.

[87] Ibid., 154.

[88] Ibid.

[89] Ibid.

[90] Pangle, *Spirit of Modern Republicanism*, 34. Pangle here is drawing on the definitive work of Herbert Storing. See Storing's "The 'Other' Federalist Papers," *Political Science Reviewer* 6 (Fall 1976): 215–47, and *The Complete Anti-Federalist*. 7 vols. (Chicago: University of Chicago Press, 1981). As Pangle convincingly argues, some modern scholars, most notably Gordon Wood, have attempted to "wring out of the Anti-Federalist writings an anti-liberty or anti-

alists, as Levy reports, believed that the Constitution's grant of specifically enumerated powers to the federal government "could be abused at the expense of fundamental liberties."[91] Anti-Federalists were particularly concerned with Congress's power to tax and with the "necessary and proper" clause.[92]

In agreeing to add the Bill of Rights, the Federalists faced a conceptual problem. They had originally argued that a Bill of Rights was unnecessary, because the federal government was a government of enumerated powers only; no government would have the power to infringe natural rights.[93] They did not abandon this fundamental position when agreeing to add a Bill of Rights, thus leaving unclear the distinction between rights listed and rights unlisted. The Bill of Rights would make explicit *some* of the limitations and procedures necessary to the protection of natural rights, they believed, but there was still a general large category of natural rights existing beyond the text of the Constitution.

The solution to this problem was the Ninth Amendment, which states that "[t]he enumeration in the Constitution, of certain rights, shall not be construed to deny or disparage others retained by the people." The Ninth Amendment "served as a definitive solution to the ratificationists' problem of how to enumerate the rights of the people without endangering those that might be omitted."[94]

Lockean conception of republicanism." *Spirit of Modern Republicanism*, 33. Their effort to do so, however, is based on the fundamental error of confusing ancient, or classical republicanism with the republicanism of Machiavelli. Cato, who had a wide influence on American Anti-Federalists, drew upon a "ruthlessly Machiavellian" psychology and not upon ancient conceptions of classical virtues; this Machiavellianism was completely at home with "repeated invocations of Hobbesian and Lockean political principles." *Ibid.*, 32. See also Kramnick, *Republicanism and Bourgeois Radicalism*, 163–70, 261–62; Sinopoli, "Liberalism, Republicanism and the Constitution." For a reading of the Anti-Federalists different from Storing's, see Cecelia Kenyon, "Introduction" in Cecelia Kenyon (ed.), *The Antifederalists* (Indianapolis: Bobbs-Merrill, 1985), xxi–cxvi.

[91] Levy, *Original Intent*, 159.

[92] *Ibid.*, 159–60.

[93] As Suzanna Sherry has argued, the delegates to the constitutional convention "did not intend to enact positively all existing fundamental law, instead relying on unwritten natural rights to supplement the enacted constitution." The founders "envisioned multiple sources of fundamental law." "Founders Unwritten Constitution," 1127, 1158.

[94] Levy, *Original Intent*, 274. See also Laurence H. Tribe and Michael Dorf, *On Reading the Constitution* (Cambridge, Mass.: Harvard University Press, 1991), 54.

The Ninth Amendment "proves" beyond a doubt that the constitutional framers operated within a general philosophy of natural, unenumerated rights.[95] Moreover, as Levy conclusively argues, "[i]n addition to rights then known, the Ninth Amendment might have had the purpose of providing the basis for rights then unknown, which time alone might disclose. Nothing in the thought of the Framers foreclosed the possibility that new rights might claim the loyalties of succeeding generations."[96]

VIII.

In summary, what can we say about the understanding of liberty embodied in the American Constitution?

Methodologically, we can say that although highly abstract, the Constitution's liberty is not indeterminate. That is, although we cannot specify the content of that liberty with scientific precision, we can,

[95] This conclusion is shared by any number of commentators; see the essays collected in Randy A. Barnett (ed.), *The Rights Retained by the People: The History and Meaning of the Ninth Amendment* (Fairfax, Va.: George Mason University Press, 1989). See also Richards, *Foundations of American Constitutionalism*, 220ff.

[96] *Original Intent*, 279. Levy argues that the natural rights meant to be protected by the Ninth Amendment included the right to pursue happiness and the right to equality of treatment before the law, as well as "the right, then important, to hunt and fish, the right to travel, and very likely the right to intimate association or privacy in matters concerning family and sex, at least within the bounds of marriage." *Ibid.*, 278. These rights, Levy says, "were fundamental to the pursuit of happiness." *Ibid.* (Levy here cites Kenneth L. Karst, "Freedom of Intimate Association," *Yale Law Journal* 89 [March 1980]: 624–92, and David H. Flaherty, *Privacy in Colonial New England* [Charlottesville: University Press of Virginia, 1967], chapters 2 and 6.) See also Richards, *Foundations of American Constitutionalism*, 224–25.

In addition to these natural rights, Levy says, "the unenumerated rights of the people included positive rights, those deriving from the social compact that creates government." Among such positive, unenumerated rights "familiar" at the time, Levy lists the right to vote and hold office; the right to free elections; the right not to be taxed except by consent through representatives of one's choice, the right to be free from monopolies, the right to be free from standing armies in time of peace; the right to refuse military service on grounds of religious conscience; the right to bail; the right to be presumed innocent, and the right to have the prosecution shoulder the responsibility to proving guilt beyond a reasonable doubt. *Ibid.*, 278–79. "All these," Levy writes, "were among existing positive rights protected by various state laws, state constitutions, and the common law." *Ibid.*, 279.

nevertheless, develop propositions that match the historical record with sufficient clarity to be of use to constitutional decision making.

There are at least four such propositions:

(1) "Liberty" was protected when citizens were protected from arbitrary government action.

(2) Liberty was to be the rule, its restriction the exception.

(3) The liberty of an individual could be restricted only for agreed, limited purposes: to protect another individual, or the public, from harm.

(4) The purpose of government, and of the Constitution, was to protect man's natural rights, including unenumerated rights. The most important of these rights were personal security and property, broadly understood.

These propositions, as subsequent chapters will argue, can provide a starting point to a modern Supreme Court wrestling with concrete dilemmas of which the framers were unaware. As such, these propositions represent the Constitution's most basic "intent"—but an intent understood at a level of abstraction much higher than the "intent" the framers may have had in framing any particular constitutional clause. This is "intent" at the level of political theory, of ideology. With a sufficient supplemental theoretical structure, this is "intent" at a level that allows the Constitution's meaning to change with the development of society—yet without becoming completely subjective.

IX.

Between the ratification of the Constitution and the passage and ratification of the Fourteenth Amendment in the 1860s, several trends contributed to the "constitutionalization" of a vague but very real natural rights philosophy, and are thus worthy of note. The first is the development of the doctrine of "vested rights." A right or interest was said to be "vested" in an individual if it belonged to him absolutely; that is, if he was entitled to it, and if it could not be removed or "divested" by the government. It was simply assumed that the general concept of vested rights was incorporated into the constitutional document—although judges often did not bother to point to a particular constitutional clause as the basis of a decision to that effect.[97] The Supreme Court used the idea of vested rights in a "nonchalant" man-

---

[97] See Tribe, *American Constitutional Law*, 546, 587–88, 613–14; and Paul Brest and Sanford Levinson, *Processes of Constitutional Decisionmaking*, 2nd ed. (Boston: Little, Brown, 1983), 116.

ner,[98] usually to protect property rights, often blending the concept with general natural law reasoning. A good example of the fuzziness with which judges applied the doctrine of vested rights is John Marshall's opinion in Fletcher v. Peck.[99] The case originated in the Yazoo land grant scandal in Georgia. In 1795, a majority of the Georgia legislature had been bribed to sell thousands of acres of state land to private companies at rock-bottom prices. A year later, the legislature rescinded the grant, but by then, large portions had been sold to out-of-state investors.[100]

The Supreme Court in *Fletcher* was faced with the question of whether a legislature could rescind its own action. In his opinion for the Court, Marshall declares that it cannot; he concludes that "[t]he lands in controversy vested absolutely,"[101] and that "the state of Georgia was restrained, *either* by general principles which are common to our free institutions, *or* by the particular provisions of the constitution of the United States. . . ."[102] In effect, Marshall is saying that he just simply knows that this particular legislative action is unconstitutional, even though he cannot pinpoint exactly why this is the case—much as a later Supreme Court will have trouble indicating exactly where the right of privacy is to be found.[103] Marshall's opinion in *Fletcher* is full of natural law reasoning:

> The legislature of Georgia was a party to this transaction; and for a party to pronounce its own deed invalid, whatever cause may be assigned for its invalidity, must be considered as a mere act of power, which must find its vindication in a train of reasoning not often heard in courts of justice. . . . [I]f an act be done under a law, a succeeding legislature cannot undo it. The past cannot be recalled by the most absolute power.[104]

That property rights, once "vested," were absolute, was the key tenet of American constitutional doctrine for much of the nineteenth century; it was, as Corwin reported long ago, the single doctrine that "gradually operated to give legal reality to the notion of governmental power as limited power."[105]

[98] Tribe, *American Constitutional Law*, 588.
[99] 10 U.S. 87 (1810).
[100] Brest and Levinson, *Processes of Constitutional Decisionmaking*, 108.
[101] 10 U.S. at 132.
[102] 10 U.S. at 139; emphasis added.
[103] See pp. 72–73 below.
[104] 10 U.S. at 132–33.
[105] Edward S. Corwin, "The Basic Doctrine of American Constitutional Law," *Michigan Law Review* 12 (February 1914): 257. See also Dartmouth

A second major development in the first half of the nineteenth century was the increasing use of the due process clauses of *state* constitutions as the peg for the substantive protection of "natural" rights. Most state constitutions contained some sort of due process clause, deriving ultimately from chapter 29 of Magna Carta, which had declared that no person should be deprived of his "estate" "except by the law of the land or a judgment of his peers."[106] Following the passage of the federal constitution, including the Fifth Amendment's due process clause, more and more state constitutions came to contain a clause declaring that "no person shall be deprived of life, liberty, or property without due process of law."[107]

During the period of Jacksonian democracy, the politically and economically conservative bench and bar increasingly seized on these state due process clauses as the ultimate guarantee of property rights; these clauses, as Michael Perry comments, "were general enough to bear added meaning."[108] These clauses "were associated in the judicial and popular mind with the principle that 'rulers and ruled alike are beneath the law, not above it'; that the arbitrary exercise of power, serving no public good, is not binding law."[109] Thus state constitutions were interpreted to protect property rights.

The third, and most significant trend during this period was the growing controversy over slavery and abolition. The debate over slavery resonated deeply in the American psyche, for the "slavery" of the colonies to the British empire had been a key part of the American ideology. As Bailyn reports, " 'slavery' was a central concept in eighteenth-century political discourse. As the absolute political evil, it ap-

---

College v. Woodward, 17 U.S. 518 (1819), holding that New Hampshire could not unilaterally place a private institution under public control.

[106] Corwin, *Liberty Against Government*, 173. On the importance of Magna Carta in America, see Howard, *Road from Runnymede*, 301–7.

[107] Corwin, *Liberty Against Government*, 174.

[108] Michael J. Perry, "Abortion, the Public Morals, and the Police Power: The Ethical Function of Substantive Due Process," *UCLA Law Review* 23 (April 1976): 698.

[109] *Ibid.*, quoting Howard, *Road from Runnymede*, 306. Similarly, Corwin commented:

> The essential fact is quite plain, namely, a feeling on the part of the judges that to leave the legislature free to pass arbitrary or harsh laws, so long as all the formalities be observed in enforcing such laws, were [sic] to yield the substance while contending for the shadow. "The Doctrine of Due Process of Law Before the Civil War," *Harvard Law Review* 24 (March 1911): 374, quoted in Perry, "Abortion, Public Morals, and Police Power," 698, n.49.

pear[ed] in every statement of political principle, in every discussion of constitutionalism or legal rights, in every exhortation to resistance."[110] Slavery was a term "referring to a specific political condition," a condition characteristic of some European peoples as well as Africans in the American South.[111] Slavery was "[b]oth symptom and consequence of disease in the body politic."[112] After 1789, the contradiction "between what political leaders in the colonies sought for themselves and what they imposed on, or at least tolerated in, others became too glaring to be ignored. . . ."[113]

Increasingly, exponents of one side of the slavery question or the other seized upon due process as "a weapon ideally suited to their needs."[114] According to Graham, the major historian of this trend, there was during this period "considerable substantive 'due processing' of natural law, and powerful pressure . . . for expansion of judicial review—far more indeed, than has generally been credited."[115] Graham reports both Abolitionists and anti-Abolitionists developed " 'common sense' lay interpretations" of due process, which "not only exploited prevalent Lockean, natural rights interpretations of the key words 'life,' 'liberty' and 'property,' but also benefited by the inherent textual advantages of the phrase 'due [i.e., just] process' as a means of 'constitutionalizing' their earlier natural rights arguments."[116] Due process, Graham concludes,

> was snatched up, bandied about, "corrupted and corroded," if you please, for more than thirty years prior to 1866. For every black letter usage in court there were perhaps hundreds or thousands in the press, red schoolhouse and on the stump. Zealots, reformers, and politicians—not jurists—blazed the paths of substantive due process.[117]

Thus, by the time of the Civil War, a vague but very real natural rights philosophy had been cemented into the Constitution, residing more or

---

[110] Bailyn, *Ideological Origins*, 232.
[111] *Ibid.*, 234.
[112] *Ibid.*, 233.
[113] *Ibid.*, 235.
[114] Howard J. Graham, "Procedure to Substance—Extra-Judicial Rise of Due Process, 1830–1860," *California Law Review* 40 (Winter 1952–53): 488.
[115] *Ibid.*
[116] *Ibid.*, 488–89.
[117] *Ibid.* See also Perry, "Abortion, Public Morals, and Police Power," 698.

less in the general notion of "due process of law."[118] As Graham says, "substantivized due process is essentially constitutionalized natural law."[119] Or, as Perry puts it, "[o]n the eve of the Civil War, 'due process of law' had come to signify more than 'customary legal procedure'; the notion was abroad that it also signified law that serves the public good—law that is not discriminatory or hostile or even irrelevant to the public welfare."[120]

X.

Much of the remainder of our story—indeed, much of the rest of American constitutional history—turns on Section 1 of the Fourteenth Amendment:

> All persons born or naturalized in the United States, and subject to the jurisdiction thereof, are citizens of the United States and of the State wherein they reside. No state shall make or enforce any law which shall abridge the privileges or immunities of citizens of the United States; nor shall any State deprive any person of life, liberty, or property, without due process of law; nor deny to any person within its jurisdiction the equal protection of the laws.

14th

To begin to understand the meaning of these words, we must look to two bodies of evidence: the legislative history of the amendment itself, and the ideological and political climate out of which it grew. Much has been written about both. Despite exhaustive scholarly examination, the legislative history of the amendment, alone, while highly suggestive, reveals no definitive answers. I will argue, however, that this lack of clear "proof" of specific framers' intent is itself highly revealing, and that, together with an understanding of the general ideology of the period, this can guide us in seeking to interpret the amendment in a manner not wholly subjective and ungrounded. Once again, we seek a middle course, rejecting the arguments of both those who claim narrow

Social Pret

---

[118] The Supreme Court invoked substantive due process in Dred Scott v. Sanford, declaring that "an act of Congress which deprives a citizen . . . of his . . . property, merely because he came himself or brought his property into a particular Territory . . . could hardly be dignified with the name of due process of law." 60 U.S. 393, 450 (1857).

[119] Graham, "Procedure to Substance," 488.

[120] Perry, "Abortion, Public Morals, and Police Power," 698–99.

scope for the amendment, based on framers' (supposed) intent, on the one hand, and those who claim the amendment can mean "anything," on the other.[121]

The legislative history of the Fourteenth Amendment begins with the highly charged atmosphere in the 39th Congress at the close of the Civil War. The previous Congress had outlawed slavery in the Thirteenth Amendment; the response of many southern states were the Black Codes.[122] The first response of the 39th Congress to the codes was simple legislation: the Freedman's Bureau Bill[123] and then the Civil Rights Act of 1866. There is unanimous scholarly agreement that an understanding of the Fourteenth Amendment must begin with this Civil Rights Act. The act had been vetoed by President Andrew Johnson, and

---

[121] In this section I have borrowed very heavily from Brest and Levinson, *Processes of Constitutional Decisionmaking*, 408–416, and from Judith A. Baer, *Equality Under the Constitution: Reclaiming the Fourteenth Amendment* (Ithaca: Cornell University Press, 1983). See also Michael Kent Curtis, *No State Shall Abridge: The Fourteenth Amendment and the Bill of Rights* (Durham, N.C.: Duke University Press, 1986).

[122] The codes assigned freed Negroes second-class legal status in most criminal and civil matters. They were assigned harsher penalties for specific offenses, and new offenses were specified for Negroes only, for example, laws prohibiting them from keeping weapons. Severe restrictions were applied to contracts for service. John Frank and Robert Munro, "The Original Understanding of 'Equal Protection of the Laws,' " *Washington University Law Quarterly* (1972): 445–46, quoted in Brest and Levinson, *Processes of Constitutional Decisionmaking*, 408.

> Many statutes called for specific enforcement of labor contracts against freedmen, with provisions to facilitate capture should a freedman try to escape. Vagrancy laws made it a misdemeanor for a Negro to be without a long-term contract of employment; conviction was followed by a fine, payable by a white man who could then set the criminal to work for him until the benefactor had been completely reimbursed. . . . *Ibid.*

See also Curtis, *No State Shall Abridge*, 35.

[123] According to Brest and Levinson,

> [t]he Freedman's Bureau Bill required the president to "extend military protection" in the rebellious states whenever Negroes were denied, inter alia, "civil rights or immunities belonging to white persons." The paucity of debate over the formula is probably explained by the bill's geographic limitation. It posed no danger to northern Democrats and conservative Republicans who, indeed, hoped that they could appease the Radical Republicans by acceding to the measure and avoiding a confrontation between President Johnson and the Congress. Their effort failed. Johnson vetoed the bill and the conservatives refused to override the veto. *Processes of Constitutional Decisionmaking*, 408–09, n.5.

preparation of the Fourteenth Amendment began before the veto was overridden.[124]

Both of these Congressional enactments contained a "civil rights formula," prohibiting discrimination in "civil rights or immunities."[125] Supporters of the act—"almost without exception"[126]—claimed that the only rights meant to be protected by the statute were those specifically listed in its Section 1 "and that a broader construction was not intended." Those rights listed were the right to make and enforce contracts; to sue; be parties to suits and give evidence; to inherit, purchase, and lease property; "to full and equal benefit of all laws and proceedings for the security of person and property;" and to be subject to "like punishment."[127]

At the same time as Congress was considering and passing the Civil Rights Act—and sustaining it over a presidential veto—the Joint Committee on Reconstruction, or Committee of 15, was also meeting, and considering a constitutional amendment to supplement the Thirteenth.[128] This committee wrote the Fourteenth Amendment.

Once again there is general scholarly agreement that the House and Senate debates over the committee's reported amendment paid little attention to the meaning of the amendment's Section 1.[129] "Other provisions of the proposed amendment, dis[en]franchising much of the

---

[124] Baer, *Equality Under the Constitution*, 76.

[125] The Civil Rights bill declared "[t]hat there shall be no discrimination in civil rights or immunities among the inhabitants of any State or Territory of the United States on account of race, color, or previous condition of slavery. . . ." Brest and Levinson, *Processes of Constitutional Decisionmaking*, 409.

[126] *Ibid.*

[127] *Ibid.*

[128] The committee was appointed in December 1865, "primarily at the insistence of the famous Radical Republican . . . Thaddeus Stevens. This step was a victory for Stevens over the president, whose Reconstruction plans were more moderate, or at least less aggressive." Baer, *Equality Under the Constitution*, 76.

[129] Brest and Levinson, *Processes of Constitutional Decisionmaking*, 414. Brest and Levinson are relying on Alexander Bickel, "The Original Understanding and the Segregation Decision," *Harvard Law Review* 69 (November 1955): 1–65; Charles Fairman, *Reconstruction and Reunion, 1864–1888*, Part 1, in *History of the Supreme Court of the United States*, vol. 6 (New York: Macmillan, 1971); Alfred Kelly, "The Fourteenth Amendment Reconsidered: The Segregation Question," *Michigan Law Review* 54 (June 1956): 1049–86. See also Baer, *Equality Under the Constitution*, 73–104, esp. 92, 96; Nelson, *Fourteenth Amendment*, 104–08, 115–16, 133; Earl M. Maltz, *Civil Rights, the Constitution, and Congress: 1863–1869* (Lawrence, Kans.: University Press of Kansas, 1990).

white southern electorate, were far more controversial. Apparently, most legislators identified Section 1 with the Civil Rights Act, which they had only recently enacted after lengthy debate."[130] Many Republicans in Congress asserted that Section 1 "merely constitutionalized the Civil Rights Act."[131] These claims have led some modern scholars to argue that an expansive reading of the Fourteenth Amendment—for example, using it to desegregate schools in 1954—is a violation of framers' intent and thereby unconstitutional.[132]

However, such a conservative argument ignores too much. It ignores, first, the several speeches in Congress that *did* give Section 1 of the proposed amendment a broad reading. For example, Congressman John Bingham of Ohio, a Radical Republican and the principle architect of the amendment, when discussing the meaning of "privileges and immunities," was careful to say that these "include, *among other privileges*, the right to bear true allegiance to the Constitution and laws of the United States, and to be protected in life, liberty, and property. . . ."[133] Similarly, opponents of the proposed Section 1 were quick to point out that its words could have far-reaching implications:

> What are privileges and immunities? Why, sir, all the rights we have under the laws of the country are embraced under the definition of privileges and immunities. The right to vote is a privilege. The right to marry is a privilege. The right to contract is a privilege. The right to be a juror is a privilege. The right to be a judge or President of the United States is a privilege. I hold if that ever becomes a part of the fundamental law of the land it will prevent any State from refusing to allow anything to anybody embraced under this term of privileges and immunities. . . . It will result in a revolution worse than that through which we have just passed.[134]

[130] Brest and Levinson, *Processes of Constitutional Decisionmaking*, 414; see also Maltz, *Civil Rights, Constitution, and Congress*, 93.

[131] Brest and Levinson, *Processes of Constitutional Decisionmaking*, 414.

[132] See, most notably, Raoul Berger, *Government by Judiciary: The Transformation of the Fourteenth Amendment* (Cambridge, Mass.: Harvard University Press, 1977), 117–33, 231–32, 243–45, 286, 288, 342. See also James F. Byrnes, "The Supreme Court Must be Curbed," *U.S. News and World Report*, 18 May 1956, reprinted in Arnold Paul (ed.), *Black Americans and the Supreme Court Since Emancipation: Betrayal or Protection?* (New York: Holt, Rinehart and Winston, 1972).

[133] Brest and Levinson, *Processes of Constitutional Decisionmaking*, 415; emphasis added.

[134] The remarks of Andrew Jackson Rogers, quoted in *ibid.*, 414–15. See also Maltz, *Civil Rights, Constitution, and Congress*, 107.

One contemporary scholar concludes that "the debates are shot through with the sort of language" modern conservatives discount.[135]

Moreover, as William Nelson, the most recent and meticulous historian of the Fourteenth Amendment points out, there *was* some discussion of specific applications of Section 1, often including a quotation from Corfield v. Coryell,[136] an 1823 case construing the privileges and immunities clause of Article IV ("The citizens of each state shall be entitled to all privileges and immunities of citizens in the several states.") The interpretation of this case would, by the 1870s, become crucial to the Supreme Court's explication of the Fourteenth Amendment.

In *Corfield*, Justice Washington had said that "privileges and immunities" should be "confin[ed] . . . to those privileges and immunities which are *fundamental*; which belong of right to the citizens of all free governments, and which have at all times been enjoyed by citizens of the several States which compose this Union. . . ." Washington continues in vague and majestic rhetoric typical of natural law thinking:

> What these fundamental principles are, it would be more tedious than difficult to enumerate. They may all, however, be comprehended under the following general heads: protection by the government, with the right to acquire and possess property of every kind, and to pursue and obtain happiness and safety, subject, nevertheless, to such restraints as the government may prescribe for the general good of the whole.[137]

A further argument, related to the presence of language and citations such as these, can be made: If members of the 39th Congress *had* clearly intended Section 1 of the Fourteenth Amendment to be limited to a specific catalog of rights, they would have said so; they were perfectly capable of using specific language. Thus the absence of evidence of this sort becomes, itself, an argument for a broader interpretation. The language of the amendment is broad; it contains no specific list of rights, as the Civil Rights Act had. The language of the Fourteenth Amendment is not the language of the Civil Rights Act; if it were, the modern conservative case would be stronger.

[135] Baer, *Equality Under the Constitution*, 82.

[136] 6 Fed. Cas. 546 (C.C.E.D.Pa. 1823). *Corfield* was the first major case decided under Article IV, section 2. See also Tribe, *American Constitutional Law*, 529; Curtis, *No State Shall Abridge*, 66–67, 73–74, 88, 168.

[137] Brest and Levinson, *Processes of Constitutional Decisionmaking*, 200–01, quoting the Slaughter-House Cases, 83 U.S. 36, 76 (1873); emphasis in original.

All of these arguments point us toward the need to examine a second body of evidence beyond narrow legislative history—the general ideology of the Republican party in the decades leading up to the passage of the amendment.

Several generations of legal historians have concluded from such an inquiry that the overarching purpose of the Fourteenth Amendment was to "incorporate" a broad natural rights philosophy—that is, to prevent the states from abridging fundamental rights in the same manner that the federal government had previously been constrained by the original Constitution. Corwin concluded in the 1940s that

> [t]he debates in Congress on the amendment leave one in little doubt of the intention of its framers to nationalize civil liberty in the United States, primarily for the benefit of the freedmen, to be sure, but incidentally for the benefit of all. This would be done, it was calculated, by converting State citizenship and its privileges and immunities into privileges and immunities of national citizenship.[138]

The next group of scholars, in the 1950s, were, in part, responding to the Supreme Court's request for historical guidance in deciding Brown v. Board of Education. The work of three men, in particular, was (and still is) regarded as seminal—Jacobus TenBroek, Howard Jay Graham, and Alfred H. Kelly.[139] These scholars concluded that the Fourteenth Amendment was "intended" to write into the Constitution broad principles of equality and natural rights.[140] TenBroek wrote:

> The clause on equal protection of the laws had almost exclusively a substantive content. . . . Protection of men in their fundamental or natural rights was the basic idea of the clause. . . . The clause was a confirmatory reference to the affirmative duty of government to protect men in their natural rights. . . .[T]he whole clause is . . . understood to mean: "Each State

---

[138] Corwin, *Liberty Against Government*, 118. Corwin sites Horace Edgar Flack, *The Adoption of the Fourteenth Amendment* (Baltimore: Johns Hopkins University Press, 1908), 55–97, 210–77.

[139] cf. Baer, *Equality Under the Constitution*, 80. See Jacobus TenBroek, *Equal Under Law*, Rev. ed. (London: Collior, 1965); Howard Jay Graham, *Everyman's Constitution* (Madison: State Historical Society of Wisconsin, 1968); Alfred H. Kelly, "The Fourteenth Amendment Reconsidered."

[140] Baer, *Equality Under the Constitution*, 80.

shall supply the protection of the laws to men in their natural rights, and the protection shall always be equal to all men."[141]

Alexander Bickel was at the time of *Brown* a law clerk to Felix Frankfurter, and was assigned by him to prepare a memorandum on legislative history; he reached a similar though more guarded conclusion.[142] "May it not be," Bickel wrote, "that the Moderates and the Radicals reached a compromise permitting them to go to the country with language which they could, where necessary, defend against damaging alarms raised by the opposition, but which at the same time was sufficiently elastic to permit reasonable future advances?"[143]

Most recently, Nelson concludes that Section 1 of the Fourteenth Amendment "was not a trivial matter designed merely to remove doubts about the constitutionality of the Civil Rights Act," but was "a declaration of fundamental principle."[144] The amendment, Nelson writes, had a "political" rather than a narrow legal purpose; it was "the Republican party's plan for securing the fruits both of the war and of the three decades of antislavery agitation preceding it."[145]

In examining Republican ideology and its precursors in those decades preceding the Civil War, Nelson, like those before him, finds that natural law thinking predominates.[146] Such natural law thinking—as it had been for the generation of the founding—was "imprecise, flexible, multisided,"[147] and was closely linked to a "deep religiosity."[148] The closest anyone ever came to an articulation of the content of "natural rights" was to quote Justice Washington in *Corfield*, or to cite common law maxims, such as the extraordinarily vague phrase, "enactments contrary to reason are void."[149] Such imprecise higher law thinking served a rhetorical and political function; it enabled politicians "to retain the support of political coalitions whose individuals members shared an agreement only about vague ideas. . . ."[150]

---

[141] TenBroek, *Equal Under Law*, 237, quoted in Baer, *Equality Under the Constitution*, 81.
[142] Baer, *Equality Under the Constitution*, 81.
[143] Bickel, "Original Understanding," 61, quoted in *ibid.* and in Brest and Levinson, *Processes of Constitutional Decisionmaking*, 425.
[144] Nelson, *Fourteenth Amendment*, 60.
[145] *Ibid.*, 61.
[146] *Ibid.*, see esp. 22.
[147] *Ibid.*, 23.
[148] *Ibid.*, 21; see also 65.
[149] *Ibid.*, 25.
[150] *Ibid.*, 38–39.

Thus Nelson, like other legal historians before him, concludes that the drafting and ratification of the Fourteenth Amendment had as its grand purpose the protection of "natural rights" from abridgment by the states.[151] Nelson, however, takes this point further than many historians when he asks the question: What exactly does such a conclusion signify for legal *doctrine*? The startling fact is that the vague natural rights philosophy meant to be incorporated by the Fourteenth Amendment had never been applied by the courts to specific issues and legal disputes, with the exception of the broad protection of property rights in cases such as Fletcher v. Peck. No court had ever considered "the scope of state power to regulate the economy, to arrest and prosecute criminals, or to control the sexual behavior of its citizens"[152]—specific and difficult legal disputes that would require an interpretation of the Fourteenth Amendment in later decades.

Moreover, Nelson finds a significant ambiguity in the debate over the Fourteenth Amendment, between those who saw it as an *absolute* guarantee against the infringement of "specific fundamental rights deriving from higher law or from the nature of citizenship in a republic,"[153] on the one hand, and those who saw it as merely guaranteeing equal, rather than absolute rights—that is, those who did not see it as preventing the state from regulating any subject so long as the state acted reasonably and without arbitrariness. According to this latter view, "as long as the state treated its citizens equally, distinguishing between them only when there was a basis in reason for doing so, the state would remain immune from federal intervention. . . ."[154]

Such was the imprecision of the debate, however, that, having introduced this distinction between "absolute" and "equal" protection, Nelson points out that it was a distinction that "was only beginning to emerge" in legal thinking in 1866,[155] and that some individuals made both arguments at the same time.[156]

But even if we choose to emphasize the second, more limited view of the scope of the Fourteenth Amendment—as modern conservatives do—we are still left pondering the meaning of "reasonable" state regulation, and "the fact is that no one in 1866 was engaging in precise

[151] *Ibid.*, esp. 22–39. See also Curtis, *No State Shall Abridge*, esp. 41, 49–56, and chapter 3.
[152] *Ibid.*, 110.
[153] *Ibid.*, 119.
[154] *Ibid.*, 115.
[155] *Ibid.*, 122–23.
[156] *Ibid.*, 123.

doctrinal analysis of what the concept of reasonableness might mean. . . ."[157]

XI.

It is important to pause and reflect upon what we have found concerning the Fourteenth Amendment. We have found, first, that there is considerable evidence to support the contention that the Fourteenth Amendment was meant to constitutionally incorporate—that is, make applicable against the states—the protection of some (largely unspecified) natural rights. We might label this the "black box" theory of rights. The framers and ratifiers of the Fourteenth Amendment believed that the original constitutional document protected a group of natural rights—unspecified, vaguely delineated—"what these fundamental principles are, it would be more tedious than difficult to enumerate . . . those privileges and immunities . . . which belong of right to the citizens of all free governments. . . ."[158]—against federal encroachment. That is, there is some group of natural rights contained within a black box. Black because we don't know exactly what's in the box, although we know *some* things are there: the right to own property, for example, and the right to the fruit of one's labor; the right of access to court. If we shake the box, we know it rattles. Further, we know that whatever is a fundamental right is within the box.

The original Constitution prevented the federal government from abridging the rights inside the black box. Now, the Fourteenth Amendment will protect these same rights—whatever they are—against abridgment by the states. In other words, the box now does double duty; the expansion of its function was the overarching purpose of the Fourteenth Amendment.

The black box, however, leaves two gigantic puzzles. First, exactly what is, and is not, inside the box? And second, does the amendment prevent the states from acting on such matters *at all*, or does the amendment only prevent the states from acting unreasonably and arbitrarily? And, if it only prevents the states from acting unreasonably and arbitrarily, what exactly *is* unreasonable or arbitrary? If we accept what several generations of historians tell us, then we must accept the conclusion that the framers of the Fourteenth Amendment *expected*

---

[157] *Ibid.*
[158] See above, p. 59.

these questions to be answered in case-by-case adjudication,[159] just as the founding generation expected the meaning of other constitutional clauses to be adjudicated on a case-by-case basis.[160]

We can, in fact, go further. If we accept that the framers of both the Constitution and the Fourteenth Amendment operated from natural law premises, then we must accept "active" judicial power. This is so for two reasons independent of the fact that the framers themselves expected it: first, because only an "active" judiciary could convert vague natural rights sentiment into enforceable legal doctrine; second, because the entire philosophical premise of American thinking about natural law is countermajoritarian.[161]

It is especially important to note that, even if we accept the more limited historical reading of the Fourteenth Amendment—that it was not meant to protect certain rights absolutely, but only to prevent the states from engaging in "unreasonable" or arbitrary legislation—we are still driven inexorably to embrace judicial power—for where else but the courts are we to obtain our definition of what is, and is not, "unreasonable"? Thus, unless we ignore a great deal of historical evidence, and entirely identify Section 1 of the Fourteenth Amendment with Section 1 of the Civil Rights Act of 1866—which, as we have seen, it is impossible to do—we are left with the conclusion that the Supreme Court, when it interprets the Fourteenth Amendment or applies it to controversies unimagined by Congress or the states in 1866, is, in fact, obeying the most basic "intent" of the framers of the amendment.

But we are not only forced to embrace judicial power by the Fourteenth Amendment; we are also forced to embrace judicial subjectivity and legal uncertainty, for, as we have seen, the ideology of natural rights meant to be constitutionalized by the Fourteenth Amendment was vague, unspecific, open to myriad interpretations. There *was* wide agreement that *some* things *were* natural rights—the right to own and enjoy property, most importantly; there was also wide agreement that *some* forms of state regulation—overt racial classifications that denied outright the enjoyment of some rights—were definitely arbitrary. But there was also widespread belief that these obvious examples were merely illustrations, examples of what the Fourteenth Amendment was meant to protect, and that such examples were not exhaustive.

---

[159] Nelson, *Fourteenth Amendment*, 124.
[160] See Powell, "Original Understanding," and text above, p. 35.
[161] See above, pp. 45–50.

Moreover, even when the framers of the amendment did talk of specific examples, they demonstrated that there was no precise *legal* or constitutional basis for their judgment. As Nelson reports, once they moved beyond the unconstitutionality of "obviously defective racial criteria,"[162] the framers of the amendment swam in murky waters. They could, and did, specify examples of illegal state regulations, "but were persistently unable to elaborate how their conclusions were derived. . . ."[163] These men—like many judges and justices in the years to come—"simply knew an arbitrary exercise of power when they saw one."[164] Nelson supplies a telling example. Thaddeus Stevens, the Radical Republican, is known to have argued that two married women—one black and one white—were members of the same legal class and therefore entitled to equal treatment, whereas two black women—one married and one unmarried—were members of different legal classes who could be treated differently without running afoul of the Fourteenth Amendment.[165]

Now, how is it possible for Stevens, or any judge, to reach such a judgment—a judgment which would be necessary to adjudicate the validity of any number of state laws? Only through a subjective judgment about the nature of the society in which he lived. Stevens *believed* that race was a legally irrelevant criterion, but marital status was not, and he believed these things because he was situated in American society at a particular time and place and subscribed to some ideas current in that society and not to others. No doubt he believed his judgments were based on the best available evidence and were therefore "rational."

Of course, a different man at a different time or place might well disagree. What the Supreme Court ought to do when men *do* disagree about such classifications is, obviously, an important question, as is the question of what the Supreme Court ought to do when even widespread social agreement is based on prejudice (for example) or is contradicted by some types of evidence (scientific evidence, for example). For the moment, however, it is sufficient to note that there is nothing inevitable about the *content* of any such judgments—and, ultimately, nothing "textual" or constitutional about them either; they are based more in sociology and psychology than in law. But the *need* for such judg-

---

[162] Nelson, *Fourteenth Amendment*, 138.
[163] *Ibid.*, 139.
[164] *Ibid.*
[165] *Ibid.*

ments—in the Stevens example, whether a woman's marital status is a characteristic relevant to state law making—*is* a part of the law, for it is required by the Fourteenth Amendment.

We have, in a sense, returned to an earlier part of the argument. The Constitution's "liberty," I argued previously, was meant to be unabridged "except for agreed, limited purposes." Such "agreements," like the judgment of what classifications are "reasonable" under the Fourteenth Amendment, are sometimes fluid; judgments about them are bound to be subjective. There will be a complex and at times difficult-to-gauge relationship between such judgments and social arrangements. However, what *is* clear is that negotiating these difficulties is what the Supreme Court is required to do when it "interprets" the constitution. What the law "is" thus cannot be divorced from social questions, for the nation's fundamental law—the Constitution—contains premises that depend upon judgments about social relations. In this sense, the original Constitution is (among other things) a set of instructions to future Supreme Courts to strike down laws that abridge liberty unnecessarily, and the Fourteenth Amendment is a set of instructions to the Court to (at a minimum) strike down legislation that abridges fundamental rights unreasonably or arbitrarily. But the judgment about what is or is not an arbitrary abridgment of liberty is a judgment that the text of the Constitution does not, by itself, make.

XII.

In the decades following the ratification of the Fourteenth Amendment, the Supreme Court began the arduous process of applying the amendment's "instructions" to specific legal disputes. Early on, it had little difficulty striking down some forms of overt racial discrimination, as in Strauder v. West Virginia, where a black man had been convicted of murder in state court by a jury from which blacks were totally excluded.[166]

The most important interpretation of the Fourteenth Amendment, however, came not in a case involving race but rather in the *Slaughter-House* cases, involving disgruntled butchers in New Orleans.[167] In 1869, the Louisiana legislature, "a corrupt, carpetbag government," enacted a statute granting a twenty-five-year monopoly to an incorpo-

---

[166] 100 U.S. 303 (1880).
[167] 83 U.S. 36 (1873). For a different analysis of *Slaughter-House*, see Gary J. Jacobsohn, *Pragmatism, Statesmanship, and the Supreme Court* (Ithaca, N.Y.: Cornell University Press, 1977), 23–77.

rated group of seventeen butchers; this gave them the right to construct and operate the only slaughterhouse in and around the city of New Orleans.[168] Any butcher in the city could use the slaughterhouse if he paid a set fee. The measure was justified as a health regulation; the city "had long faced the problem of contamination of the Mississippi River caused by the dumping of animal carcasses into the river north of the city limits."[169]

Other butchers who were, in effect, deprived of work by the law (because they could not afford to pay the fee) sued, arguing that they had been denied the right to practice their profession under the Fourteenth Amendment. Represented before the Supreme Court by a former justice,[170] their case forced the Court to address the question of whether the Fourteenth Amendment protected any substantive rights beyond the right to be free from overt racial discrimination. In a five-to-four decision the Supreme Court held against the butchers; within a few years, however, the justices in the minority had won majority adherence to their views, and the doctrine of "substantive" due process began its long entrenchment in federal constitutional law. Also as a result of this case, the "privileges and immunities" clause lost whatever chance it had of being interpreted in a substantively meaningful manner; henceforth, debate would shift completely to the meaning of "liberty" and "property" in the due process clause. But whatever the textual peg of the argument, Justices in these years were arguing about the same thing: what was, and was not, included within the black box of fundamental rights.

Writing for the five-member majority in *Slaughter-House*, Justice Miller seeks to limit the scope of the amendment as much as possible to the protection of former slaves.[171] To do so, he introduces the concept of dual citizenship—individuals have separate rights originating in either their national or state citizenship. On the all-important question of what rights are a result of national citizenship—and hence protected by the Fourteenth Amendment and unabridgable by state action—Miller provides a highly limited answer. "Was it the purpose of the fourteenth amendment . . . to transfer the security and protection of all . . . civil rights . . . from the States to the Federal government?"

[168] Joel B. Grossman and Richard S. Wells, *Constitutional Law and Judicial Policy Making*, 3rd ed. (White Plains, N.Y.: Longman, 1988), 182.
[169] *Ibid.*
[170] John Campbell, a southerner, who had resigned at the start of the Civil War.
[171] See Nelson, *Fourteenth Amendment*, 162.

Miller asks; his answer is an emphatic "no."[172] With the inevitable quotation from Justice Washington in Corfield v. Coryell, Miller limits "fundamental" rights to a highly limited list: the right "to come to the seat of government to assert any claim"; the right "to demand the care and protection of the Federal government . . . when on the high seas or within the jurisdiction of a foreign government"; the right to use the navigable waters of the United States; the right peaceably to assemble and petition for redress of grievances (a First Amendment right); the "privilege of the writ of *habeas corpus*" (protected in the original constitution).[173]

In contrast, Justices Field and Bradley in dissent find the black box of fundamental rights to contain much more. Armed with the same quotations from *Corfield*, they find that the New Orleans monopoly violates the rights of the suing butchers to lawfully pursue their occupation. "The question presented is . . . one of the gravest importance," Justice Field declares, "not merely to the parties here, but to the whole country. It is nothing less than the question whether the recent amendments to the Federal Constitution protects the citizens of the United States against the deprivation of their common rights by State legislation."[174] Field finds that "all monopolies in any known trade or manufacture are an invasion of these common rights, for they encroach upon the liberty of citizens to acquire property and pursue happiness. . . ."[175] The Fourteenth Amendment "was intended to give practical effect to the declaration of 1776 of inalienable rights, rights which are the gift of the Creator, which the laws does not confer, but only recognizes."[176]

Similarly, Justice Bradley reads the Fourteenth Amendment as a broad protection of civil rights, including the "right to choose one's calling" which he sees as "an essential part of that liberty which it is the object of government to protect"; a calling, "when chosen, is a man's property and right. Liberty and property are not protected when these rights are arbitrarily assailed. . . ."[177] Harkening back to the "rights of Englishmen; the rights which had been wrested from English sovereigns at various periods of the nation's history," and to Blackstone, Bradley speaks the language of fundamental rights, rights "which can only be taken away . . . [or] interfered with, or the enjoy-

---

[172] 83 U.S. at 77.
[173] *Ibid.* at 79.
[174] *Ibid.* at 89.
[175] *Ibid.* at 101.
[176] *Ibid.* at 105.
[177] *Ibid.* at 116.

ment of which can only be modified, by lawful regulations necessary or proper for the mutual good of all. . . ."[178]

Together with these broad principles, Field points out that the grant of the monopoly to seventeen New Orleans butchers is not, in itself, necessarily a *health* regulation; the only law which could properly be labeled a health law would be "one which requires the landing and slaughtering of animals below the city," and one "which requires the inspection of the animals before they are slaughtered."[179] *Who* does the slaughtering, or the number of butchers who do it, is irrelevant to the public health.

In this argument—which makes a great deal of intrinsic sense—Bradley and Field are examining the relationship between the state's stated goals and the means it chooses to reach those goals, an inquiry that will become central to much Fourteenth Amendment litigation. Here, they are asking for a better "fit" between means and ends than the state has provided; that is, although the state's goal is laudable (protecting the public health), the means it has chosen to achieve that goal (the monopoly) is too broad and too loosely connected to the stated goal to survive the scrutiny of the Fourteenth Amendment.[180]

Field and Bradley soon commanded a majority for their expansive reading of fundamental rights. Within a few years in the mid-1870s, the Court reached broad agreement on the basic framework of Fourteenth Amendment litigation.[181] Nelson lists three elements of this agreement: (1) Section 1 of the Fourteenth Amendment "protected property and, by implication other rights . . ."; (2) the states "could regulate protected rights as long as their regulations were reasonable"; (3) reasonable regulations were "those that furthered the public good and were equal in their impact."[182] These last two points are, of course, crucial,

---

[178] *Ibid.* at 114, 116.

[179] *Ibid.* at 87. See also Justice Bradley's dissent at 120.

[180] This form of Fourteenth Amendment analysis turns upon one interpretation of what is "reasonable"—a law is "reasonable" if there is a sufficiently close relationship between a state's means and the legislative ends. A different Fourteenth Amendment methodology would equate "reasonable" with "that which is traditional," as in Plessy v. Ferguson, 163 U.S. 537 (1896), where the Court sustained the constitutionality of separate but "equal" facilities for whites and blacks. See Nelson, *Fourteenth Amendment*, 176. The logical flaw of the latter definition is clear: "tradition" may well include the persecution of a minority. Equating "reasonable" with "that which is traditional" gives carte blanche to a political majority, and eviscerates any protection of a minority against mistreatment or exploitation. See below, pp. 128–31.

[181] Nelson, *Fourteenth Amendment*, 174.

[182] *Ibid.*

for the definition of what is "reasonable," or of what exactly furthered the public good, could be answered either in an expansive or in a highly limited manner. In a very indirect sense, the monopoly granted in New Orleans contributed to the public health; whether *this amount* of indirection ran afoul of the Fourteenth Amendment was a question different justices could (and did) answer differently.

These doctrinal developments in the 1870s coincided, of course, with rapid industrialization. As a number of historians of the period have documented, "the relative influence of lawyers and courts on the character of public policy notably expanded during the years of America's industrialization," as "neither the party system, nor the state or national legislatures, nor a still primitive structure of public administration could respond" to the changing economy.[183] Into this void stepped a conservative bench and bar, armed with an "increasingly elaborate apparatus of journals and treatises, legal theory, and legal professionalism."[184] Thomas Cooley published his *Constitutional Limitations* in 1868, the same year as the ratification of the Fourteenth Amendment. Arguing strenuously that courts ought to actively protect personal rights, especially economic rights, Cooley's book was the best-selling legal treatise of its generation.[185]

This economic conservatism slid easily into the already entrenched ideology of natural rights under which the Constitution and Fourteenth Amendment had been written. The black box had long been in place, and now would be "revealed" to have new items within. The idea that state and federal regulatory laws, emerging during this period of rapid economic change, were invading the sacred rights of liberty and property, without adequate constitutional justification, gave the formerly vague ideology of natural rights its first real and organized substantive meaning. The blackness of the box faded to a more subtle gray; the contents became clearer.

It is easy to view this development as inevitable given the economic realities of the age. But Morton Keller argues that, at least for some justices, such as Field and Brewer, this development "was something more than subservience to vested interests."[186] Field "adhered to old American values of private right and individual freedom that led him

---

[183] Morton Keller, *Affairs of State: Public Life in Late Nineteenth Century America* (Cambridge, Mass.: Belknap Press of Harvard University Press, 1977), 343.
[184] *Ibid.*, 344.
[185] *Ibid.*, 345–46.
[186] *Ibid.*, 367.

to be as ill at ease with corporate power as he was with legislative activism."[187] Other justices, however, had no difficulty embracing corporate capitalism, leading to the eventual definition of a corporation as a legal "person" entitled to Fourteenth Amendment protection.[188]

The result of these developments was, from the late 1880s on, a judicial "revolution,"[189] as state and federal regulations increasingly fell to the Court's definition of "substantive" due process. Although the Court had declared only two federal laws unconstitutional before 1864, it struck down ten between 1864 and 1875, and eleven between 1875 and 1898.[190] Of 217 state laws struck down by the Court before 1910, 48 were struck down during the 1880s, the "peak" decade of economic due process.[191]

This reading of laissez-faire economics into the due process clause, however, was not inevitable. At every step, some justices dissented vigorously from the Court's holdings. A more expansive reading of the states' "police" powers (to be taken up in the next chapter) would have allowed the Court to sustain much of the regulatory legislation it struck down. What this economically conservative reading of due process demonstrates, above all, is the extraordinary "embeddedness" of Supreme Court doctrine in larger social and intellectual developments.

To reflect further on this phenomenon and its jurisprudential implications, and to answer the quandary with which we began—can the Fourteenth Amendment be said to protect abortion rights in the late twentieth century—we must examine more closely several things: the manner in which the Supreme Court manipulated doctrine to achieve laissez-faire results; the abandonment of laissez-faire in the New Deal; the "rebirth" of substantive due process in the 1960s and 1970s, this time redefined to protect privacy. Although the black box has remained in place, its contents have been radically redefined over the course of American history. We should not forget, however, that the box itself was put in place by the Constitution, the original document and the Fourteenth Amendment.

---

[187] *Ibid.*
[188] See Santa Clara County v. Southern Pacific Railroad, 118 U.S. 394 (1886).
[189] Keller, *Affairs of State*, 369.
[190] *Ibid.*
[191] *Ibid.*

CHAPTER 3

POLICE POWERS, NEUTRAL PRINCIPLES, AND CONSTITUTIONAL CHANGE

I.

In 1905 the Supreme Court declared that the state of New York could not regulate the number of hours bakers could work.[1] The law in question had limited bakers to ten hours a day and sixty hours a week. Writing for the majority, Justice Peckham found that the statute "necessarily interferes with the right of contract between the employer and employes [sic]."[2] The "general right to make a contract in relation to his business," Peckham continues, "is part of the liberty of the individual protected by the Fourteenth Amendment of the Federal Constitution."[3]

In 1965 the Supreme Court struck down a Connecticut statute which made it a crime to use or to assist individuals in the use of "any drug, medicinal article or instrument for the purpose of preventing conception." Justice Douglas, writing for the majority, found the statute to be a violation to a right of privacy, a right that, he said, originates in the "penumbras" and "emanations" of the "specific guarantees in the Bill of Rights." The Connecticut case, Douglas says, "concerns a relationship lying within the zone of privacy created by several fundamental constitutional guarantees."[4]

---

[1] Lochner v. New York, 198 U.S. 45 (1905).
[2] *Ibid.* at 53.
[3] *Ibid.*
[4] Griswold v. Connecticut, 381 U.S. 479, 480–85 (1965).

A few years later, in 1973, the Court found the right of privacy "broad enough to encompass a woman's decision whether or not to terminate her pregnancy." The right of privacy, Justice Blackmun wrote for the majority, can be found either "in the Fourteenth Amendment's concept of personal liberty and restrictions upon state action," or "as the District Court determined, in the Ninth Amendment's reservation of rights to the people. . . ."[5]

Much of modern jurisprudential thought has been taken up with these three cases and the relation among them.[6] *Lochner* and its philosophy, of course, were renounced by the Court in the wake of the New Deal. "Rejection of the *Lochner* heritage," as Gerald Gunther comments, "is a common starting point for modern Justices. . . ."[7]; the term *Lochnerizing*[8] is used by many commentators as a shorthand expression for the action of a judge who mistakenly finds his own values in the Constitution. "For critics and proponents alike," Paul Brest and Sanford Levinson comment, "Lochner v. New York symbolizes the dark side of fundamental rights adjudication."[9]

We might say, then, that modern constitutional discourse has been dominated by a question and a quest. The question is relatively straightforward: Can we, today, accept the legitimacy of the Supreme Court's decisions in *Griswold* and *Roe* while at the same time condemning *Lochner?* More generally, if we reject the jurisprudence of *Lochner*—a jurisprudence that enshrined a now-outmoded theory of economic relationships—can we, at the same time, accept the modern court's decision making based upon "fundamental" rights? Both kinds of decision rest upon some understanding of "liberty," and the kind of liberty the due process clause was meant to protect; both depend on the declaration of a constitutional value ("liberty of contract" in *Lochner;* "privacy" in *Griswold* and *Roe*) nowhere mentioned in the document.

The stakes are high in posing this question, for more rights are at issue than privacy rights; implicated in this question is any constitu-

---

[5] Roe v. Wade, 410 U.S. 113, 153 (1973).

[6] See, for example, Laurence H. Tribe and Michael C. Dorf, "Levels of Generality in the Definition of Rights," *University of Chicago Law Review* 57 (Fall 1990): 1060–66.

[7] Gerald Gunther, *Constitutional Law,* 11th ed. (Mineola, N.Y.: Foundation Press, 1985), 454.

[8] The term is John Hart Ely's in "The Wages of Crying Wolf: A Comment on Roe v. Wade," *Yale Law Journal* 82 (April 1973): 944.

[9] Paul Brest and Sanford Levinson, *Processes of Constitutional Decisionmaking,* 2nd ed. (Boston: Little, Brown, 1983), 691.

tional decision that rests upon a "modern" reading of constitutional values. For example, if Justice Peckham and his brethren were "wrong" to find liberty of contract in the due process clause (and to find the New York statute in *Lochner* to be in violation of that liberty) can we say that Chief Justice Warren was "right" to find segregated schools a violation of equal protection—a decision that rested on the concept of "stigmatic" injury derived from modern social science? Thus Brown v. Board,[10] no less than *Griswold* and *Roe,* becomes problematic when the analogy to *Lochner* is made.

The Court itself in *Griswold* was extraordinarily nervous about the analogy that might be made to *Lochner.* "Overtones of some arguments," Justice Douglas wrote in his majority opinion, "suggest that Lochner v. New York . . . should be our guide. But we decline that invitation. . . . We do not sit as a super-legislature to determine the wisdom, need, and propriety of laws that touch economic problems, business affairs, or social conditions."[11] But, in the very next sentence, Douglas presents us with one of the most charmingly contradictory non sequiturs in all of constitutional discourse: "This law, however, operates directly on an intimate relation of husband and wife and their physician's role in one aspect of that relation."[12] Without admitting it, Douglas is invoking the methodology of substantive due process; he is saying that the intimacy of a husband and wife are within the black box of fundamental rights.

These questions about *Brown, Griswold,* and *Roe* point to the "quest" of modern jurisprudence—at least its mainstream academic branch—the quest for "neutral" principles. No criticism of a controversial decision is more common than the Court "violated" such principles; the critical literature in the wake of both *Brown* and *Griswold*—not to mention Roe v. Wade—is replete with such criticisms. Herbert Wechsler, the scholar most responsible for the use of the phrase "neutral principles" in modern commentary, says, in essence, that the Court, in *Brown,* ignored them.[13] "To be sure," Wechsler says,

---

[10] Brown v. Board of Education, 347 U.S. 483 (1954). For a discussion of stigma, see below, pp. 91–92.
[11] 381 U.S. at 481–82. Also see the comments of Justice White in Bowers v. Hardwick, 478 U.S. 193, 194–95 (1986). As Kenneth Karst has commented, the Court "labors" to avoid the rhetoric of substantive due process. "Freedom of Intimate Association," *Yale Law Journal* 89 (March 1980): 653, 664.
[12] 381 U.S. at 482.
[13] Herbert Wechsler, "Toward Neutral Principles of Constitutional Law," *Harvard Law Review* 73 (November 1959): 31–34.

the courts decide, or should decide, only the case they have before them. But must they not decide on grounds of adequate neutrality and generality, tested not only by the instant application but by others that the principles imply? Is it not the very essence of judicial method to insist upon attending to such other cases, preferably those involving an opposing interest, in evaluating any principle avowed?[14]

Other scholars have similarly made "neutrality" a key test of constitutional soundness. Robert Bork warned us as early as 1971 that "[w]e have not carried the idea of neutrality far enough"; not only must principles be applied neutrally, he wrote, but "if judges are to avoid imposing their own values upon the rest of us . . . they must be neutral as well in the *definition* and the *derivation* of principles."[15] Otherwise, we are left with a Court "that makes rather than implements value choices" and this, Bork tells us, is equivalent to "limited coups d'etat."[16]

It is not only the extremely conservative commentator who embraces neutrality as a desirable goal; John Ely seems to endorse the general idea of neutrality as well, as when he writes, in his criticism of Roe v. Wade, that "[a] neutral and durable principle may be a thing of beauty and a joy forever," so long as the principle in question has sufficient "connection" with "any value the Constitution marks as special."[17]

As these brief quotations suggest, the quest for neutral principles is a symptom of an even larger theoretical problem. In fact, modern jurisprudence is preoccupied with the idea of neutrality and with the *Lochner* analogy because it is still seeking to define the appropriate relationship between law and politics. In whatever form this dichotomy is expressed—law versus politics, judicial review versus democracy— it is the issue that runs like a red thread through a great deal of what is said by, and about, the Court. Americans want to believe that they are governed not by men but by law—immutable law, knowable and durable (if not quite unchangeable), sanctified by the document and the

---

[14] *Ibid.,* 15.

[15] Robert H. Bork, "Neutral Principles and Some First Amendment Problems," *Indiana Law Journal* 47 (Fall 1971): 7; emphasis in original.

[16] *Ibid.,* 6. Bork has recently expanded on these themes in *The Tempting of America: The Political Seduction of the Law* (New York: Free Press, 1990).

[17] Ely, "Wages of Crying Wolf," 949. See also Ely's discussion in *Democracy and Distrust: A Theory of Judicial Review* (Cambridge, Mass.: Harvard University Press, 1980), 54–55.

nobility of the framers. Those who seek "neutrality" are uncomfortable with the idea that the law might be tainted by politics.

But, as we saw in the previous chapter, there is an inevitable connection between law and politics, for (among other reasons) we cannot interpret the Constitution's "liberty" without reference to the liberty theorem, which states that liberty can be restricted only for agreed, limited purposes. And such "agreement" about restrictions of liberty will be, in a very basic sense, "political"—and subject to change. We have also seen that the Fourteenth Amendment requires a similar connection between law and politics, for it calls for judgment about what state classifications are "reasonable," and such judgments can only be made with reference to relevant social data.[18]

This chapter explores in further detail those relationships between law and politics. It begins with an anthropological discussion of the law/fact distinction, which provides a useful theoretical starting point. Next, we examine one particularly important constitutional mechanism—the police powers doctrine—that the Supreme Court uses to implement changes in America's underlying "agreement" about liberty. This leads to a consideration of the place of social "facts" in constitutional decision making, with examples drawn from different types of cases.

II.

The first step in the argument is to understand why law and politics cannot be kept separate—are in fact not separate things—and a useful place to begin is with the law/fact distinction, and with a comparative perspective on that distinction. The Western legal tradition assumes a sharp distinction between rules and judgments—the law—and events in the real world—the facts. The facts—who did what to whom, who promised what, with what sort of conditions attached—are matters of evidence; in many types of case, juries are left to decide what really "happened." But a comparative perspective challenges this strict conceptual distinction between law and facts. And, in a more general sense, if there is no such thing as "pure law" separate from particular sets of facts, then the distinction between law and politics—between law and how things "are" in the world—becomes more difficult to maintain. Moreover, when one sees what counts as a "law" in other cultural contexts, one begins to wonder whether law can be said to exist apart from a specific social context.

[18] See above, pp. 63–66.

The most useful perspective on this issue is that offered by legal anthropology.[19] Clifford Geertz points out that anthropology and jurisprudence are similar; they both "see . . . broad principles in parochial facts."[20] Geertz examines the law/fact distinction and points out that there is a fact "problem" in modern legal analysis. We face the "[e]xplosion of fact, fear of fact, and, in response to these, sterilization of fact"—and this is a "chronic focus of legal anxiety."[21] In other words, modern law sometimes has great difficulty deciding what is "true" about the world.[22] The difficulty that modern legal analysis has absorbing and using "facts" is a reflection, Geertz says, of

[19] For another discussion of the relation between law and facts, see Kim Lane Scheppele, *Legal Secrets: Equality and Efficiency in the Common Law* (Chicago: University of Chicago Press, 1988), esp. 95–105.

[20] Clifford Geertz, *Local Knowledge: Further Essays in Interpretive Anthropology* (New York: Basic Books, 1983), 167.

[21] *Ibid.*, 171.

[22] Geertz is worth quoting at length:
> The explosion of fact can be seen on all sides. There are the discovery procedures that produce paper warriors dispatching documents to each other in wheelbarrows and taking depositions from anyone capable of talking into a tape recorder. There is the enormous intricacy of commercial cases through which not even the treasurer of IBM much less a poor judge or juror could find his way. There is the vast increase in the use of expert witnesses; not just the icy pathologist and bubbling psychiatrist of long acquaintance but people who are supposed to know all about Indian burial grounds, Bayesian probability, the literary quality of erotic novels, the settlement history of Cape Cod, Filipino speech styles, or the conceptual mysteries—"What is a chicken? Anything that is not a duck, a turkey, or a goose"—of the poultry trade. There is the growth of public law litigation—class action, institutional advocacy, *amicus* pleading, special masters, and so on—which has gotten judges involved in knowing more about mental hospitals in Alabama, real estate in Chicago, police in Philadelphia, or anthropology departments in Providence than they might care to know. There is the technical restlessness, a sort of rage to invent, of contemporary life which brings such uncertain sciences as electronic bugging, voice printing, public opinion polling, intelligence testing, lie detecting and, in a famous instance, doll play under judicial scrutiny alongside the more settled ones of ballistics and fingerprinting. But most of all there is the general revolution of rising expectations as to the possibilities of fact determination and its power to settle intractable issues that the general culture of scientism has induced in us all; the sort of thing that perhaps led Mr. Justice Blackmun into the labyrinths of embryology (and now following him with less dispassionate intent, various congressmen) in search of an answer to the question of abortion. *Ibid.*, 171.

a rather more fundamental phenomenon, the one in fact upon which all culture rests: namely, that of representation. The rendering of fact so that lawyers can plead it, judges can hear it, and juries can settle it is just that, a rendering: as any other trade, science, cult or art, law, which is a bit of all of these, propounds the world in which its descriptions make sense.[23]

What Geertz is saying here is that the law depends upon construing how things "are" in the world, and that deciding how things "are" in the world varies from culture to culture. Law always has a particular, and peculiar, manner of rendering "facts." Law, Geertz says, "is not a bounded set of norms, rules, principles, values, or whatever from which jural responses to distilled events can be drawn, but part of a distinctive manner of imagining the real."[24] The key word here is *imagining;* how "facts" and "law" are "imagined" is a process that varies from culture to culture. Legal facts, Geertz says, "are socially constructed . . . by everything from evidence rules, courtroom etiquette, and law reporting traditions, to advocacy techniques, the rhetoric of judges, and the scholasticisms of law school education. . . ." Law, Geertz tells us, is "a distinctive manner of imagining the real"—it is a form of "local knowledge."[25]

Look closely at any society, Geertz is saying, and we can say that what counts as a "fact" and what counts as a legal "rule" or "principle" are difficult to separate. Moreover, they bear a direct relationship to the organizing ideology of a society—to what people believe is good and bad, right and wrong, just and unjust. And such beliefs, of course, are "political" to their very core. Law is one way in which people give meaning to the world around them; a society with private property will have a different concept of "right" than one without; a religious society will have a different concept of "duty" than a secular one; different cultures will have different ideas of "truth" and "proof"— and so on. These ideas will determine not merely the *content* of legal rules, but what *counts* as a legal rule, or a legal fact, in the first place.[26]

---

[23] *Ibid.,* 173.

[24] *Ibid.*

[25] *Ibid.*

[26] In one sense, Geertz's insights may seem to undercut an important part of my overall argument—that we can "know" social facts that are relevant to deciding constitutional cases. But Geertz's analysis implies only that what we do or do not "count" as a "fact" is culturally and normatively determined; he does not make the more radical argument that there can be no such thing as a legal or social "fact." Without "facts," Geertz clearly implies, there can be no law.

Adjudication, Geertz says, proceeds back and forth between two kinds of statements: "If-then" statements of general precept, and "as-therefore" statements of concrete application. The first is a language of "general coherence"; the latter, a language of "specific consequence." The task of anyone who wishes to understand a particular legal system—a legal "sensibility"—is to elucidate those crucial words that carry these cultural messages. These words will carry "coherence images"—that is, they will tell us much about what that society believes, about how the members of that society make their world coherent. Geertz illustrates his argument by examining three such words in three different cultures; a word meaning (very roughly) "truth" in the Islamic world; a word meaning "duty" (and more) in Indic culture; and a word meaning (roughly) "practice" in Malaysian society.[27]

Geertz does not venture into American constitutional discourse, but his insights are useful nonetheless. If we direct our attention to constitutional language,[28] we will find buried in the use of various terms and phrases many of the "coherence images" that constitutional law embodies—beliefs about right and wrong, good and bad, just and unjust, and—in many cases, the ultimate question—the proper role of government. This point can be illustrated by focusing upon one set of terms in particular—those surrounding the idea of the state's "police power" (which includes the concept of the "general" or "public" "welfare"); it is within the contours of this phrase that a great deal that really matters to constitutional decision making takes place.

III.

The "police powers" are usually defined generically by the Supreme Court as the power of a state "to promote the health, safety, morals and general welfare" of the population.[29] The Court defined it in one case as "the power of the State to establish all regulations that are reasonably necessary to secure the health, safety, good order, comfort, or general welfare of the community"[30]—the verbiage varies a little from case to case, but usually follows this fairly standard form. It is

---

[27] *Ibid.*, 174–75 and 183ff.

[28] For an excellent discussion, see John Brigham, *Constitutional Language: An Interpretation of Judicial Decision* (Westport, Conn.: Greenwood Press, 1978).

[29] See Edward S. Corwin's *The Constitution and What It Means Today* (Princeton: Princeton University Press, 1973), 77.

[30] Atlantic Coast Line Co. v. Goldsboro, 232 U.S. 548 (1914), quoted in *ibid.*, 140, n.20.

the power, the Court once candidly admitted, "to govern men and things."[31] The police power, the Court said in the *Slaughter-House* case, "is, and must be from its very nature, incapable of any very exact definition or limitation"[32]; it is, "to use the old phrase . . . an inherent attribute of sovereignty at all levels of government."[33]

Police power allows states to regulate the content of food and drugs; it allows the states to compel education to a certain age and to require schoolchildren to have certain kinds of inoculations; it allows the states to pass licensing requirements for numerous professions; it allows the state to regulate the age at which one may drink, marry, drive an automobile, make informed and knowing decisions (intimate or otherwise) about the direction of one's life; it allows countless regulations of industry—in short, it allows the state to proceed with much of what it does to govern day-to-day life.

More specifically, the phrase "police powers" is the way Americans designate the realm of normally acceptable restrictions of liberty; generally, we say that the state can exercise its police powers only to protect the "general welfare." Thus "police powers" is the phrase that captures the constitutionally acceptable *exceptions* to the liberty theorem. The Constitution, we may say, "contains" the idea of police powers (although they are not, literally, mentioned in the text; they must be derived from the Constitution's overall structure) as well as the idea of the general welfare (which *is* mentioned, twice: in the preamble, and in the list of general congressional powers in Article 1, section 8).

There are many things to notice about this concept of police power; that it always contains some concept of "harm" that the state may reasonably prevent; that, however it be defined, it will contain ideas about the proper scope of government authority—the spheres of life the government may and may not enter; that where one puts the burden of proof—on those who challenge the state's exercise of the power, or upon the state itself in the first instance—will make an enormous difference to the outcome of any particular case.

More importantly, when one examines the cases in which the Supreme Court has invoked the police power—either in overturning or in sustaining legislation—one is struck by two things: the fact that its substantive content has changed over time, and, furthermore, that the

[31] License Cases, 5 U.S. 504, 583 (1847).

[32] 83 U.S. 36, 62 (1873).

[33] Richard A. Epstein, *Takings: Private Property and the Power of Eminent Domain* (Cambridge, Mass.: Harvard University Press, 1985), 107.

generic term is never really defined or defended—it is simply invoked, usually in vague language, seldom with anything so much as a footnote attached to it. The state's police power is just one of those things that is somehow *there;* there is no equivalent of Marbury v. Madison or McCulloch v. Maryland, magisterially established, once and for all, a clear and unequivocal precedent; there is no single clause to hitch it to; there is no single ancient provision of British common law, no clause of Magna Carta, to which we can confidently point to prove its existence.

If we take the long historical view, we see several more things of interest about the police power. First, that it seems to have gained importance over the course of the nineteenth century as a "meta-" doctrine that could limit another "meta-"doctrine, that of vested rights.[34] In its own turn, the idea of vested rights had arisen as one of the principal judicial means of limiting popular sovereignty.[35] In fact, the closer one looks the more the whole thing seems extraordinarily Hegelian; as Michael Perry puts it, "[s]overeign state legislative power was the thesis; the doctrine of vested rights, limiting the sovereign power, was the antithesis; and the doctrine of police power, which sanctioned the invasion of vested rights for the sake of the public welfare, was the synthesis."[36] At the same time as the police powers doctrine was working to undermine the theory of vested rights, other forces[37] were working to turn the due process clause of the Fourteenth Amendment into the new locus of fundamental rights (which the concept of vested rights had originally been elaborated to protect). Thus, early in the nineteenth century, the contest was between vested rights and the police power; by the close of the century, the contest was between substantive due process and the police power.

The back-and-forth character of these doctrines—police powers on one side, vested rights or substantive due process on the other—points to an important conclusion. "Police powers" are really the ultimate elastic doctrine in constitutional analysis; whatever the Court's notion of the sphere of fundamental personal rights at any given point in time, "the" police powers are adjusted, like an accordion, to account for

---

[34] See pp. 51–55.

[35] See Michael Perry, "Abortion, the Public Morals, and the Police Power: The Ethical Function of Substantive Due Process," *UCLA Law Review* 23 (April 1976): 697. Perry draws extensively upon the work of Corwin; see esp. Corwin's *Liberty Against Government* (Baton Rouge: Louisiana State University Press, 1948).

[36] Perry, "Abortion, Public Morals, and Police Power," 697–98, n.44.

[37] See above, pp. 66–71.

what—according to the Court—society is willing to regard as reasonable invasions of those rights for the public good. An examination of what the Court says about police powers thus becomes a key component of fundamental rights analysis; just as a virus can sometimes be detected only by the presence of antibodies, there will be times when the best measure of how the Court is defining fundamental rights will be to look at what the Court says about police powers.

Thus, whether explicitly mentioned or not, different accounts of the police power can be found at the root of any number of major controversial cases, past and present. In fact, one begins to suspect that this vague concept is the key to what is really happening in a vast majority of important constitutional cases that bring significant changes to constitutional doctrine. This is true, for example, of *Lochner*, the case that sends shudders through contemporary defenders of fundamental-rights adjudication.

IV.

Lochner is usually discussed as an example of a now-discredited theory of substantive due process. That it may be, but it is discredited as due process *because* our underlying ideas about appropriate police powers have changed. To recall the facts for a moment, New York had passed legislation limiting the number of hours a baker could work. The state said that this was a health measure—and thus a justified exercise of its police power—although the majority of the Court suspected that it was really a labor law masquerading as a health measure. "Clean and wholesome bread," Justice Peckham wrote, "does not depend upon whether the baker works but ten hours per day or only sixty hours a week." And, if the law *is* a health law, the state's chosen means of pursuing "health" are not sufficiently related to its stated goal: "The mere assertion that the subject relates though but in a remote degree to the public health does not necessarily render the enactment valid. The act must have a more direct relation, as a means to an end, and the end itself must be appropriate and legitimate. . . ."[38] There can be "no fair doubt," according to Peckham, "that the trade of a baker, in and of itself, is not an unhealthy one to that degree which would authorize the legislature to interfere. . . ."[39]

As for "the question whether this act is valid as a labor law," Peckham writes, this

[38] 198 U.S. at 57.
[39] *Ibid.* at 59.

may be dismissed in a few words. There is no reasonable ground for interfering with the liberty of person or the right of free contract. . . . There is no contention that bakers as a class are not equal in intelligence and capacity to men in other trades or manual occupations, or that they are not able to assert their rights and care for themselves without the protecting arm of the State, interfering with their independence of judgment and of action. They are in no sense wards of the State.[40]

Statutes such as this, "limiting the hours in which grown and intelligent men may labor to earn their living, are mere meddlesome interferences with the rights of the individual," and such laws are "not saved from condemnation by the claim that they are passed in the exercise of the police power and upon the subject of the health of the individual . . . unless there be some fair ground, reasonable in and of itself, to say that there is material danger to the public health or to the health of the employes [sic]."[41] Given the state's inadequate grounds for action, the statute's interference with "liberty" renders it unconstitutional under the Fourteenth Amendment. "The right to purchase or to sell labor is part of the liberty protected by this amendment, unless there are circumstances which exclude the right."[42]

The majority in *Lochner* is usually criticized for *finding* a "liberty of contract" in the due process clause.[43] But is it not far more accurate to say that the majority erred (if it erred at all) in not construing New York's police powers broadly enough to *allow* this particular invasion of the liberty of contract to stand? Would anyone candidly deny that

[40] *Ibid.* at 57.
[41] *Ibid.* at 61.
[42] *Ibid.* at 53.
[43] For example, one commentator speaks of the "naive" assumption that "the individual employee of a great industrial corporation" could be said to possess "full liberty of contract . . . [to] dicker with his employer upon equal terms." Robert F. Cushman, *Leading Constitutional Decisions,* 16th ed. (Englewood Cliffs, N.J.: Prentice-Hall, 1982), 150. Another says that the Court's "program of defining rights" in cases such as Lochner was "an attempt to deal with the problem of the perceived illegitimacy of forms of domination by making them seem to *disappear,* i.e., by making all coercion seem to be the result of . . . consent. . . ." Robert Gordon, "Legal Thought and Legal Practice in the Age of American Enterprise, 1870–1920," in Gerald Greison (ed.), *Professions and Professional Ideologies in America* (Chapel Hill: University of North Carolina Press, 1983), quoted in Brest and Levinson, *Processes of Constitutional Decisionmaking,* 233.

the right to make a contract *is* a fundamental right in Anglo-American law? Away from discussions of this particular notorious case, probably not.[44]

In this particular weighing of police powers versus vested rights now residing in the due process clause, the Court's majority (we would say today) did not rank the constitutional values correctly. This is, in fact, what Justice Harlan says in his dissent in the case, making his opinion far superior than the more famous dissent by Justice Holmes. Harlan grants that liberty of contract exists, and weighs it against the state's police power. He finds that there is a "real . . . substantial" relationship between the New York statute and health. Examining the scientific basis for the legislature's enactment of the law, he quotes a Professor Hirt, who, "in his treatise on the 'Diseases of the Workers,' has said: 'The labor of the bakers is among the hardest and most laborious imaginable,' " as well as another author who writes that "the constant inhaling of flour dust causes inflammation of the lungs and of the bronchial tubes. The eyes also suffer through this dust. . . . The long hours of toil to which all bakers are subjected produces rheumatism, cramps, and swollen legs." Thus "it is plain," Harlan writes, "that this statute was enacted in order to protect the physical well-being of those who work in bakery and confectionery establishments."[45]

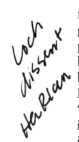

For his part, Justice Holmes ignores the police powers question, and states that "this case is decided upon an economic theory which a large part of the country does not entertain." On economic questions, he says, the Court should not interfere with "the right of a majority to embody their opinions in law."[46] In effect, Holmes is saying that state legislatures can do what they please; he avoids the real choice between legitimate constitutional values that the case presents.

Lochner has come to stand for a discredited generation of constitutional law; modern commentators speak of the "stench . . . surrounding the whole concept of substantive due process,"[47] and the Court itself has explicitly discussed its reluctance to base decisions on such grounds.[48] But we should not lose sight of why *Lochner* is a "bad"

---

[44] On the existence of a right to contract see Stephen Mecedo, *Liberal Virtues: Citizenship, Virtue, and Community in Liberal Constitutionalism* (Oxford: Clarendon Press, 1990), 180.

[45] 198 U.S. at 69, 70.

[46] *Ibid.* at 75.

[47] Henry Paul Monaghan, "Of 'Liberty' and 'Property,' " *Cornell Law Review* 62 (March 1977): 417.

[48] See, for example, Justice Stewart's concurrence in Zablocki v. Redhail, 434 U.S. 374, 395–96 (1978).

decision. It is not because the majority of the Court gave substantive content to "liberty," but rather because the majority stubbornly refused to take seriously the social and scientific facts supporting New York's exercise of its police powers. New York had good reasons for its actions, even by the standards of 1905, as Justice Harlan's citations from relevant authorities make clear. The "stench" of *Lochner* is created by a Supreme Court that refused to see the world as it is. We can, today, be even more confident than Justice Harlan that New York had good reason for acting, not merely to protect the health of bakers but also to redress the inequalities of bargaining position between employer and employee.

For the majority of the Court in 1905, however, the "agreement" of American society protected by the Fourteenth Amendment was this: that liberty could be curtailed only to protect the *total* public good;[49] a given occupation could not be singled out for special legislative solicitude, either on matters of health or on matters of economics.

V.

Our judgment that the Court erred in *Lochner* is one we can make confidently today (especially on the question of the bakers' bargaining position) only because of intervening political events. If we look at those cases that constitute the revolution in constitutional law that allowed the New Deal to go forward, what is really going on is a change in the underlying concept of the state's police powers. In the wake of a major sea change in American politics—and Roosevelt's Court-packing threat—the Supreme Court in the late 1930s found adequate constitutional grounds for congressional and state legislative action aimed at promoting a kind of economic "welfare" previously believed to lie outside the realm of governmental power. Thus the New Deal, we can say, changed the basic "agreement" of the American people about the reasons the state could legitimately offer for the curtailment of liberty.

As a result of this political change, the Supreme Court began to use a completely new rhetoric. For example, in one case sustaining the constitutionality of a mortgage moratorium law passed by the Minnesota legislature, Chief Justice Hughes writes words that would have been unthinkable ten years previously. "The policy of protecting contracts against impairment," Chief Justice Hughes tells us,

[49] See Laurence H. Tribe, *American Constitutional Law*, 2nd ed. (Mineola, N.Y.: Foundation Press, 1988), 571.

presupposes the maintenance of a government by virtue of which contractual relations are worth while,—a government which retains adequate authority to secure the peace and good order of society. This principle of harmonizing the constitutional prohibition with the necessary residuum of state power has had progressive recognition in the decisions of this Court.[50]

The law passed by the Minnesota legislature granted temporary relief from mortgage foreclosures; Minnesota, of course, is a farm state, and hundreds of family farms were threatened.

The moratorium passed by the Minnesota legislature, without question, violated, in a strict sense, the clause of the Constitution forbidding states to "impair the obligation of contracts"[51]—*unless* we graft onto the case something like Hughes's statement that all constitutional provisions must be read in light of a larger state power—a police power, really—to maintain the very existence of the state. Hughes's statement, we should remember, constitutes a deft political maneuver—there is nothing in the text of the document that requires such a reading of the contract clause.

Moreover, Hughes is engaging in hyperbole—does anyone really believe that the state of Minnesota would have fallen into civil war if the mortgage foreclosures had been allowed to go forward? There would have been some unpleasantness, much true suffering, certainly; a few bank managers shot at, some agitation in St. Paul—but would the government of the state really have ceased to *exist?* What Hughes is really saying—but could not say, in so many words, for fear of revealing just how "political" and extra-constitutional his decision was—is that now, today, in the wake of our recent experience, we believe different things about the correct role of government vis-a-vis the economy; we now believe that protecting the sanctity of individual contracts (despite the clause of the Constitution that seemingly requires the states to keep their hands off) is not the state's highest duty; that the state has obligations to protect the general welfare that go beyond protecting their private, individual contracts.

In his dissent in the Minnesota case Justice Sutherland points out— quite correctly—that the contract clause was originally written against a background of various kinds of state legislation passed for the relief of

---

[50] Home Building and Loan Assoc. v. Blaisdell, 290 U.S. 398, 435 (1934). For an alternative reading of this case, see Gary J. Jacobsohn, *Pragmatism, Statesmanship, and the Supreme Court* (Ithaca, N.Y.: Cornell University Press, 1977), 183–93.

[51] U.S. Constitution, Article I, Section 10, Clause 1.

debtors in the 1780s, quite similar to the Minnesota legislation at issue here. Numerous historians have emphasized the contribution such legislation made to the growing desire in the years preceding 1787 to call a constitutional convention.[52] Contemporary academic defenders of Hughes's opinion, such as Charles Miller, attempt to alleviate the burden of this historical record by arguing that the earlier relief legislation (in the 1780s) "exacerbated economic instability," whereas the Minnesota law was in keeping with the "large purpose" of the contract clause, "the smooth functioning of the economy." In Minnesota, Miller writes, "economic conditions were completely different."[53] This is, of course, hindsight; in 1934, no one could say with any certainty what course of action would "exacerbate economic instability."

Choosing between Hughes and Sutherland in this case would not be an easy task. And whatever the choice, there is no way to make it on purely legal or textual grounds. Deciding the case required attention either to the historical background of the contract clause (for Sutherland) and a *judgment* that the economic situation of the 1780s was sufficiently similar to the situation of the 1930s to be controlling, or attention (for Hughes) to recent cataclysmic political and economic events, and a *judgment* about the relevance of these events to the action of the Minnesota legislature. A bare majority of the Court chose to interpret the contract clause as Hughes did, but, again, there is nothing inevitable about such a choice.

Other clauses of the Constitution were similarly reinterpreted in the late 1930s; the New Deal accelerated a process, begun earlier in the century, by which the commerce clause, in particular, became a kind of *federal* police power clause, permitting (by previous standards) extraordinarily broad congressional action. Once again, such changes could take place only because a majority of the Supreme Court admitted into its decision making process certain "facts" about the economy it had previously chosen to cast as irrelevant.

[52] See above, pp. 45–46.

[53] Charles A. Miller, *The Supreme Court and the Uses of History* (Cambridge, Mass.: Belknap Press of Harvard University Press, 1969), 45–46.

[54] See below, pp. xx. See also Tribe, *American Constitutional Law*, 437, and C. Herman Pritchett, *Constitutional Law of the Federal System* (Englewood Cliffs, N.J.: Prentice-Hall, 1984), 222–39.

[55] For example, in sustaining the Wagner Act, the Court found adequate basis for Congressional action to forbid any person from engaging in any unfair labor practice "affecting commerce." Ignoring the Court's standing doctrine—that Congress could legislate only on matters having a "direct" effect on interstate commerce—the Court sustained action against unfair labor practices at the Pennsylvania plants of the Jones and Laughlin Steel Company.

VI.

What does all of this tell us about the nature of constitutional interpretation, the quest for neutral principles, and the relationship between law and politics?

It tells us quite a bit, for what becomes clear the longer one looks at cases dealing with police powers (or with substantive due process) is that the only thing the text of the Constitution can be said to "say" about these cases is that it provides the broad *categories* in which their issues are framed. The Constitution—its structure, its history—gives us the *idea* of state police power; it gives us the due process clause. The Supreme Court fills in the rest.

In the process of filling in this content it looks—where? Out there, somewhere, to some amalgamation of public opinion, current social morality, contemporary "experience," current perceptions—in short, the Court looks to politics, to prevailing ideas of political morality, and tells us what the "general welfare" requires—and hence what the Constitution allows the state to do under its police powers. As Perry puts it, "[t]he scope of the 'public welfare' is a function *of social conventions;* the basic determinants of the public welfare are the conventional attitudes of the socio-political culture."[56]

In the language of Clifford Geertz, what the Supreme Court is doing is what some institution or process must accomplish in all legal cultures—it is providing the "coherence images"—those notions of reality that blend the empirical, the moral, and the political—that are the real stuff of the law—any law, anywhere.

Once this becomes clear, several interesting conclusions follow. The first is that, quite simply, there is no such thing as a "neutral" principle in cases such as this, for the outcome will always ultimately depend upon some reading of American values—some "coherence image"—and such value judgments cannot be "neutral." Police powers can have

---

Chief Justice Hughes wrote of the company—one of the nation's largest steel producers:

> In view of . . . [their] far-flung activities, it is idle to say that the effect [on interstate commerce] would be indirect or remote. It is obvious that it would be immediate and might be catastrophic. We are asked to shut our eyes to the plainest facts of our national life and to deal with the question of direct and indirect effects in an intellectual vacuum. National Labor Relations Board v. Jones & Laughlin Corp., 301 U.S. 1, 41 (1937), quoted in Pritchett, *Constitutional Law,* 231.

[56] Perry, "Abortion, Public Morals, and Police Power," 735; emphasis added.

no meaning apart from some understanding of what the general welfare requires; and, unless we wish to adopt a ruthlessly intentionalist stance—that the "general welfare" must always mean no more than it meant in 1789, when (to take the most obvious difficulties) medicine, education, and industry were rudimentary—we have no choice but to allow the Court to fill in the blanks. Those who advocate neutrality are often confusing it with the idea of *generality*—that is, that the law must treat all the members of a particular category in the same manner. But the decision as to how to divide up reality into categories, or how to treat the categories themselves, cannot be "neutral," for, by their very nature, these are value-laden decisions.

The quest for neutral principles is a symptom, really, of the fear of judicial subjectivity. "Why should the Court, a committee of nine lawyers, be the sole agents of change?" Robert Bork demands to know.[57] But to pose the question this way is to misread much of our constitutional history. Judgment is not naked and arbitrary power, no matter how much it may look that way to those who disagree with a particular decision (or cluster of decisions). "Nine lawyers" were not the "sole agents of change" during the *Lochner* era, nor during the New Deal; in fact, in these cases it looks far more as if the Court was somewhat passively reflecting various aspects of mainstream political opinion.

If the Constitution does grant the states police powers, and those powers must be tied to some understanding of what the general welfare requires, then judicial subjectivity is inevitable, and neutral principles— principles that do not draw fine lines or make specific judgments about particular things, principles that do not have some moral dimension, some notion of what kind of society this is or should be—will be hard to come by.[58]

A second conclusion that flows from this line of reasoning is that the current debate among constitutional scholars—about "interpretivism" versus "non-interpretivism"—is quite beside the point, at least in cases concerning a police power–substantive due process conflict (which is many cases indeed).

Ely defines interpretivism as the stance that "judges deciding constitutional issues should confine themselves to enforcing norms that are stated or clearly implicit in the written Constitution," and non-inter-

[57] Bork, "Neutral Principles," 6.
[58] For a somewhat similar argument made in the context of the First Amendment, see Laurence H. Tribe, *Constitutional Choices* (Cambridge, Mass.: Harvard University Press, 1985), chapter 13.

pretivism as "the contrary view that courts should go beyond that set of references and enforce norms that cannot be discovered within the four corners of the document."[59]

But what could be said, within such a framework, of *Lochner,* or the Minnesota mortgage case? Once we say that the "error" of *Lochner* was not the sudden discovery of a liberty of contract in the due process clause, but rather the particular *weighing* of that value against the state's police power, and the limited *definition* of the police power propounded by the majority, then making a distinction between a value "in" the Constitution and one "beyond" it no longer makes a great deal of sense.

In this light, the important question about *Lochner* is no longer political (in the conventional sense, i.e., "should judges exercise so much power?"; however they decided the case, they would have been exercising enormous power), nor jurisprudential ("should judges look 'in' the Constitution or 'beyond' it") but epistemological—how can judges gauge and measure what society at any given time believes to be necessary to the public welfare? What kind of materials should judges examine to make such judgments? What if there is conflicting public opinion? At what point in the development of public opinion can judges say a new consensus exists? What contribution should judges make to the development of that consensus? What if there *is* no consensus?

These are all, to be sure, enormously difficult questions, but they are the relevant questions that diatribes about judicial imperialism and debates about interpretivism only obscure. And, if we recall the liberty theorem, they are the most important questions the Supreme Court faces. In any era, the premier constitutional question will be what exceptions to the liberty theorem the Supreme Court allows. Furthermore, this is a question that cannot be avoided, except perhaps by those who would tie the Court's hands, in all particulars, to original understandings of how society functions.[60]

Thus, what is often happening beneath the surface in an unusually controversial case is one of two things: either (as many commentators

---

[59] Ely, *Democracy and Distrust,* 1. See also Thomas C. Grey, "Do We Have an Unwritten Constitution?," *Stanford Law Review* 27 (February 1975): 703–18.

[60] Moreover, those who would tie the Court's hands to "original understandings" must still cope with the evidence that the framers *intended* constitutional development through case-by-case adjudication. See H. Jefferson Powell, "The Original Understanding of Original Intent," *Harvard Law Review* 98 (March 1985): 885–948. See also pp. 35, 63–64.

have told us)[61] the Court is far behind or far ahead of public opinion (and the new "coherence image" the public will, or has, embrace[d]); or, as seems increasingly the case today, the Court is reflecting the opinion on one side of an issue on which the public is severely divided—an issue, in other words, on which two contradictory coherence images coexist in society.

A final point flows from this line of analysis. As we have seen, the Court cannot help but interpret the Constitution in the light of two kinds of "data": general beliefs about what the public welfare requires, on the one hand, and social "facts" on the other. At times, the two will coincide, making the Court's task relatively easy—that is, society's judgments will be based on the relevant "facts." But at other times, societal consensus will be somehow out of whack with the "facts." What, then, should the Court do? Or what should it do when there is no societal consensus? With these questions in mind, we turn to a discussion of several relevant cases.

VII.

Brown v. Board of Education is perhaps as close as America will ever come to a revolution from above. The case turned, of course, on the equal protection clause; police powers lurk only in the background of the case, in that public education is itself the classic expression of a state's legitimate exercise of its police powers.

But I want to suggest that *Brown* significantly depended on ideas much more directly linked to the police power question, at least as I have described it here. In its concept of "stigmatic" injury—the damage done to the hearts and minds of black schoolchildren about which Chief Justice Warren wrote so eloquently—the Court was announcing yet a further addition to the list of the types of public welfare for which the state is responsible. "Psychological harm is harm the state cannot inflict as it goes about exercising its traditional police power functions"—that, in a sense, is what *Brown* establishes.

Brown says, in effect, that the equal protection clause requires that

[61] See Robert Dahl's classic article, "Decision-Making in a Democracy: The Supreme Court as a National Policy-Maker," *Journal of Public Law* 6 (Fall 1957): 279–95; see also David Adamany, "Legitimacy, Realigning Elections, and the Supreme Court," *Wisconsin Law Review* 1973: 790–846; Jonathan Casper, "The Supreme Court and National Policy-Making," *American Political Science Review* 70 (March 1976): 50–63; Richard Funston, "The Supreme Court and Critical Elections," *American Political Science Review* 69 (September 1975): 795–811.

such police powers be exercised only in certain ways. And how does the Court *know* that's what the equal protection clause requires? How does the Court *know* that sigmatic harm is constitutionally relevant harm?

By "modern authority,"[62] which in this case means the findings of social science. We know things about human beings we did not know at the time of Plessy v. Ferguson,[63] the Warren Court is saying; we know that people are hurt in ways other than physical violence; we know, further, that we now live in a society where education plays a vastly more important role in the lives of these individuals than it did a century before, at the time of the adoption of the Fourteenth Amendment. *Brown* turns, in the end, on what we know—about people, about education. We should not lose sight of the fact that, once again, there is nothing in the text of the Constitution that requires— or prevents—the Supreme Court from making the determination of "fact" upon which *Brown* ultimately depends.[64]

If *Brown* can be viewed as turning on what we "know," Roe v. Wade can be viewed as turning on what we cannot know. We cannot know whether the fetus, in its earliest stages of development, is a human being—a "person." Given that we cannot know, scientifically,[65]

---

[62] 347 U.S. at 494.

[63] 163 U.S. 537 (1896). This case establishes the doctrine of "separate but equal."

[64] This same conclusion would follow even if the Court had chosen alternate, non-social-science-based grounds for the holding in *Brown*. For example, had the Court chosen to view school segregation as a "badge" of slavery prohibited by the Thirteenth Amendment, it would have still been required to "read" the social reality of segregation in a particular manner; its interpretation would still depend on social "fact." As Justice Harlan's dissent in the original *Plessy* case makes clear, "separate but equal" can be interpreted as constitutional only by the most stubborn refusal to face social facts. "Every one knows that the statute in question," Harlan wrote in *Plessy*, "had its origin in the purpose, not so much to exclude white persons from railroad cars occupied by blacks, as to exclude colored people from coaches occupied by or assigned to white persons." *Ibid.* at 557. Harlan's reference to what "every one knows" is exactly to the point; the constitutionality of social practices cannot be determined without reference to social "facts." Racial discrimination depends, ultimately, on social stigma, not the constitutional text.

[65] To the extent that science does have anything to say about the "personhood" of the fetus, an emerging consensus seems to suggest that "the neural equipment for personhood is not present prior" to the seventh month of pregnancy, *if* we regard the brain as "the seat of personhood." See Michael V. L. Bennett, "Personhood from a Neuroscientific Perspective," in Edd Doerr and James W. Prescott (eds.), *Abortion Rights and Fetal 'Personhood'* (Long Beach, Calif.: Centerline Press, 1989), 85.

that the fetus is a person, the status of the fetus becomes a matter of belief; under the First Amendment, matters of belief belong to the individual.

Saying this, of course, does not end the inquiry. Under the First Amendment one may believe anything, including that God commands human sacrifice of one's children; under the state's police power, an individual may be prevented from putting such beliefs into practice. Can the state similarly and legitimately legislate to protect the fetus?

Before answering that question directly, we should examine what else we know and don't know about abortion. We know that, on most matters, we allow individuals to control their own bodies[66] as well as their own decisions about whether they will or won't have a child. We know that when it is illegal, millions of women still procure abortions, often putting themselves at grave physical risk to do so. We also know—and this is a highly relevant fact—that a properly performed abortion, early in pregnancy, is medically safer than carrying the fetus to term.[67]

Legally, all of these social and medical facts are embedded in a certain understanding of liberty. In Perry's words, "whatever its original meaning might have been, 'liberty' has come to signify to us—it has come to mean—the freedom of the individual to shape the most fundamental aspects of his or her life according to the dictates of his or her informed and conscientious judgment."[68] Moreover, the debate about abortion takes place in a legal context of substantive due process, and—again to quote Perry—"whatever the original meaning of 'due process of law' . . . [it] has come to mean to us . . . the principle or ideal that government may not deprive us of our precious liberty to shape our lives unless government *must* do so in order to secure some *overriding good.*"[69]

---

[66] The right to bodily integrity has been upheld by courts in contexts other than abortion. For example, a man dying of bone cancer in Pittsburgh in 1978 sought to force his cousin to donate bone marrow; the courts, however, upheld the right of the cousin to refuse. See the discussion in Marjorie Reily Maguire, "Symbiosis, Biology, and Personalization," in *ibid.*, 12.

[67] See Roe v. Wade, 410 U.S. at 163. See also Thomas W. Hilgers, "The Medical Hazards of Legally Induced Abortion," in Hilgers and Dennis J. Horan (eds.), *Abortion and Social Justice* (New York: Sheed and Ward, 1972), 57; Hilgers writes that "the medical procedure of abortion . . . is potentially 23.3 . . . times as safe as the process of going through ordinary childbirth." See also Doerr and Prescott, *Abortion Rights,* 2.

[68] Michael J. Perry, *Morality, Politics and Law* (New York: Oxford University Press, 1988), 173.

[69] *Ibid.,* 174; emphasis added.

Is the protection of the fetus such an "overriding good"? Perry asserts that it may be, and thus that the states should be free to proscribe abortion, but offers no argument or evidence about the fetus to support his conclusion.[70] Indeed he could not, for to do so he would be driven back ultimately to the inescapable conclusion that the "personhood" of the fetus is a matter of belief, and not a matter of overriding importance for the state. He would also be driven to the evidence that there is certainly no *consensus* in American society that the fetus is a person deserving legal protection, equivalent to the societal consensus that murder is wrong.

Absent clear evidence of harm to another person, how can we *not* see abortion as a matter for the woman to decide for herself, given the things that the law, today, holds about individual autonomy, things reflected in the view that family planning and contraception are matters beyond the realm of legitimate state interest?[71]

[70] *Ibid.,* 174–75. He does say the state is always required to carve out exceptions to a restrictive abortion law: the state must allow abortions to protect maternal health, to terminate a pregnancy caused by rape or incest, or to terminate a pregnancy that would result in the birth of "a genetically defective child whose life would be short and painful." *Ibid.,* 175.

[71] It is important to recall that *Roe* was decided against a background of precedent including not only Griswold v. Connecticut, but several other cases, stretching back to the 1920s, protective of the privacy of the American family and the rights of parents. In Meyer v. Nebraska, 262 U.S. 390 (1923), the Court struck down a state law which prohibited teaching a foreign language to any child not yet in the eighth grade. The Court used the case to make a general statement about the Constitution's "liberty":

> While this Court has not attempted to define with exactness the liberty . . . guaranteed [by the Fourteenth Amendment], the term has received much consideration and some of the included things have been definitely stated. Without doubt, it denotes not merely freedom from bodily restraint but also the right of the individual to contract, to engage in any of the common occupations of life, to acquire useful knowledge, to marry, establish a home and bring up children, to worship God according to the dictates of his own conscience, and generally to enjoy those privileges long recognized at common law as essential to the orderly pursuit of happiness by free men. . . . The established doctrine is that this liberty may not be interfered with, under the guise of protecting the public interest, by legislative action which is arbitrary or without reasonable relation to some purpose within the competency of the State to effect. Determination by the legislature of what constitutes proper exercise of police power is not final or conclusive but is subject to supervision by the courts. . . .
> Practically, education of the young is only possible in schools conducted by especially qualified persons who devote themselves

Once we are sure that a fetal "person" does exist, in the later stages of pregnancy, the state's police powers come into play, of course, and the woman's right to privacy must be weighed against the legitimate state interest in the welfare of the fetus. Quite sensibly, the Court allows this state interest to enter legislative decision making at the point of fetal viability—the point at which we can be sure we are dealing with a separate "person." But to allow the state to legislate on behalf of the fetus much earlier than the point of viability is to allow

> thereto. The calling always has been regarded as useful and honorable, essential, indeed, to the public welfare. Mere knowledge of the German language cannot reasonably be regarded as harmful. 262 U.S. at 399, 400.

In Pierce v. Society of Sisters, 268 U.S. 510 (1925), the Court struck down an Oregon law requiring children to attend public schools:

> Under the doctrine of Meyer v. Nebraska . . . , we think it entirely plain that the Act . . . unreasonably interferes with the liberty of parents and guardians to direct the upbringing and education of children under their control. As often heretofore pointed out, rights guaranteed by the Constitution may not be abridged by legislation which has no reasonable relation to some purpose within the competency of the State. The fundamental theory of liberty upon which all governments in this Union repose excludes any general power of the State to standardize its children by forcing them to accept instruction from public teachers only. The child is not the mere creature of the State; those who nurture him and direct his destiny have the right, coupled with the high duty, to recognize and prepare him for additional obligations. 268 U.S. at 534, 535.

In 1942, the Court in Skinner v. Oklahoma, 316 U.S. 535 (1942), overturned the Habitual Criminal Sterilization Act of Oklahoma, which forced sterilization of a criminal offender convicted for a third time of a felony "involving moral turpitude." The particular defendant had been convicted of one chicken theft and two armed robberies, and was sentenced to sterilization. Justice Douglas wrote in overturning the law:

> We are dealing here with legislation which involves one of the basic civil rights of man. Marriage and procreation are fundamental to the very existence and survival of the race. The power to sterilize, if exercised, may have subtle, far-reaching and devastating effects. In evil or reckless hands it can cause races or types which are inimical to the dominant group to wither and disappear. There is no redemption for the individual whom the law touches. Any experiment which the State conducts is to his irreparable injury. He is forever deprived of a basic liberty. 316 U.S. at 541.

For all three cases, see Brest and Levinson, *Processes of Constitutional Decisionmaking,* 657–61. These cases, like *Griswold,* can be viewed as turning on the acceptance by the Court of the constitutional relevance of certain social "facts" concerning the centrality of the family and family intimacy to American life. For a fuller discussion, see below, pp. 134–46.

the state to embody in its law a moral guess—one that violates the much more firmly established right of the woman to her own moral beliefs and to control of her own body. Construing such protection of the fetus as an "overriding good" the state can legitimately pursue simply ignores too much reality, including the reality of a lack of consensus on these questions in American society. Unless the state can convincingly argue that it *is* a matter of overriding importance that the fetus be protected early in pregnancy, then the woman's fundamental right to bodily privacy must prevail.

The debate about abortion is a debate about the moral relevance of certain physical facts (the number of chromosomes in a fertilized egg; the brain capacity of a fetus or its ability to feel pain; the ability of a viable fetus to exist outside the mother's womb). There *is* a sufficiently strong moral consensus that separate, "viable" beings are "persons" the state must protect; beyond this point, however, consensus does not exist, and the debate is truly a moral debate, about which reasonable persons may disagree. As with all other moral debates, the Court must protect individual autonomy of belief as a paramount constitutional value. If a woman chooses to believe that the first-trimester fetus within her womb is not a "person," and that her own life would be significantly harmed by continuing to be pregnant, what compelling interest of the state can override her belief and her determination of her own good?

In *Roe,* as in *Brown, Lochner,* and the New Deal cases, what the Court ultimately must measure is the closeness of fit between the moral and political judgments embodied in state legislation, on the one hand, and social "facts" on the other. The "fact" that stigmatic injury is a real thing to the Warren Court (in *Brown*); the "fact" that we cannot know at what point in pregnancy before viability the fetus becomes a person; the "fact" that industrial employees do not make free choices in the contracts they make (in *Lochner*); the "facts" of a modern industrial economy as the post-1937 Court interpreted them in the New Deal decisions—the Court's reading of all of these "facts" is what these landmark cases turn upon.

What all of this points toward is a jurisprudence rooted in the admittedly sloppy process of reconciling constitutional doctrine to societal consensus, and, especially, the social facts upon which such consensus ought to be based. It points toward a jurisprudence in which epistemological questions concerning social facts are the Court's most important questions. This will be, admittedly, a sloppy jurisprudence, because the kinds of social facts needed do not lend themselves to exacting scientific specification.

Moreover, we are pointed toward a jurisprudence in which the Court will, from time to time, seem undemocratic, for it will be telling us that the moral judgment embodied in some piece of legislation is based on an outmoded or inaccurate reading of social facts. But, to recall Geertz's perspective, this kind of messy reconciliation between what a society defines as fact and what a society judges to be moral is what lies at the base of all law. What creates this sloppy indeterminacy is the nature of social and political life, and not the nature of the judicial process or the actions of the Supreme Court.

VIII.

The remainder of this chapter, as well as the next several, are devoted to examining concrete constitutional dilemmas that fall into various categories of social "fact." My underlying argument is that viewing concrete cases within this framework, and within the context of the liberty theorem, sheds considerable light on difficult constitutional choices, particularly questions concerning the rights of minorities and the "creation" of "new" rights. More fundamentally, my basic argument is that the most important questions raised by these cases are epistemological questions about relevant social facts.

We begin with the fundamental social fact of ethical pluralism. In the previous section, the argument for a woman's right to choose an abortion early in her pregnancy turned, in part, on the lack of societal consensus concerning the status of the fetus. Remembering that our fundamental principle is that "liberty can be restricted only for agreed, limited purposes," we were driven to conclude that the status of the fetus is a matter of belief, something each individual is allowed to decide for herself.

This argument can be generalized and applied to different kinds of First Amendment problems. When deciding the constitutionality of various kinds of laws that restrict liberty of speech and thought, the Supreme Court must always remember that the United States is a large, diverse, heterogeneous society, in which people believe many different things about many different subjects and pursue many different kinds of lives; in short, the Court must accept pluralism as a fundamental social fact and accept ethical diversity as its necessary moral corollary. Furthermore, the Court must remember that liberty is the rule and its restriction the exception.

What restrictions on liberty of speech are allowable? Taking the idea of "clear and present danger" as our cue, we can say that the Constitution requires that speech (and all matters of belief) be protected so long as they do not cause immediate physical harm to persons or property.

How do we justify using this as our First Amendment touchstone? In particular, how do we justify applying such a doctrine to types of speech, such as sexually explicit speech, which the framers of the First Amendment would surely have condemned?

The answer a Supreme Court justice might give to this question would look something like this. We have stated that the constitutional framers accepted the notion that "liberty can be restricted only for agreed, limited purposes." At the time at which the First Amendment was written, there *was* widespread agreement that certain forms of speech—including sedition and blasphemy—caused harm that the state had every right to prevent. We, however, live in a pluralist world, in which we believe in the fundamental principle that "under the First Amendment, there is no such thing as a false idea."[72] That is, there is no restriction on ideas, or the circulation of ideas, that would not be an imposition of belief on some group of people—those who purchase and peruse pornographic literature; those who detest organized religion; those who hold the government in contempt. Although these groups are minorities, they are not tiny; but even if they were exceedingly small minorities, many in American society who do not share their inclinations would nevertheless be offended by the state's restriction of their liberty, for they do no real, concrete harm.[73]

The societal consensus over the harmfulness of sedition—present when the First Amendment was written, perhaps—broke down quickly, in the closing years of the eighteenth century, as political parties developed in Congress and debate raged over the Alien and Sedition Acts.[74] After that debate, we could no longer say there was a basic agreement in American society that criticism of the government—the "intent to defame" the government or to "excite against [it] the

---

[72] Gertz v. Robert Welsh, Inc., 418 U.S. 323, 339 (1974). For a similar argument about laws against blasphemy, see David Edwards, "Toleration and the English Blasphemy Law," in John Horton and Susan Mendus (eds.) *Aspects of Toleration* (New York: Methuen, 1985), 82.

[73] Cf. Ronald Dworkin, *Taking Rights Seriously* (Cambridge, Mass.: Harvard University Press, 1977), 254: "The belief that prejudices, personal aversions and rationalizations do not justify restricting another's freedom . . . occupies a critical and fundamental position in our popular morality."

[74] See James Q. Wilson, *American Government: Institutions and Policies*, 1st ed. (Lexington, Mass.: D.C. Health, 1980), 487–89, and the sources cited therein.

hatred of the people," in the language of the Sedition Act—could be punishable offenses.

The consensus over blasphemy and other forms of "immoral" speech broke down more slowly; there is no single event we can point to as a major turning point.[75] But we can say, with total confidence, that, as a result of complex and accumulating social change, there is no unanimous or nearly unanimous consensus in American society today that blasphemy and pornography cause "harm" the state has a right to prevent. Nor is there any reliable empirical evidence that they do cause any form of concrete harm.[76] Hence, we are justified in applying the idea of clear and present danger to these types of speech even though the framers would not themselves have done so. Moral "harm," absent physical harm, is not something the state can prevent without trampling upon constitutionally protected liberty.

In this argument I have used the phrase "unanimous or nearly unanimous" to describe the level of consensus that would be necessary to justify the state's restriction of liberty. What I have in mind is something equivalent to the level of societal consensus over the belief that murder is wrong, or the belief that incest is wrong (even if it is, on some level, "consensual"). The belief, even the strong belief, of a large majority that (for example) pornography is harmful, or that the fetus is a person, without empirical proof of concrete harm, is insufficient.[77]

Why set the barrier to state action so high? The answer to that question turns on perhaps the most basic social fact of the American polity, and the one most central to the framers' understanding of society: the tendency of men to divide into disagreeing and hostile

---

[75] William Nelson has carefully documented "the breakdown of ethical unity" in Massachusetts beginning in the 1780s. This social and legal process included a deemphasis on prosecutions for "sin," the development of associational pluralism, and religious disestablishment; it involved a "fundamental shift in man's understanding of the nature of truth." Truth came to be regarded as plural, something sought not by a unified community but by pluralistic institutions. See *Americanization of the Common Law: The Impact of Legal Change on Massachusetts Society, 1760–1830* (Cambridge, Mass.: Harvard University Press, 1975), 109–15.

[76] See below, p. 103.

[77] For similar arguments, see Bruce Ackerman's comments about "extraordinary consensus" in "The Storrs Lectures: Discovering the Constitution," *Yale Law Journal* 93 (May 1984): 1013–72; see also David A. J. Richards, *Foundations of American Constitutionalism* (New York: Oxford University Press, 1989), 234; Macedo, *Liberal Virtues*, 21, 30.

factions. When we ask, "why make it difficult for the state to abridge First Amendment rights?" we should always remember the hostility of factions; we should make an analogy to freedom of religion, and recall the framers' clear-sighted recognition that the tendency to intolerance is a characteristic of human nature—a social fact—of which we must remain especially cognizant. That a majority of Americans may despise a particular minority or a particular activity or a particular belief was not an unknown or merely hypothetical possibility to the framers; generalizing from this, we can say that, in today's secular world, on all matters of belief, the Constitution demands that liberty be the rule and its restriction the exception, and that restrictions need extraordinary justification. Such justification can only come in the form of (a) reliable empirical evidence of concrete harm, or (b) a unanimous or nearly unanimous moral sentiment.

IX.

Another way of justifying a high standard for restrictions of liberty is to consider what the alternative would be. In this light, it is useful to examine some of the Supreme Court's obscenity decisions.

The Supreme Court has struggled mightily for over thirty years to derive a definition of "obscenity" that is not unconstitutionally vague and that does not suppress erotic literature or art perceived to have "artistic" content. This struggle has produced a "flood of divided rulings and groping decisions."[78] In the words of Justice Harlan (in 1968), "the subject of obscenity has produced a variety of views among the members of the Court unmatched in any other course of constitutional adjudication."[79]

Within this confusion, a general line of attack has been to focus on whether the work in question has any content apart from its appeal to "prurient" interest. Until relatively recently, works of art needed to be "*utterly* without redeeming social importance" to be classified as obscene; recent decisions have broadened the state's power to allow suppression of material lacking "*serious* literary, artistic, political, or scientific value."[80] What state interests justify such suppression?

[78] Gunther, *Constitutional Law*, 1065.
[79] Ginsberg v. New York, 390 U.S. 629 (1968), quoted in Gunther, *Constitutional Law*, 1065, n.1.
[80] Roth v. United States, 354 U.S. 476, 484 (1957), and Miller v. California, 413 U.S. 15, 24 (1973), quoted in Brest and Levinson, *Processes of Constitutional Decisionmaking*, 1195–96; emphasis added.

Although conceding "that the State has *no legitimate interest* in control [of] the moral content of a person's thoughts," Chief Justice Burger nevertheless authored a number of opinions significantly broadening the states' authority to regulate obscenity. Burger and five other members of the Court held in 1973 that "there are legitimate state interests at stake in stemming the tide of commercialized obscenity, even assuming it is feasible to enforce effective safeguards against exposure to juveniles and to passersby." Such interests "include the interest of the public in the quality of life and the total community environment, the tone of commerce in the great city centers, and possibly, the public safety itself." Burger then quotes approvingly a passage from the writing of Alexander Bickel,[81] who justifies the suppression of obscenity because of "the tone of the society, the mode, to use terms that have perhaps greater currency, the style and quality of life, now and in the future."[82]

Such sentiments stand in stark contrast to the standards the Court has promulgated in other types of First Amendment litigation, such as cases governing the regulation of "subversive" political groups or the publication of information dangerous or embarrassing to the government. In such cases, the reigning standard is the clear and present danger test, interpreted to mean that the state must demonstrate that speech incites "immanent lawlessness" before it can be suppressed, or that publication of information must "inevitably, directly, and immediately cause the occurrence of an event kindred to imperiling the safety of a transport already at sea."[83] In these cases, the *time* element is crucial; a "present" danger is an immediate danger.

Throughout its long struggle to define obscenity, the Court has not been able to come up with any justification for treating speech about sex differently than speech about other subjects, other than the kind of vague pronouncements Burger offers in the quotations above. What is remarkable about Burger's justification is that it is completely non-specific—it concerns a state's—i.e., a majority's—right to protect the "tone" of society and the "quality of life." What if Mormons in Utah decided that the presence of other religious sects degraded their "quality of life" and the "tone" of their society? What if the white majority

---

[81] "On Pornography: II, Dissenting and Concurring Opinions," *Public Opinion* 22 (Winter 1971): 25–26.

[82] Paris Adult Theatre I v. Slaton, 413 U.S. 49, 67, 57–59 (1973), quoted in Brest and Levinson, *Processes of Constitutional Decisionmaking*, 1202, 1199; emphasis added.

[83] New York Times v. United States, 403 U.S. 713, 726–27 (1971).

of a southern state decided that allowing blacks to move freely in their cities adversely affected the "tone of commerce"? Would such sentiments matter? To pose the question is to reveal the weakness of the argument.

Similarly, when speculating about the supposed link between obscenity and crime, Burger is driven to speak of "possible" and "arguable" links, and to quote from the *minority* report of a national commission;[84] he also speaks of the Court's responsibility to defer to the legislative determination of such "facts." Again, this is a far cry from the Court's requirement of demonstrable immediacy when other types of speech are suppressed, and the Court's refusal to defer to the legislative judgment on virtually any First Amendment matter.

Supreme Court justices, however, are not alone in their willingness to bend the First Amendment when it comes to sex; the condemnation of pornography has become an important political issue for many feminist scholars,[85] as well as sympathetic political theorists. Jean Elshtain, for example, correctly points out that the "reigning ethos" of our attitude toward speech is well captured by "Jefferson's pronouncement that it mattered not to him whether his neighbor believed in twenty gods or no god—it neither picked his pocket nor broke his leg."[86] Yet

---

[84] *Ibid.*, n.6.

[85] The leading figures here are Andrea Dworkin and Catherine MacKinnon. See Dworkin, *Pornography: Men Possessing Women* (New York: Perigee Books, 1981); MacKinnon, "Feminism, Marxism, Method, and the State: Toward Feminist Jurisprudence: Viewpoint," *Signs* 8 (Summer 1983): 635–58; and "Feminism, Marxism, Method, and the State: An Agenda for Theory," *Signs* 7 (Spring 1982): 515–44; see also MacKinnon, "Pornography, Civil Rights and Speech," *Harvard Civil Rights–Civil Liberties Law Review* 20 (Winter 1985): 1–70.

Feminists and their allies succeeded in gaining passage of an ordinance in Indianapolis defining pornography as "a practice that discriminates against women," a definition significantly broader than the traditional definition of obscenity. In the Indianapolis statute, "pornography" is "the graphic sexually explicit subordination of women, whether in pictures or in words," that includes one of a long list of characteristics, including presentations in which "women are presented as sexual objects for domination, conquest, violation, exploitation, or possession, or use, through postures or positions of servility or submission of display." The Indianapolis ordinance was declared unconstitutional in American Bookseller's Association v. Hudnut, 771 F. 2d. 323 (7th Cir. 1975). The Supreme Court summarily affirmed, 475 U.S. 1001 (1986). A similar ordinance in Minneapolis was vetoed by that city's mayor. See the discussion in David Bryden, "Between Two Constitutions: Feminism and Pornography," *Constitutional Commentary* 2 (Winter 1985): 147–89.

[86] "The New Porn Wars," *The New Republic*, 25 June 1984, 18.

she nevertheless goes on to speak of the right of "communities" to regulate the flow of obscenity: "Communities should have the power to regulate and to curb open and visible assaults on human dignity. . . ." "Clearly," she says, "the idea of 'rights' cannot bear all the weight being placed upon it."[87] Yet if we allow the state to suppress "assaults on human dignity" on matters sexual, why not on matters political? Why not declare that socialism (or capitalism) represents an "assault on human dignity" and outlaw political parties or suppress the speech of individuals who preach its virtues?

My aim here is not to present a comprehensive analysis of the debate over obscenity, but rather to use this as an example of the difficulty of justifying the suppression of liberty in the name of the "morality" of society's majority, and the need for far more than a simple or even strong majority consensus before liberty is curtailed. Chief Justice Burger and Jean Elshtain may not like it, but there are people in American society—and more than a handful—who enjoy sexually explicit books and films, who would feel their freedom curtailed if such material were unavailable. And, try as they might, Burger and Elshtain cannot prove that exposure to such material causes immediate crime or other concrete harm.[88] If this is a society that believes that "under

[87] *Ibid.*, 20, 18. This comment comes in an attack on the idea of a "right" to masturbate. Yet if sexual privacy is a constitutional right, does that not include masturbation? Does Elshtain wish to allow the state the power to specify acceptable and unacceptable sexual practices? She does not say.

[88] Most empirical evidence concerning the effects of obscenity on its viewers demonstrates the adoption of negative *attitudes*—not behavior—toward women; moreover, even that evidence is highly tentative. As Joel Grossman reports:

> Much of this evidence comes from experimental research by social psychologists. . . . In brief summary, the results indicate that prolonged exposure to filmed sexual violence resulted in diminished sensitivity to such violence, increased acceptance of aggression, increased belief in rape myths, and fantasies of sexual aggression. Some subjects reported an increased propensity toward aggressive behavior. It must be emphasized that all of these reported effects were attitudinal and not behavioral. [Moreover] exposure to nonviolent—so-called "ordinary"—pornography did not produce the same results. . . . "The First Amendment and the New Anti-Pornography Statutes," *News for Teachers of Political Science* 45 (Spring 1985), 21 n.33.

Grossman cites Neil Malamuth and Edward Donnerstein (eds.), *Pornography and Sexual Aggression* (Orlando, Fla.: Academic Press, 1984); Malamuth and Donnerstein, "The Effects of Aggressive-Pornographic Mass Media Stimuli," *Advances in Experimental Social Psychology* 15 (1982), 103–36; Daniel Linz, Edward Donerstein and Steven Penrod, "The Effect of Long Term Exposure

the First Amendment there is no such thing as a false idea," then the dislike of Burger and Elshtain for pornography is no different from the hatred of a religious fanatic for "heretics" or the smug superiority of a white supremacist. Commentators can fulminate all they like about "moral tone" and "assaults on human dignity," but the fact remains that "obscene" books are still books; "obscene" films are still films. The kind of theoretical waffling Burger and Elshtain do—quoting Jefferson and then ignoring him; conceding that the mind of man is sacrosanct and then ignoring that tenet—is a good sign of an argument gone awry. When we legislate against "filth" we are ignoring the fundamental social fact of diversity; we are forgetting the fundamental truth of ethical pluralism.[89]

X.

I have argued that restrictions of liberty under the state's police power require either (a) reliable empirical evidence of concrete harm, or (b) a unanimous or nearly unanimous moral consensus. Promulgating such a standard raises many new questions. What constitutes "reliable" evidence? How is the Court to judge the level of agreement necessary to satisfy the second criterion?

My purpose is not necessarily to answer such questions definitively, but rather to point out their relevance for constitutional decision making, as well as their implications for larger jurisprudential questions. I do not want to argue that constitutional questions necessarily have single "correct" solutions flowing from these standards (although these standards do, in some cases, strongly incline us toward one position or another), but rather that it is possible to generate a coherent intellectual position by using them—an intellectual position true to the notion of liberty underlying the Constitution. I also want to make it clear that such questions are implicit in much of what the Court does; making these questions more explicit clarifies the manner in which law and politics inevitably blend in constitutional discourse.

---

to Filmed Violence Against Women," (unpublished paper, 1984). See also Louis Henkin, "Morals and the Constitution: The Sin of Obscenity," *Columbia Law Review* 63 (March 1963): 391–414; and Bryden, "Between Two Constitutions." For a discussion of feminist arguments, see Dorchen Leidholdt and Janice G. Raymond (eds.), *The Sexual Liberals and the Attack on Feminism* (New York: Pergamon Press, 1990).

[89] For a somewhat similar argument see Dworkin's criticisms of Patrick Devlin in *Taking Rights Seriously*, chapter 10. See also Perry, *Morality, Politics and Law*, 95–97.

We have seen that adopting these standards provides a coherent justification for a "liberal" position on several questions of personal rights; later chapters will extend this analysis. But what of the question with which this chapter began and with which much contemporary jurisprudence has been preoccupied: Is it possible to reconcile such a liberal position on civil liberties issues with the abandonment by the Court of the substantive protection of economic rights?

What is at stake in many of the cases that pose this question is the level of scrutiny the Court brings to its judgments. In the late 1930s and early 1940s the Court developed its doctrine of "preferred" freedoms and its "two-track" theory of judicial review. After the Court's about-face over the constitutionality of the New Deal in 1937, it began to subject state and federal laws regulating the economy to the "rational relation" test; that is, statutes would be declared unconstitutional only if the Court could not (literally) dream up some rational reason for the law or speak of deferring to the "wisdom" of the legislature.[90] Needless to say, granting such benefit of the doubt to the state meant—and continues to mean—that virtually any statute will pass constitutional muster. The Court's deference to the legislative branches on matters of economic policy reflected their assumption that legislatures and

rational basis [handwritten marginal note]

[90] Typical of the Court's action is Williamson v. Lee Optical, 348 U.S. 483 (1955), sustaining an Oklahoma law which, in effect, forbade opticians from fitting or duplicating lenses without a prescription from an opthalmologist or optometrist. "In practical effect," the Court said, the statute "means that no optician can fit old glasses into new frames or supply a lens, whether it be a new lens or one to duplicate a lost or broken lens, without a prescription." *Ibid.* at 486. The district court had overturned the law, finding that "through mechanical devices and ordinary skills, the optician could take a broken lens or a fragment thereof, measure its power, and reduce it to prescriptive terms." *Ibid.* Justice Douglas for the Supreme Court sustains the law, even though "it may exact a needless, wasteful regulation in many cases." But, Douglas says, "it is for the legislature, not the courts, to balance the advantages and disadvantages" of the law. "In some cases," the Court says, "the directions contained in the prescription are essential. . . . The legislature *might* have concluded that the frequency of occasions when a prescription is necessary was sufficient to justify this regulation. . . ." *Ibid.* at 487; emphasis added.

In another case, Douglas again wrote for the Court sustaining a New York law prohibiting advertising on the sides of trucks unless the owner of the truck was advertising his own business. Once again, the Court speculated about the possible justifications for the law: "The local authorities may well have concluded that those who advertise their own wares on their trucks do not present the same traffic problem in view of the nature or extent of the advertisement which they use. It would take a degree of omniscience which we lack to say that such is not the case." Railway Express Agency v. New York, 336 U.S. 106, 110 (1949).

not courts were competent to gather the information—the "facts"—necessary to decide policy questions on complex and technical economic subjects.

At the same time, the Court developed the idea of a "preferred" position for "fundamental" rights and "suspect" classes.[91] When laws touched the Bill of Rights, or abridged the rights of "discrete and insular" minorities, state action would lose its benefit of the doubt, and the statute would have to pass the "strict scrutiny" test.[92] Under strict scrutiny, the law would be declared constitutional only if it were "necessary" to achieve a "compelling" state goal. Such a standard requires a weighing of both legislative means and legislative ends, and, in practice, virtually every statute subjected to it is declared unconstitutional. Although a number of legislative goals have been thought to be sufficiently "compelling," very few statutes are thought to be "necessary" means to achieve those ends; to be adjudged "necessary," the state would have to prove that it had no other means available to it to achieve the same goal.

Earlier we saw that the advent of the New Deal brought to the Supreme Court a new kind of rhetoric about the state's police power to protect the public welfare. Such rhetoric often was framed within an explicit discussion of the political and economic crises of the 1930s; in a number of cases the Court came perilously close to a complete abandonment of any power to review acts of the legislative branches and to accepting a crude "ends justify the means" philosophy. The Court justified its action on the ground that Congress had adequate *factual* bases for its far-reaching actions. It did so by incorporating into constitutional law a number of economic concepts, most impor-

---

[91] The starting point of the preferred freedoms doctrine is the famous footnote in the Carolene Products case of 1938, in which Chief Justice Stone spoke of the "narrower scope for operation of the presumption of constitutionality" for legislation touching the Bill of Rights, restricting the political process, or "directed at particular . . . minorities. . . ." United States v. Carolene Products Co., 304 U.S. 144, 152, n. 4 (1938). The text to which this footnote is attached speaks of the importance of judicial deference to "legislative facts"—explicit or implicit—in cases dealing with "ordinary" economic legislation. *Ibid.* See Robert Cover, "The Origins of Judicial Activism in the Protection of Minorities," *Yale Law Journal* 91 (June 1982): 1290, n.10. For a fuller discussion, see below, pp. 194–98.

[92] To be sure, there were a number of decisions protective of civil liberties, particularly First Amendment liberties, before 1937. See, e.g., Fiske v. Kansas, 274 U.S. 380 (1927); and Near v. Minnesota, 283 U.S. 697 (1931). Such cases, however, were generally isolated instances of judicial action, and were not justified in any systematic manner.

tantly the "aggregation" doctrine and the concept of a "national market" for commerce. Since the Constitution grants to Congress only the power to regulate *interstate* commerce, the Court could only sustain a number of New Deal measures (such as the prohibition of unfair labor practices) if they could be found to have "a substantial economic effect on interstate commerce."[93]

In one celebrated case, the Court ruled that Congress could regulate the size of the wheat crop of an Ohio farmer, even though the crop was intended solely for home consumption, because "commerce among the states in wheat is large and important," and the "wheat industry has been a problem industry for some years." The Court accepts Congress's conclusion—as a matter of economic "fact"—that "the effect of consumption of homegrown wheat on interstate commerce is due to the fact that it constitutes the most variable factor in the disappearance of the wheat crop." Congress can legitimately regulate the price of wheat, and it can do this "as effectively by sustaining or increasing the demand as by limiting the supply." Thus one farmer's *demand* for wheat is a fit subject of Congressional concern; "that [his] own contribution to the demand for wheat may be trivial by itself is not enough to remove him from the scope of federal regulations where, as here, his contribution, taken together with that of many others similarly situated, is far from trivial." It can "hardly be denied," the Court says, "that a factor of such volume and variability as home-consumed wheat would have a substantial influence on price and market conditions. . . . Homegrown wheat . . . competes with wheat in commerce."[94]

Similarly, Congress can constitutionally regulate labor practices because of the effect of such practices on commerce; this reflects "the Congressional conception of public policy that interstate commerce should not be made the instrument of competition in the distribution of goods produced under substandard labor conditions, which competition is injurious to the commerce and to the states from and to which the commerce flows."[95]

Such acceptance by the Court of economic "facts" took place in a highly charged political atmosphere, an atmosphere which included

---

[93] Wickard v. Filburn, 317 U.S. 111, 115 (1942), quoted in Gunther, *Constitutional Law,* 136.

[94] 317 U.S. at 125, 127–128, quoted in Gunther, *Constitutional Law,* 136–37.

[95] United States v. Darby, 312 U.S. 100, 115 (1941), quoted in Gunther, *Constitutional Law,* 140.

FDR's court-packing plan.[96] A number of Supreme Court opinions at the time drew explicit attention to the political situation. When judging the constitutionality of the unemployment scheme created by the Social Security Act of 1935, Justice Cardozo candidly wrote that to decide the case "there is need to remind ourselves of facts as to the problem of unemployment that are now matters of common knowledge. . . ."[97] The individual states, Cardozo says, "were unable to give" relief to unemployment:

> The problem had become national in area and dimensions. There was need of help from the nation if the people were not to starve. It is too late today for the argument to be heard with tolerance that in a crisis so extreme the use of the moneys of the nation to relieve the unemployed and their dependents is a use for any purpose narrower than the promotion of the general welfare.[98]

Whether we regard as legitimate the Court's current "two-track" approach—heightened scrutiny for civil liberties; great deference to the legislature on economic questions—must depend on how we evaluate the Court's acceptance and use of economic and political "facts" in these cases, and the extension of such logic far beyond the economic crisis of the 1930s. It is worth noting that the holdings of these New Deal opinions have extraordinarily far-reaching, and chilling implications. Could *any* legislation be justified in the name of economic survival? If homegrown wheat affects interstate commerce with sufficient force to be a fit subject for Congressional legislation, what of homemade food? If the restaurant industry were suddenly in sufficient trouble, could Congress outlaw home-cooked meals? What of home-sewn clothes (if the apparel industry were in dire straights)? The logic of such laws—the existence of a national market; the aggregation of many individual acts—would be no different from the logic of the constitutional acceptance of the New Deal.[99]

Although these examples may seem farfetched, the Court in a num-

---

[96] See William E. Leuchtenburg, *Franklin D. Roosevelt and the New Deal, 1932–1940* (New York: Harper and Row, 1963), 231–38.

[97] Steward Machine Company v. Davis, 301 U.S. 548, 586 (1937).

[98] *Ibid.* at 586–87.

[99] Cf. Macedo, *Liberal Virtues,* 183–86. For a defense of the Court's actions in the New Deal cases, see Bruce Ackerman, "Beyond Carolene Products," *Harvard Law Review* 98 (February 1985): 713–46.

ber of real cases has extended the New Deal logic extraordinarily far. In Perez v. United States[100] the Court sustained federal conviction of a loan shark under the Consumer Credit Protection Act. Conviction of criminals who do not cross state lines had been considered, until this case, the paradigmatic example of *state police power*. The Court, however, found that Perez, although not himself involved in interstate crime, was engaged in a "class of activities" having substantial interstate effects, and therefore a fit subject for Congressional legislation. Explicitly citing New Deal cases—which have nothing to do with crime—Justice Douglas wrote that "extortionate credit transactions, though purely intrastate, may in the judgment of Congress affect interstate commerce."[101] Douglas quotes from the substantial Congressional debate over passage of the law in question, including Senator William Proxmire's candid remarks that "because of *the importance of the problem,* the Senate conferees agreed to the House provision. Organized crime operates on a national scale. . . . The problem simply cannot be solved by the States alone."[102]

The leap of logic in this case—from a national economic market to a national market in crime—is substantial. As Justice Stewart points out in his sole dissent in the case, "under the statute before us a man can be convicted without any proof of interstate movement, of the use of the facilities of interstate commerce, or of facts showing that his conduct affected interstate commerce." Unless Congress "could rationally have concluded that loan sharking is an activity with interstate attributes that distinguish it in some substantial respect from other local crime," Stewart writes, the law should be judged unconstitutional. "It is not enough to say that loan sharking is a national problem, for all crime is a national problem."[103]

A logic similar to *Perez* was used to sustain several sections of the Civil Rights Act of 1964 and its applicability to restaurants serving food that had traveled in interstate commerce. In Katzenbach v. McClung,[104] the Court held that Congress could forbid racial discrimination at Ollie's Barbeque in Birmingham, Alabama, under the commerce clause, "*The absence of direct evidence* connecting discrimina-

---

[100] 402 U.S. 146 (1971).
[101] 402 U.S. at 154, quoted in Gunther, *Constitutional Law,* 150.
[102] 402 U.S. at 150, quoted in Gunther, *Constitutional Law,* 149; emphasis added.
[103] 402 U.S. at 157, quoted in Gunther, *Constitutional Law,* 150.
[104] 379 U.S. 294 (1964).

tory restaurant service with the flow of interstate food," the Court said, "is not . . . a crucial matter. . . ."[105] Congress "had ample basis upon which to find that racial discrimination at restaurants which receive from out of state a substantial portion of the food served does, in fact, impose commercial burdens of national magnitude upon interstate commerce."[106] Testimony in Congress "afforded ample basis for the conclusion that established restaurants in such areas sold less interstate goods because of the discrimination, that interstate travel was obstructed directly by it, that business in general suffered and that many new businesses refrained from establishing there as a result of it."[107] Ollie's claim that he would *lose* business (and therefore buy less food) if forced to integrate—perfectly plausible given his time and place—was regarded by the Court as irrelevant.

A few years later, the Court extended the holding of *Katzenbach* to cover the snack bar of a small, isolated Arkansas club, despite the fact that it could be reached only by country roads and that the district court (sustained by the court of appeals) had found no evidence that the food sold had moved in interstate commerce.[108] This was, finally, too much for Justice Black, a staunch defender of the New Deal commerce and police power cases, but himself the product of rural southern upbringing. "There is not a word of evidence," he wrote in his lone dissent, "showing that . . . an interstate traveler was ever there or ever invited there or ever dreamed of going there."[109] The record was also "totally devoid of evidence" to show that a "substantial portion" of the "small amount of food sold had previously moved in interstate commerce."[110] While the Civil Rights Act was important, "we are not called on to hold nor should we hold subject to that Act this country people's recreation center, lying in what may be, so far as we know, a little 'sleepy hollow' between Arkansas hills miles away from any interstate highway."[111] This, Black says, "would be stretching the Commerce Clause so as to give the Federal Government complete control

[105] *Ibid.* at 304–5, quoted in Brest and Levinson, *Processes of Constitutional Decisionmaking,* 327; emphasis added.

[106] 379 U.S. at 299, quoted in Brest and Levinson, *Processes of Constitutional Decisionmaking,* 327.

[107] 379 U.S. at 300, quoted in Brest and Levinson, *Processes of Constitutional Decisionmaking,* 327.

[108] Daniel v. Paul, 395 U.S. 298 (1969).

[109] *Ibid.* at 310.

[110] *Ibid.* at 312.

[111] *Ibid.* at 315.

over every little remote country place of recreation in every nook and cranny of every precinct and county in every one of the fifty states."[112]

These cases underline the extent to which the Court has interpreted legislative power to regulate the economy, and any activities touching the economy, as plenary, and has surrendered any real substantial review of such legislative power. Once again, we should notice the extent to which these readings of the commerce power and the police power depend upon incorporation into the Constitution of various interpretations of economic and social reality—the aggregation doctrine; the national market—interpretations that have nothing whatever to do with the text of the Constitution. Moreover, these cases turn on the level of review the Court chooses to exercise—a very loosely defined "rational relation" test—which is itself a political judgment based upon a theory of reality: that legislatures and not courts are competent to assess complex economic reality.

The problem with this justification for the rational relation test is that the Court chooses *not* to defer to this competence of the legislature when a law touches any civil liberties matter; then, the Court demands that the state explain itself fully and justify completely its action. There is no intrinsic reason why the Court could not apply a higher standard of review—perhaps an intermediate standard—to economic matters. Under such a standard, when a legitimate claim is made that economic rights are at stake, the Court would demand that the state's chosen means be "substantially related" to the achievement of an "important" governmental objective.[113] Such an intermediate standard would be just as "constitutional" as the standard the Court now employs. Whatever standard is applied is a purely political judgment—it reflects the extent to which the Court wishes to defer to Congress on any given subject. Nothing in the text of the Constitution tells the Court how much to defer, or on what subjects.

The answer to the question "can we condemn *Lochner* but accept

---

[112] *Ibid.* It is worth noting that alternate, non-commerce-based grounds were perhaps available to sustain the Civil Rights Act, but that the Justice Department under Robert Kennedy believed the commerce clause decisions of the New Deal period to be the strongest available legal precedent. See the excerpts from the congressional testimony reprinted in Gunther, *Constitutional Law*, 159–62. Kennedy was right, of course; the New Deal cases contain language and reasoning that support an extraordinarily broad reading of congressional power.

[113] On the intermediate standard, see Gunther, *Constitutional Law*, 472; and Epstein, *Takings*, 136–37.

Griswold and *Roe*" thus turns out to be "it depends"; it depends on our construction of social reality, on what we are and are not willing to regard as a "fact." Fundamentally, it depends upon how we evaluate the Court's hands-off approach to the economy, which originated during the crisis of the 1930s, and whether we regard as valid the Court's extension of that approach to more and more areas of the law (crime, civil rights).

Contemporary liberals should not kid themselves, however; when the Court abridges an "economic" right, it is still abridging a right,[114] and when the Court gives plenary power to Congress under the police powers doctrine or the commerce clause, it is opening up a breathtaking domain of regulation in which few principled distinctions can be made. Whether the "facts" of economic life support such a broad reading of legislative power is debatable; because it is debatable, the Court should examine more closely than it currently does the validity of the legislature's reasons for acting. Simply citing congressional findings without examining them, and then trotting out the bête noire of Lochner v.

---

[114] After decades of complete deference to the judgment of Congress on economic matters, there were some signs that some justices in the 1970s and 1980s wanted to pull back and begin exercising some level of substantive review of economic decisions. For example, Justice Stewart wrote in 1972 that

> The dichotomy between personal liberties and property rights is a false one. Property does not have rights. People have rights. The right to enjoy property without unlawful deprivation, no less than the right to speak or the right to travel, is, in truth, a "personal" right, whether the "property" in question be a welfare check, a home or a savings account. In fact, a fundamental interdependence exists between the personal right to liberty and the personal right in property. Neither could have meaning without the other. That rights in property are basic civil rights has long been recognized.

Stewart then sites Blackstone, Locke, and John Adams. Lynch v. Household Finance Corporation, 405 U.S. 538, 552 (1972), quoted in Gunther, *Constitutional Law*, 474.

Similar sentiments underlie recent renewed interest in the "takings" clause. See, for example, Justice Scalia's dissent in Pennell v. City of San Jose, 485 U.S. 1 (1988); see also Nollan v. California Coastal Commission, 483 U.S. 825 (1987) and First English Evangelical Lutheran Church of Glendale v. Los Angeles, 482 U.S. 304 (1987). For a discussion, see Jennifer Nedelsky, *Private Property and the Limits of American Constitutionalism* (Chicago: University of Chicago Press, 1990), 231–46; see also Epstein, *Takings, passim*, as well as the articles in Ellen Frankel Paul and Howard Dickman (eds.), *Liberty, Property, and the Future of Constitutional Development* (Albany: SUNY Press, 1990), esp. the article by William Riker, "Civil Rights and Property Rights," 49–64. See also the symposium, "Rediscovering Economic Liberties," *Rutgers Law Review* 41 (Spring 1989): 753–864.

New York or citing the importance of judicial deference on such matters, does little to fulfill the Court's mandate. The New Deal and the depression which spawned it ended a long time ago.

XI.

This chapter began with a consideration of the manner in which the police powers doctrine functions as an adjustable, elastic clause, allowing the Court to incorporate into the Constitution various "coherence images." Such "images" include notions of what restrictions of liberty are allowable. This led to the conclusion that there is no such thing as a "neutral" constitutional principle, for important constitutional decisions about restrictions of liberty will always turn on the Court's judgment about the relevance of certain social "facts," or the Court's assessment of what restrictions of liberty the American public fundamentally "agrees" are necessary for the public welfare. This led to the proposition that restrictions of liberty are justified only when the Court is satisfied that there is empirical evidence of concrete harm, or a unanimous (or nearly unanimous) moral sentiment.

There are many different kinds of social "fact." There is science and economics; there is social science (relevant, for example, to Brown v. Board). There is the fundamental social fact of ethical pluralism (relevant to the abortion question—in the absence of definitive scientific answers—and also to the question of obscenity). We turn in the next chapters to an elaboration of the ways in which some of these kinds of social "facts" are relevant to cases involving the rights of minorities.

The argument about the relevance of moral consensus to some constitutional decisions, as well as the observation that the Court's reading of "facts" can be heavily influenced by politics (as it was during the New Deal), points toward some interesting theoretical conclusions about the relationship between judicial review and democracy. There is a direct relationship between some democratic judgments and constitutional decisions; when a majority speaks loudly enough, the Court may suddenly discover the relevance of new "facts" (for example, the aggregation doctrine); when the majority speaks in unison, that itself may become the basis for the Court's actions. And when the majority does not speak in unison, *that* is highly relevant (as in the debate about abortion). Those who worry (both on and off the bench) that judicial review is undemocratic (Felix Frankfurter, William Rehnquist, Alexander Bickel, John Ely, to name just a few) miss what is most fundamental about the Supreme Court and the Constitution. The Court cannot help but be democratic in an ultimate sense, for it cannot decide its most important cases without reference to social knowledge—-"facts"—or social judgments. Such knowledge and judgments derive from democratic sources; the Court does not pull them out of thin air.

To be sure, the Court does not act in accordance with the wishes of a simple political majority. That is because the Constitution's most fundamental commitment is to liberty, liberty that can be restricted only with good cause and for certain purposes. But a "super"-majority, with "facts" backing it up, or with near-unanimous agreement, would not long be ignored by the Court.

Those who worry about the undemocratic nature of judicial review should take comfort from this. Those who worry about society's irrationality and tendency to hysteria and prejudice must take comfort in a vigilant Court, willing and able to look openly and skeptically at the majority's "facts."

CHAPTER 4

"THE MOST WILLFUL BLINDNESS": THE SUPREME COURT AND SOCIAL FACTS

I.

In the previous chapter we found that the most fundamental error of Lochner v. New York (and, by implication, the error of the jurisprudence this single case symbolizes) was the stubborn refusal of the Court's majority to take seriously the social and scientific facts supporting New York's exercise of its police powers. In previous chapters we found that liberty, understood as a right to be free from arbitrary government action, is a fundamental constitutional value, and, further, that the protection of minorities is a central purpose of American constitutionalism. We also found that it is impossible to engage in constitutional interpretation without reference to fundamental social "facts," as when it is necessary to judge the relevance of certain social categories and traits to arrive at a judgment concerning the "reasonableness" of state legislation under the due process clause of the Fourteenth Amendment.

This chapter and the next will combine these lines of analysis in a discussion of several current issues concerning the rights of "marginal" persons. Viewed within the appropriate frame of analysis, these cases do not concern the presentation of novel claims or the discovery of "new" rights;[1] rather, they represent cases in which litigants are seeking the protection of their most basic liberty. When a conservatively inclined Court refuses to honor the claims of litigants in these cases, it is

---

[1] For an example of the charge that the Court in these types of cases is "creating" new rights, see Justice White's dissent in Moore v. East Cleveland, 431 U.S. 494 (1977). For a discussion of Moore, see below, pp. 138–40.

refusing to see the relevance of the most basic social facts at issue in the case, in a manner no less stubborn than the majority in *Lochner*. When the Court *is* willing to accept the relevance of certain social facts, it is not inventing new rights, but enforcing the oldest, most basic constitutional right—the right to be free from arbitrary government action.

As we will see, "facts" enter into constitutional decision making in different ways. Often the construction of facts is crucial—that is, how the Court chooses to characterize a given social situation has a major influence on the outcome. Sometimes crucial in such cases is the Court's willingness or unwillingness to inject a note of social realism into legal formulas. Thus, for example, a number of social institutions are designed to "treat" certain categories of individuals but, in fact, do little more than house them, and the Court's willingness or unwillingness to recognize that fact—and to make an explicit analogy to incarceration in prison—becomes crucial to the outcome of a case. At other times, what is crucial is the Court's willingness to accept scientific evidence in a given case, or social scientific conclusions about a given issue. We begin with three seemingly unrelated, but important, cases.

II.

In the first case, DeShaney v. Winnebago County,[2] the petitioner was a child, Joshua DeShaney, who had been beaten and permanently damaged by his father. The respondents, the county department of social services and several of its social workers, had received complaints that Joshua was being abused; they "had reason to believe that this was the case, but nonetheless did not act to remove petitioner from his father's custody."[3] Joshua and his mother sued, claiming that the county's failure to protect him deprived him of his liberty in violation of the due process clause of the Fourteenth Amendment.

The Supreme Court, in a six-to-three vote, held for the county, in an opinion written by Chief Justice Rehnquist. While conceding that the facts of the case were "undeniably tragic," Rehnquist held that "nothing in the language of the Due Process Clause itself requires the State to protect the life, liberty, and property of its citizens against invasion by private actors." It was Joshua's father, not an agent of the state, who inflicted harm. The due process clause, Rehnquist says, "is phrased as a limitation on the State's power to act, not as a guarantee

---

[2] 109 S.Ct. 998 (1989).
[3] *Ibid.* at 1001.

of certain minimal levels of safety and security."[4] Since the state had no affirmative duty or obligation to guarantee Joshua anything, and did not inflict any harm on him, his rights cannot have been violated.

Thus, according to the majority, due process generally requires no affirmative protection from the infliction of harm by private actors. Having put forth this general principle, the question then shifts to whether any "special relationship" can be said to exist between the petitioner and the state which would require the government to act in his particular case.[5] Answering *that* question turns on the interpretation of precedent, about which the Court's majority and the three dissenters disagree; they also disagree about how to interpret the facts of Joshua's case in relation to those precedents.

The precedents in question concern the rights of prisoners and mental patients. In Estelle v. Gamble,[6] the Court had held that the state must provide adequate medical care to incarcerated prisoners. In Youngberg v. Romeo the Court held that due process requires the state to provide involuntarily committed mental patients with whatever services are necessary to guarantee their "reasonable safety" from themselves and others.[7]

According to the majority in *DeShaney*, these and similar cases "afford . . . no help" to Joshua; "taken together, they stand only for the proposition that when the State takes a person into its custody and holds him there against his will, the Constitution imposes upon it a corresponding duty to assume some responsibility for his safety and general well-being." The crucial fact is custody; custody leads to the "affirmative duty to protect."[8] This duty "arises not from the State's knowledge of the individual's predicament or from its expressions of intent to help him," but rather "from the limitation which it has imposed on his freedom to act on his own behalf."[9] When the state has *already* restricted someone's liberty, "through incarceration, institutionalization, or other similar restraint," the protection of the due process clause is triggered, and not before. Thus, according to Rehnquist, the relevant precedents have "no applicability" to Joshua DeShaney. Indeed, the petitioners "concede that the harms Joshua suffered did not occur while he was in the State's custody, but while he was in

custody

---

[4] *Ibid.* at 1001, 1003.
[5] *Ibid.* at 1004.
[6] 429 U.S. 97 (1976).
[7] 457 U.S. 307, 314–25 (1982). For a discussion of *Youngberg*, see below, pp. 178–83.
[8] 109 S.Ct. at 1005–6.
[9] *Ibid.* at 1006.

the custody of his natural father."[10] The situation might be different, the Court says in a footnote, "had the State by the affirmative exercise of its power removed Joshua from free society and placed him in a foster home operated by its agents."[11] But, "[w]hile the State may have been aware of the dangers that Joshua faced in the free world, it played no part in their creation, nor did it do anything to render him any more vulnerable to them."[12]

This construction of the facts is crucial, for *had* the state rendered Joshua more vulnerable to his father, the state could be said to have engaged in some affirmative "action" and not merely in neutral "inaction," and the majority's argument would begin to collapse. In light of this, it is useful to review in greater detail the sequence of steps leading to Joshua's ultimate injury.

Joshua was born in 1979 in Wyoming; in 1980 his parents were divorced in a Wyoming court and his father was granted custody. Soon thereafter father and son moved to Winnebago County, Wisconsin; the father remarried, and that marriage also ended in divorce.

Authorities in Winnebago County learned that Joshua might be a victim of child abuse in January 1982, "when his father's second wife complained to the police, at the time of their divorce, that he had previously 'hit the boy causing marks and [was] a prime case for child abuse.' " The county's Department of Social Services (DSS) "interviewed the father, but he denied the accusations, and DSS did not pursue them further."[13]

A year later "Joshua was admitted to a local hospital with multiple bruises and abrasions." The physician "suspected child abuse and notified DSS, which immediately obtained an order from a Wisconsin juvenile court placing Joshua in the temporary custody of the hospital." A few days later "the county convened an ad hoc 'Child Protection Team' "; this group consisted of "a pediatrician, a psychologist, a police detective, the county's lawyer, several DSS caseworkers, and various hospital personnel." This group "decided that there was insufficient evidence of child abuse to retain Joshua in the custody of the court." Instead, the team "recommend[ed] several measures to protect Joshua," such as "enrolling him in a preschool program, providing his father with certain counselling services, and encouraging his father's girlfriend to move out of the home." The father "entered into a volun-

[10] *Ibid.*
[11] *Ibid.* at 1006, n.9.
[12] *Ibid.* at 1006.
[13] *Ibid.* at 1001.

tary agreement with DSS in which he promised to cooperate with them in accomplishing these goals." Thus the child protection case was dismissed and Joshua was returned to the custody of his father.[14]

Within a month, "emergency room personnel called the DSS case-worker handling Joshua's case to report that he had once again been treated for suspicious injuries." Still "the caseworker concluded that there was no basis for action." Over the next six months, "the case-worker made monthly visits to the DeShaney home, during which she observed a number of suspicious injuries on Joshua's head; she also noticed that he had not been enrolled in school and that the girlfriend had not moved out." The caseworker "dutifully recorded these inci-dents in her files, along with her continuing suspicions that someone in the DeShaney household was physically abusing Joshua, but she did nothing more."[15]

Soon thereafter, "the emergency room notified DSS that Joshua had been treated once again for injuries that they believed to be caused by child abuse." The caseworker visited the DeShaney home two more times, but was told on these occasions that Joshua "was too ill to see her."[16] DSS still took no action. Finally, his father "beat four-year-old Joshua so severely that he fell into a life-threatening coma." Emergency surgery "revealed a series of hemorrhages caused by traumatic injuries to the head inflicted over a long period of time." Although Joshua did not die, "he suffered brain damage so severe that he is expected to spend the rest of his life confined to an institution for the profoundly retarded." His father was eventually tried and convicted of child abuse.[17]

In spite of these grisly facts, the majority concludes that the state did nothing to make Joshua more vulnerable to his father's violence; it did nothing to create a situation sufficiently analogous to the depriva-tion of liberty inflicted upon a prisoner or a mental patient involuntarily committed to an institution. "That the State once took temporary custody of Joshua," Rehnquist says, "does not alter the analysis, for when it returned him to his father's custody, it placed him in no worse position than that in which he would have been had it not acted at all; the State does not become the permanent guarantor of an individual's safety by having once offered him shelter."[18]

---

[14] *Ibid.*
[15] *Ibid.*
[16] *Ibid.* at 1002.
[17] *Ibid.*
[18] *Ibid.* at 1006.

But the state did far more to Joshua than merely once offering him shelter; over a long period of time, it returned him to his father's custody, or failed to remove him from that custody, despite its almost-certain knowledge that he was being abused. Moreover, it did so within the structure of a child welfare system that made the DSS the only avenue available to Joshua for protection. The hospital could not by itself help Joshua, for it was required by law to report its suspicions to the DSS.[19] Neighbors, who had "informed the police that they had seen or heard Joshua's father or his father's lover beating or otherwise abusing Joshua," had made reports to the police, and the police— again, because of state law—"brought these reports to the attention of DSS."[20] The decision whether to remove Joshua from his father was left to the DSS at every step.

Given these facts—given this social reality—it is extremely difficult to characterize the state's action vis-à-vis Joshua as merely neutral. As Justice Brennan concludes in his dissent, "Wisconsin's child-protection program . . . effectively confined Joshua DeShaney within the walls of Randy DeShaney's violent home until such time as DSS took action to remove him." The state was not neutral; the state created a particular system that monopolized whatever relief Joshua had available to him. As Justice Brennan says, "in these circumstances a private citizen, or even a person working in a government agency other than DSS, would doubtless feel that her job was done as soon as she had reported her suspicions of child abuse to DSS." By the operation of such a program, the state "has relieved ordinary citizens and governmental bodies other than the Department of any sense of obligation to do anything more than report their suspicions of child abuse to DSS."[21]

Given this state monopoly, "if DSS ignores or dismisses these suspicions, no one will step in to fill the gap." Thus it is not true to say that the state merely " 'stood by and did nothing' with respect to Joshua"; rather, "through its child-protection program, the state actively intervened in Joshua's life."[22]

These facts, for the three dissenters, put Joshua's case "solidly within the tradition" of the relevant precedents, which, not surprisingly, they interpret differently than the Court's majority.[23] The majority had interpreted the cases concerning prisoners and mental patients as turn-

[19]   See Justice Brennan's dissent, 109 S.Ct. at 1010.
[20]   *Ibid.*
[21]   *Ibid.* at 1011.
[22]   *Ibid.*
[23]   *Ibid.*

ing on the fact of custody; this allows them to say that, absent taking custody of Joshua away from his father, the state was not responsible for what happened to him. But for the dissenters, the precedents turn less on the fact of physical custody than on the fact that the state makes it impossible for the prisoner or the mental patient to help himself; it separates him "from other sources of aid that . . . the State [is] obligated to replace."[24] The dissenters would recognize "that 'the State's knowledge of [an] individual's predicament [and] its expressions of intent to help him' can amount to a 'limitation of his freedom to act on his own behalf' or to obtain help from others." Thus, they would read the relevant precedents "to stand for the . . . more generous proposition that, if a State cuts off private sources of aid and then refuses aid itself, it cannot wash its hands of the harm that results from its inaction." The dissent then makes an analogy to other types of cases in which "a State's actions—such as the monopolization of a particular path of relief—may impose upon the State certain positive duties."[25] It refers to Boddie v. Connecticut,[26] in which the Court struck down a filing fee as applied to divorce cases brought by indigents, and Schneider v. State,[27] in which the Court decided "that a local government could not entirely foreclose the opportunity to speak in a public forum." It also refers to two race-related cases, Shelley v. Kraemer[28] and Burton v. Wilmington Parking Authority,[29] which "suggest that a State may be found complicit in an injury even if it did not create the situation that caused the harm."[30]

Although "arising as they do from constitutional contexts different from the one involved here," these cases "set a tone" for the dissenters; they "signal that a State's prior actions may be decisive in analyzing the constitutional significance of its inaction."[31] In this case, the state's "prior actions" consisted of setting up its system of child welfare and requiring that all information and decisions concerning Joshua's safety be made within that system; this system made it impossible for any

---

[24] *Ibid.* at 1009.
[25] *Ibid.*
[26] 401 U.S. 371 (1971).
[27] 308 U.S. 147 (1939).
[28] 334 U.S. 1 (1948).
[29] 365 U.S. 715 (1961).
[30] 109 S.Ct. at 1009. *Shelley* concerned restrictive real estate covenants; the Court held that such covenants could not be enforced by the state. *Burton* concerned the operation of a coffee shop leased from a city-owned parking garage; the coffee shop had refused to serve Negroes.
[31] 109 S.Ct. at 1009–10.

actor but DSS to help Joshua, and continually left him exposed to his father's violence. Given these facts, Joshua should be able to claim the protection of the due process clause, for the state of Wisconsin has "acted" in the series of events leading to his ultimate injury.

The argument that due process is relevant to Joshua's plight does not end the controversy, for the due process clause forbids only government action that is arbitrary. In previous cases, "arbitrary" had been defined as equivalent to "unprofessional" behavior on the part of a state actor resulting in injury; mere "negligence" would not mean that a violation of due process has occurred.[32] It thus becomes necessary, for Brennan and his fellow dissenters, to allow Joshua and his mother the opportunity to at least argue that the DSS's actions were so irrational as to be arbitrary, rather than based on "the sound exercise of professional judgment." If the DSS caseworker's decision to leave Joshua in the care of his father *was* based on the appropriate exercise of professional judgment, the state is not liable. In an important passage, Brennan notes that this "vision of substantive due process serves a purpose similar to that served by adherence to procedural norms, namely, requiring that a State actor stop and think before she acts in a way that may lead to a loss of liberty." The due process clause "is not violated by merely negligent conduct," which means "that a social worker who simply makes a mistake of judgment under what are admittedly complex and difficult conditions will not find herself liable. . . ." If, however, the DSS caseworker's conduct went beyond a "mistake of judgment," her behavior, and therefore the state's treatment of Joshua, becomes arbitrary, and thereby rises to constitutional significance.[33]

Because the Court majority, however, refuses to consider the DSS in any way responsible for what happened to Joshua, it is unconcerned with the exercise of professional judgment, be it appropriate, negligent, or arbitrary. But, given Brennan's alternative construction of both the facts and the precedents, if the caseworker's conduct *was* more than a negligent "mistake," then a constitutional violation has occurred, for the state of Wisconsin has treated Joshua arbitrarily.

The *DeShaney* case has implications that go far beyond child abuse or the treatment of any vulnerable group, for it raises in a dramatic

---

[32] See Justice Brennan's dissent, 109 S.Ct. at 1011–12.

[33] *Ibid.* at 1012. It is important to note that Brennan is not arguing that the caseworker's judgment in Joshua's case *was* more than merely a negligent error, but rather that it could be, and that Joshua should have an opportunity to argue and prove that it was.

manner the ways in which the state can structure, facilitate, or prevent private behavior, blurring the line between public and private action.[34] Randy DeShaney, a "private" actor, beat his son, destroyed his brain, and reduced him to a vegetable, after Joshua had been repeatedly returned to his home or left there by the state. We regard many forms of property as "private," yet it is the laws of the state that define the form and content of such property. We regard corporations for many purposes as "private" entities, yet it is the laws of the state that allow a corporation to exist and that structure its form.[35] Marriage is a "private" relationship, yet it is recognized, licensed, and, if necessary, dissolved by the state. Various professions are similarly licensed.

Where does the state end and truly private behavior begin? How deeply implicated is the state in the behavior of various private actors? If the state licenses an incompetent physician, is it liable for the damages he causes? *DeShaney* shows us (among other things) that these are complex and difficult questions that depend on the particular facts of individual cases; moreover, it shows us that characterizing a given event as the result of "private" action is not necessarily determinative of the degree of the state's responsibility.

III.

The second case concerns an issue of family law applied to a complicated set of social facts. A California law says that a child born to a married woman living with her husband is "a child of the marriage" unless the husband is impotent or sterile. In legal terminology, such a law creates a "presumption." Under the terms of the statute in question, only the husband or wife may challenge that presumption, that is, only the husband or wife may claim that the child was fathered by another party.[36] This statute has been applied to Victoria D., a child born to Carole D., who was married to Gerald D. The constitutionality of the statute was challenged both by Victoria D. and by a third party: Michael H., with whom Carole had for a time lived, while still married to Gerald. Michael H. was, according to blood tests, 98.07 percent certain of being Victoria's father. Against the claims of both Victoria

[34] For an example of similar reasoning as early as 1883, see Justice Harlan's dissent in the Civil Rights Cases, 109 U.S. 3 (1883).
[35] See the discussion in Justice White's dissent in First National Bank of Boston v. Bellotti, 435 U.S. 765, 802–22 (1978).
[36] Cal. Evid. Code Ann. sec. 621 (West Supp. 1989).

and Michael, a five-to-four majority of the Supreme Court upheld the constitutionality of the California law.[37]

The case raises fundamental questions concerning the "liberty" protected by the due process clause; it also raises fundamental questions concerning the relationship between that liberty and both social and scientific facts. The Supreme Court's judgment, most obviously, contradicts the scientific evidence of the blood tests; it also contradicts the social reality of Carole's and Victoria's life. As recited by Justice Scalia in the opinion of the Court, the complicated facts are these: Carole, "an international model," married Gerald, "a top executive in a French oil company," in the spring of 1976. They established a home in Los Angeles "in which they resided as husband and wife when one or the other was not out of the country on business." Approximately two years after the marriage, "Carole became involved in an adulterous affair with a neighbor, Michael H." In a few months she conceived a child. Gerald, the husband, "was listed as father on the birth certificate and has always held Victoria out to the world as his daughter." Carole, however, "soon after delivery of the child . . . informed Michael that she believed he might be the father."[38]

Five months after the birth of Victoria "Gerald moved to New York City to pursue his business interests, but Carole chose to remain in California." Soon after Gerald left, "Carole and Michael had blood tests of themselves and Victoria, which showed a 98.07% probability that Michael was Victoria's father." Three months later, "Carole visited Michael in St. Thomas, where his primary business interests were based. There Michael held Victoria out as his child." In a few months, "Carole left Michael and returned to California, where she took up residence with yet another man, Scott K." In the ensuing months, "Carole and Victoria spent time with Gerald in New York City, as well as on vacation in Europe." They then returned to Scott (man number three) in California.[39]

Soon after Carole's return from Europe, Michael, "rebuffed in his attempts to visit Victoria," filed a filiation action in a California court to establish his paternity and his right to visitation. The court "appointed an attorney and guardian *ad litem*[40] to represent Victoria's interests," and "Victoria then filed a cross-complaint asserting that if she had more than one psychological or *de facto* father, she was entitled

---

[37] Michael H. v. Gerald D., 109 S.Ct. 2333 (1989).
[38] *Ibid.* at 2337.
[39] *Ibid.*
[40] That is, an independent professional to represent her separate interests.

to maintain her filial relationship, with all of the attendant rights, duties, and obligations, with both." During this five-month period, "Carole was again living with Gerald in New York," and filed a motion for summary judgment, but at the end of five months "she returned to California, become involved once again with Michael, and instructed her attorneys to remove the summary judgment motion from the calendar."[41]

For the next eight months, "when Michael was not in St. Thomas, he lived with Carole and Victoria in Carole's apartment in Los Angeles, and held Victoria out as his daughter." During this period "Carole and Michael signed a stipulation that Michael was Victoria's natural father." Carole, however, "left Michael the next month . . . and instructed her attorneys not to file the stipulation." Soon thereafter "Carole reconciled with Gerald and joined him in New York, where they now live with Victoria and two other children since born into the marriage."[42]

Given these facts, Michael argues that the California statute in question contains both procedural flaws (in that it denies him the opportunity to challenge the conclusion that Victoria is the child of Gerald and Carole; under the terms of the statute, only Gerald or Carole could challenge the conclusion) and substantive flaws, in that it denies his "liberty interest" in his parental relationship with Victoria. Victoria, through her guardian, claims similarly that she has a parallel liberty interest in maintaining her relationship with both Michael and Gerald.

The Supreme Court, however, rejects all of these claims.[43] It finds that the state's interests in preserving the marital union of the husband and wife, and in preserving the legitimacy of the child, compelling. Further, it finds no support in precedent or tradition for Michael's claim of a constitutionally protected relationship with Victoria. "California law, like nature itself," according to Scalia, "makes no provision for dual fatherhood."[44] The issues of the case "reduce . . . to whether

[41] 109 S.Ct. at 2337.
[42] Ibid.
[43] The Court splits along complicated lines, as will become clear below. Five justices—Scalia, Rehnquist, O'Connor, Kennedy, and Stevens—vote to sustain the California statute against the claims of Victoria and Michael, although only Rehnquist joins all of Scalia's opinion. O'Connor and Kennedy join all but one crucial point in Scalia's opinion (see p. 128); Stevens concurs on separate grounds (see note 61 below). Thus there is no majority opinion. Four justices—Brennan, Marshall, Blackmun, and White—vote against the California statute.
[44] 109 S.Ct. at 2339.

the relationship between persons in the situation of Michael and Victoria has been treated as a protected family unit under the historic practices of our society, or whether on any other basis it has been accorded special protection."[45] Scalia "think[s] it impossible to find that it has. In fact, quite to the contrary, our traditions have protected the marital family . . . against the sort of claim Michael asserts." Scalia then goes back to the common law, where "the presumption of legitimacy was a fundamental principle."[46] Moreover, since "what Michael asserts here is a right to have himself declared the natural father *and thereby to obtain parental prerogatives*,"[47] to prevail he must establish not merely "that our society has traditionally allowed a natural father in his circumstances to establish paternity, but that it has traditionally accorded such a father parental rights. . . ."[48] Scalia finds no support for such rights for "an adulterous natural father."[49] Although conceding that the due process clause protects substantive liberty interests, "in an attempt to limit and guide interpretation of the Clause, we have insisted not merely that the interest denominated as 'liberty' be 'fundamental' . . . but also that it be an interest traditionally protected by our society."[50] The claims of an "adulterous natural father" do not qualify.

Although Michael had put forward various precedents to support his claim of a protected liberty interest,[51] Scalia reads these cases—

---

[45] *Ibid.* at 2342. Scalia gives little attention to Michael H.'s procedural argument, finding that his procedural argument—that the California law prevents him from challenging the conclusive presumption that Victoria is the child of Carole and Gerald—is dependent on his substantive argument—that he has constitutional rights at stake. See *ibid.* at 2340.

[46] *Ibid.* at 2342.

[47] *Ibid.* at 2343; emphasis in original.

[48] *Ibid.* at 2344.

[49] *Ibid.* at 2344, n.6.

[50] *Ibid.* at 2341.

[51] Michael asserts the relevance of four prior cases dealing with the relationship of unwed fathers to their children: Stanley v. Illinois, 405 U.S. 645 (1972); Quilloin v. Walcott, 434 U.S. 46 (1978); Caban v. Mohammed, 441 U.S. 380 (1979); and Lehr v. Robertson, 463 U.S. 248 (1983). In two of these cases—*Stanley* and *Caban*—the rights of the unwed fathers were upheld; in *Quilloin* and *Lehr,* such claims were rejected. Michael reads these four cases as together establishing the principle that biological parenthood, combined with an established parental relationship, is sufficient to create a protected liberty interest. *Quilloin* and *Lehr* lost their claims, according to Michael, because they had not "act[ed] as a father toward [their] children." Michael H. v. Gerald D., 109 S.Ct. at 2352 (Brennan, J., dissenting). See also Justice White's dissent at 2360–61.

wrongly—as protected only "the relationships that develop within the unitary family."[52] Such "unitary" families do not include Michael and Victoria:

> The family unit accorded traditional respect in our society, which we have referred to as the "unitary family," is typified, of course, by the marital family, but also includes the household of unmarried parents and their children. Perhaps the concept can be expanded even beyond this, but it will bear no resemblance to traditionally respected relationships—and will thus cease to have any constitutional significance—if it is stretched so far as to include the relationship established between a married woman, her lover and their child, during a three-month sojourn in St. Thomas, or during a subsequent eight-month period when, if he happened to be in Los Angeles, he stayed with her and the child.[53]

Thus, because he is defined as an "adulterous natural father," Michael's relationship to Victoria is judged to be unprotected by the due process clause. Due process does protect family relationships, according to Scalia, but only family relationships that are sufficiently "traditional." And Victoria's separate due process claim, Scalia says, "is, if anything, weaker than Michael's."[54] Victoria "claims a Due Process right to maintain filial relations with both Michael and Gerald." This claim "merits little discussion, for, whatever the merits of the guardian['s] . . . belief that such an arrangement can be of great psychological benefit to a child, the claim that a State must recognize multiple fatherhood has no support in the history or traditions of this country."[55]

The plurality's methodology in this case is thus to confine the protection of the due process clause to only the most "traditional" relationships, especially those within the "unitary" family. And in deciding what constitutes traditionally respected rights, the crucial issue quickly becomes the level of generality at which the parties to the suit are described.[56] For Justice Scalia, Michael is an adulterer; he belongs to the legal category adulterous "natural father of a child conceived within

[52] 109 S.Ct. at 2342.
[53] *Ibid.* at 2342, n.3.
[54] *Ibid.* at 2346.
[55] *Ibid.*
[56] See the discussion in Laurence H. Tribe and Michael C. Dorf, "Levels of Generality in the Definition of Rights," *University of Chicago Law Review* 57 (Fall 1990): 1085–98.

and born into an extant marital union that wishes to embrace the child."[57] For the dissenters, however, Michael is a member of the category "parent" or "biological father," or perhaps "biological father with an established relationship with his child." But Scalia insists on the narrower, more specific category. Moreover, because the law—going back to Blackstone and the common law—has never protected this narrow category, Scalia finds no constitutional merit in Michael's claim.

In a footnote, Scalia defends this use of "the most specific level at which a relevant tradition protecting, or denying protection to, the asserted right can be identified." What is at stake in this, he says, is nothing less than the rule of law itself; "a rule of law that binds neither by text nor by any particular, identifiable tradition, is no rule of law at all." Unless the Court consults the most specific tradition available, judges are left to decide cases on their subjective whim; "general traditions," as opposed to the most specific tradition, would "permit judges to dictate rather than discern society's views."[58]

For five members of the Court, however, this definition of due process—as equivalent to the most specific tradition available—is too narrow. Justice O'Connor and Kennedy concur in Scalia's result, but do not join his discussion of "tradition." In a short concurring opinion they take issue solely with his due process analysis; they correctly point out that his footnote "sketches a mode of historical analysis to be used when identifying liberty interests . . . that may be somewhat inconsistent with our past decisions in this area.` . . ." At times, "the Court has characterized relevant traditions protecting asserted rights at levels of generality that might not be 'the most specific level' available."[59] O'Connor and Kennedy then cite a number of crucial due process cases, including Griswold v. Connecticut and Eisenstadt v. Baird, the cases establishing a right of privacy, and Loving v. Virginia, the case outlawing antimiscegenation statutes in the South.[60] And in a

---

[57] 109 S.Ct. at 2344.

[58] *Ibid.* at 2344, n.6.

[59] *Ibid.* at 2346.

[60] Griswold v. Connecticut, 381 U.S. 479 (1965); Eisenstadt v. Baird, 405 U.S. 438 (1972); Loving v. Virginia, 388 U.S. 1 (1967). In *Griswold*, the Court declared unconstitutional a Connecticut statute prohibiting the use of contraceptives by married couples. It based its decision on a right of marital privacy; different justices found support for this right in different places, including the due process clause and the Ninth Amendment. The various opinions contained a great deal of broad language about marital privacy and privacy in general; the various justices did not restrict themselves to a discussion of the tradition behind the legal category "married persons wishing to use

separate concurring opinion, Justice Stevens points out that the relevant precedents "demonstrate that enduring 'family' relationships may develop in unconventional settings."[61]

In his dissent, joined by Justices Marshall and Blackmun, Justice Brennan takes direct aim at Scalia's "tradition" argument. Scalia, Brennan says, is "apparently oblivious to the fact that this concept ['tradition'] can be as malleable and as elusive as 'liberty' itself. . . ." The definition of "tradition" is not so easy; "because reasonable people can disagree about the content of particular traditions, and because they can disagree even about which traditions are relevant to the definition of 'liberty,' the plurality has not found the objective boundary that it seeks."[62]

Brennan then points out that "even if we could agree . . . on the content and significance of particular traditions, we still would be forced to identify the point at which a tradition becomes firm enough to be relevant to our definition of liberty and the moment at which it becomes too obsolete to be relevant any longer."[63] Brennan here is surely pointing to an obvious flaw in Scalia's logic; "tradition" in this country long supported the subordination of racial and religious minorities and women despite the equal protection clause, yet we no longer tolerate such discrimination; we also do not believe such discrimination to be sanctioned by the Constitution. Clearly, we are guided by more than just "tradition" when we interpret the Constitution.

Brennan goes on to fault Scalia for "citing barely a handful of this

---

contraceptives." In *Eisenstadt,* the Court extended this holding to the privacy of individuals, using similarly broad reasoning. In Loving v. Virginia, the Court struck down Virginia's antimiscegenation law. Again, it used broad language in its discussion of the issues presented by the case; it did not restrict its analysis to the question of whether "tradition" allowed states to prevent blacks from marrying whites.

[61] 109 S.Ct. at 2347. Stevens—like Michael H.—cites Stanley v. Illinois and Caban v. Mohammed, see note 51 above. In *Stanley,* the Court upheld the right of an unwed father to a hearing before his children were removed from his custody. In *Caban,* the Court upheld the right of a father to bar adoption of his illegitimate children. In both cases, the Court emphasized the importance of the relationship existing between the father and his children.

Stevens concurs in the result of the *Michael H.* plurality because of a California provision that would have allowed Michael to prove that he was an "other person having an interest in the welfare of the child" to whom "reasonable visitation rights" could be awarded at the trial judge's discretion. See 109 S. Ct. at 2347.

[62] 109 S.Ct. at 2349.

[63] *Ibid.*

Court's numerous decisions defining the scope of the liberty protected by the Due Process Clause" and ignoring cases in which the Court has given a broad definition to "property" or "liberty." If the Court had "looked to tradition" with the specificity Scalia demands, "many a decision would have reached a different result."[64] Brennan lists a number of relevant examples:

> Surely the use of contraceptives by unmarried couples . . . or even by married couples. . . ; the freedom from corporal punishment in schools. . . ; the freedom from an arbitrary transfer from a prison to a psychiatric institution. . . ; and even the right to raise one's natural but illegitimate children . . . were not "interests traditionally protected by our society" . . . at the time of their consideration by this Court.[65]

Yet, as Brennan correctly points out, these are all interests the Court has protected. It has done so by extracting broad principles—privacy; a right to be free from arbitrary government action—from relevant precedents and applying them to contemporary disputes. It is not that the Court completely ignores tradition in due process analysis; "throughout our decision-making in this important area runs the theme that certain interests and practices—freedom from physical restraint, marriage, childbearing, childrearing, and others—form the core of our definition of 'liberty.' " These interests are judged to be protected by the due process clause "partly" because "of the fact that the Due Process Clause would seem an empty promise if it did not protect them, and partly [as] the result of the historical and traditional importance of these interests in our society."[66]

Brennan here is saying that "tradition" can only form a starting point for due process analysis; it can provide evidence of the values society has always considered fundamental. What Brennan does not say, but leaves implicit, is that the delineation of these traditional values is inherently a vague and subjective judicial task; the certainty Scalia seeks is a chimera. And when he says that "the Due Process Clause would seem an empty promise if it did not protect" certain values,

[64] *Ibid.* at 2350.
[65] *Ibid.* Brennan here is referring to *Griswold* and *Eisenstadt,* see note 60, as well as to Ingraham v. Wright, 430 U.S. 651 (1977); Vitek v. Jones, 445 U.S. 480 (1980); and Stanley v. Illinois, see note 61. Brennan is quoting Scalia, 109 S.Ct. at 2341.
[66] 109 S.Ct. at 2350.

Brennan is implicitly acknowledging the ideology of natural rights that
lies at the foundation of American constitutionalism. There is for
Justice Brennan, as there had been for Justices Field and Bradley in the
Slaughter-House case in 1873,[67] a black box of fundamental rights;
the due process clause "would seem an empty promise" if there were
no such black box. Contained within the black box are the right to be
free from physical restraint, rights pertaining to marriage, childbearing,
child rearing, "and others." Due process would be an empty promise
without these fundamental rights because due process protects liberty,
and liberty can be restricted only for agreed, limited purposes. American society has always agreed, and continues to agree, that certain
rights are fundamental; it may be useful to consult "tradition" to find
out what kinds of liberty society has always valued in this way, but
judicial inquiry does not end there; tradition is a fluid thing, and
can become outmoded. Judges must, Brennan says, take notice of a
changing world. "The plurality's interpretive method is more than
novel," Brennan says, "it is misguided. It ignores the good reasons
for limiting the role of 'tradition' in interpreting the Constitution's
deliberately capacious language."[68] The plurality ignores social and
scientific facts:

> In the plurality's constitutional universe, we may not take
> notice of the fact that the original reasons for the conclusive
> presumption of paternity are out of place in a world in which
> blood tests can prove virtually beyond a shadow of a doubt
> who sired a particular child and in which the fact of illegiti-
> macy no longer plays the burdensome and stigmatizing role it
> once did.[69]

The plurality also ignores the modern social reality of nonconformist
morality, represented in this case by Carole's movement among different intimate partners. Here, Brennan's language is a bit more veiled;
he presumably does not wish to call his colleague a prude. But his point
is clear, and goes beyond the facts of this particular case. "The plurality

[67] 83 U.S. 36 (1873).
[68] 109 S. Ct. at 2351. Brennan uses the phrase "deliberately capacious
language" to make the extremely important theoretical point that the framers
of the Constitution did not intend future Supreme Courts to be bound by their
own specific applications of general legal principles and concepts. See chapter
2.
[69] *Ibid.*

ignores the kind of society in which our Constitution exists," he says. "We are not an assimilative, homogeneous society, but a facilitative, pluralistic one, in which we must be willing to abide someone else's unfamiliar or even repellant practice because the same tolerant impulse protects our own idiosyncrasies."[70] Indeed, there can be little doubt that Scalia *is* repelled by the facts of Carole's and Michael's life; his language gives him away. "The facts of this case are," Scalia says at the beginning of his opinion, "we must hope, extraordinary."[71] Such sarcasm is highly unusual for a Court long used to dealing with the rights of criminals and other unconventional people. Similarly, when describing some of the time Michael spent with Victoria, Scalia refers to an "eight-month period when, if he happened to be in Los Angeles, he stayed with" Carole and Victoria.[72] We must hope, Scalia is saying, that people live conventional lives, that they don't change their minds about the people with whom they will be intimate. And jet-setting people who travel a lot couldn't possibly care for their children, for otherwise wouldn't they stay home?[73]

Against this kind of opprobrium and sarcasm, Justice Brennan says that "[e]ven if we can agree . . . that 'family' and 'parenthood' are part of the good life, it is absurd to assume that we can agree on the content of those terms. . . . In a community such as ours, 'liberty' must include the freedom not to conform."[74] The facts of the case, for Brennan, are indisputable, and compel a conclusion. Michael H. "is almost certainly Victoria D.'s natural father," he "has lived with her as her father, has contributed to her support, and has from the beginning sought to strengthen and maintain his relationship with her. . . . The evidence is undisputed that Michael, Victoria, and Carole did live together as a family. . . ."[75]

Accordingly, Brennan finds that Michael and Victoria's interests in maintaining a parent-child relationship with each other fits squarely within well-established precedent:

> We confront an interest—that of a parent and child in their relation with each other—that was among the first that this

---

[70] *Ibid.*
[71] *Ibid.* at 2337.
[72] *Ibid.* at 2342, n.3.
[73] In a similar vein, Robert Bork wisecracks about the lives of the individuals in the case; see *The Tempting of America: The Political Seduction of the Law* (New York: Free Press, 1990), 235.
[74] 109 S.Ct. at 2351.
[75] *Ibid.* at 2352–53.

Court acknowledged in its cases defining the "liberty" protected by the Constitution. . . . The plurality's . . . pinched
conception of "the family" . . . is jarring in light of our many
cases preventing the States from denying important interests or
statuses to those whose situations do not fit the government's
narrow view. . . . Today's rhapsody on the "unitary family"
is out of tune with such decisions.[76]

Brennan here cites cases as old as 1923 and as recent as 1977 protecting
the parent-child relationship.

What Justice Brennan acknowledges in all of this and Scalia does
not is the link between the due process clause and the Constitution's
fundamental liberty. Due process does not protect merely the traditional; to claim, as Scalia does, that due process protects only those
specific rights society has always protected is to turn the Constitution
into a redundant form of majoritarianism. Due process protects liberty,
and liberty is a right to be free from arbitrary government action. In
this case, it is arbitrary for the state of California to ignore fundamental
social facts, such as the reality that some people may choose to change
their intimate partners; not every "family" consists of a man married
forever to a woman together with their children. And it is arbitrary for
California to ignore the specific facts of this case: the scientifically
indisputable fact that Michael *is* Victoria's father; the highly relevant
social fact that he has lived with her as her father and sought to
strengthen his relationship with her. Also highly relevant is the fact
that illegitimacy is not the stigma today that it was at the time the
California law was first adopted.

Scalia ignores all of this because he is afraid of judicial "subjectivity"; he is afraid the rule of law would be sacrificed to judicial whim.
But the facts upon which Justice Brennan relies—the availability of
blood tests; Michael's very real relationship with Victoria; the altered
social world in which they live—are not judicial fantasies. And, as his
opinion makes clear, the value he seeks to protect as a part of the
Constitution's fundamental liberty—the parent-child relationship—is
firmly grounded in legal principle and precedent. Scalia's willingness
to ignore these facts and these precedents in the name of traditional
morality is far more accurately characterized as judicial whim. Scalia's
approach is to ignore facts and enshrine the narrowest possible reading
of tradition.

[76] *Ibid.*

IV.

The majority decision in Bowers v. Hardwick,[77] the Georgia sodomy case decided in 1986, contains interpretive flaws similar to those made in Michael H. v. Gerald D. A five-member majority[78] there relies largely on "tradition" to say that there is no fundamental right "to engage in homosexual sodomy."[79] In doing so, they ignore the clear implications of many of the Court's own precedents; they also ignore fundamental social facts about the nature of homosexuality and homosexual relations, as well as the complete absence of any compelling interest in the regulation of private, consensual, intimate behavior.

Writing for the majority, Justice White overturns the decision of the Eleventh Circuit Court of Appeals, which had ruled that homosexual activity is "a private and intimate association" protected by the Ninth Amendment and the due process clause.[80] The circuit court relied on Griswold v. Connecticut, Eisenstadt v. Baird, Stanley v. Georgia, and Roe v. Wade.[81] But for Justice White, "none of the rights announced in those cases *bears any resemblance* to the claimed constitutional right of homosexuals to engage in acts of sodomy that is asserted in this case."[82] There is "no connection," Justice White continues, "between family, marriage, or procreation on the one hand and homosexual

---

[77] 478 U.S. 186 (1986).

[78] The majority included Justice Powell, who, after his retirement from the Court, said publicly that he made a "mistake" in the case. See the *Washington Post*, 26 October 1990.

[79] 478 U.S. at 191.

[80] Hardwick v. Bowers, 760 F.2d 1202 (1985).

[81] Griswold v. Connecticut, see note 60, declared unconstitutional a Connecticut statute criminalizing the use of contraceptives by married couples, and announced the existence of a constitutional right to privacy. Eisenstadt v. Baird, see note 60, extended this holding to nonmarried individuals. Roe v. Wade, 410 U.S. 113 (1973), extended the right of privacy to include a woman's decision to terminate a pregnancy under certain conditions. In Stanley v. Georgia, 394 U.S. 557 (1969), the Court ruled that a state could not make the strictly private possession of obscene material a crime. Although relying on the First Amendment, "the element of privacy," in the analysis of the court of appeals in *Hardwick*, "deepened Stanley's interests and limited the possible purposes of state regulation." 760 F.2d at 1212.

[82] 478 U.S. at 190–91; emphasis added. It is worth noting that in construing the facts of the case in this manner, Justice White ignores the gender-neutrality of the Georgia statute in question, which states simply that "a *person* commits the offense of sodomy when he performs or submits to any sexual act involving the sex organs of one *person* and the mouth or anus of another. . . ." *Ibid.* at 187, n.1; emphasis added. A heterosexual couple joined Michael Hardwick's

activity on the other. . . ."[83] The heart of the Court's holding is this assertion of a lack of a sufficient "connection" or "any resemblance" between the precedents in question and "homosexual activity."

This conclusion is eminently challengeable. Many judges and commentators have looked at the same precedents and concluded that, taken together, they protect "intimate association" regardless of the gender, marital status, or intent to procreate of the two individuals involved.[84] Although *Griswold v. Connecticut* concerned the use of contraceptives by married couples, it can be read as announcing a general right to privacy concerning sexual or intimate matters. *Eisenstadt* explicitly extended this right of privacy to individuals, and spoke of a couple having sex as "an association of two individuals each with a separate intellectual and emotional makeup."[85] Similarly, *Carey v. Population Services* spoke of constitutionally protected "decisions" concerning sexual relations.[86] Given these precedents—and given the equal protection clause—the burden of proof would seem to shift to the state wishing to deny Hardwick the rights it grants to heterosexuals.[87] "Decisions concerning sexual relations" would seem to be a paradigmatic example of liberty understood as the right to be let alone.

The larger methodological issue raised by this conclusion, of course, is the lack of textual support for a right to privacy. Justice White concedes that the Supreme Court has repeatedly declared the existence of rights "that have little or no textual support in the constitutional

---

original suit, alleging that they wished to engage in prohibited sexual activity in their home, "and that they had been 'chilled and deterred' from engaging in such activity by both the existence of the statute and Hardwick's arrest." *Ibid.* at 187, n.2. Their claim was dismissed by the lower courts for lack of standing.

[83] *Ibid.* at 191.

[84] Together with the opinion of the court of appeals in *Hardwick*, see the opinion of Judge Merhige in Doe v. Richmond, 403 F. Supp. 1199 (E.D. Va. 1975), reprinted in Paul Brest and Sanford Levinson, *Processes of Constitutional Decisionmaking*, 2nd ed. (Boston: Little, Brown, 1983), 680–83. See also Kenneth L. Karst, "The Freedom of Intimate Association," *Yale Law Journal* 89 (March 1980): 624–92; David A. J. Richards, *Foundations of American Constitutionalism* (New York: Oxford University Press, 1989), chapter 6; Note, "Developments in the Law: Sexual Orientation and the Law," *Harvard Law Review* 102 (May 1989); 1511–1671, and the sources cited therein.

[85] 405 U.S. at 453.

[86] 431 U.S. 678, 687–691 (1977).

[87] The argument concerning the equal protection clause is developed at greater length in the next chapter. See pp. 235–39.

language."[88] Such rights, White says, have been identified through one of two judicial formulas. The first "liberty" formula is announced in *Palko v. Connecticut*,[89] in which the Court speaks of "those fundamental liberties that are 'implicit in the concept of ordered liberty,' such that 'neither liberty nor justice would exist if [they] were sacrificed.' "[90] It is important to note that this is a straightforwardly subjective formula; whatever values are sufficiently important or "fundamental" are protected by it.[91] The second formula cited by Justice White is that of *Moore v. East Cleveland*,[92] where fundamental liberties "are characterized as those liberties that are 'deeply rooted in this Nation's history and tradition.' "[93] It is important to note that these two liberty "tests," as Justice White formulates them, are quite different; the first depends not at all on "tradition" or "history," but rather on whether a given right is a part of the concept of "fundamental liberty."[94]

After laying out these two tests, Justice White then declares for the majority that "it is obvious to us that *neither* of these formulations would extend a fundamental right to homosexuals to engage in . . . sodomy."[95] Why? Because "proscriptions against that conduct have ancient roots. . . ." Sodomy "was a criminal offense at common law and was forbidden by the laws of the original thirteen States when they ratified the Bill of Rights. In 1868, when the Fourteenth Amendment

[88] 478 U.S. at 191.

[89] 302 U.S. 319 (1937).

[90] 478 U.S. at 191–92, quoting *Palko v. Connecticut*, 302 U.S. 325, 326.

[91] The *Palko* case concerned "incorporation"—that is, the applicability of the Bill of Rights to the states under the Fourteenth Amendment. The *Palko* standard, announced by Justice Cardozo, allowed the Court to selectively incorporate only those provisions of the first eight amendments deemed most "fundamental." Critics of this approach, including Justices Black and Douglas, argued that this approach amounted to little more than a "natural law" formula, allowing judges enormous power. See Justice Black's dissenting opinion in *Adamson v. California*, 332 U.S. 46 (1947). For a discussion, see Joel B. Grossman and Richard S. Wells, *Constitutional Law and Judicial Policy-Making*, 3rd ed. (New York: Longman, 1988), 446–459; see also Laurence H. Tribe, *American Constitutional Law*, 2nd ed. (Mineola, N.Y.: Foundation Press, 1988), 773, 778, 1411.

[92] 431 U.S. 494 (1977). See the discussion below, pp. 138–40.

[93] 478 U.S. at 192, quoting *Moore v. East Cleveland*, 431 U.S. at 503.

[94] Justice White's presentation of the *Palko* and *Moore* formulations as totally distinct is slightly misleading. The *Palko* court seeks nontextual constitutional rights in the "scheme of ordered liberty" *and* in the "traditions and conscience of our people." 302 U.S. at 325. The analysis below proceeds in the terms Justice White offers.

[95] 478 U.S. at 192; emphasis added.

was ratified, all but five of the thirty-seven States in the Union had criminal sodomy laws."[96]

Thus Justice White has proven that sodomy as a fundamental right fails the second test, the test of "history" or "tradition." He is quite right, of course; there is no specific American tradition protecting sodomy, although the historical record is far more ambiguous and less condemnatory of homosexuality than Justice White indicates.[97] But White has engaged in a sleight of hand, for—even by his own stated criteria—he has ignored the other formulation used by the Supreme Court in the declaration of fundamental rights—the *Palko* test, the test of "ordered liberty." It is such a test that would require a closer look at precedent than White is willing to allow, to see if Michael Hardwick's liberty is sufficiently analogous to other protected forms of liberty.[98] This formula, this test for fundamental liberty, Justice White does not want to examine too closely, and attempts to preempt by his bald declaration that there is no "resemblance" between sodomy and other, protected activity.

But Justice White is clearly wrong, for there is more than a passing "resemblance" between Michael Hardwick's behavior and behavior the Court is willing to protect when performed by heterosexuals, behavior the Court began to protect with Griswold v. Connecticut—private, consensual, nonprocreative sex.[99] As the court of appeals in *Hardwick* was able to conclude, "[t]he Constitution prevents the States from unduly interfering in certain individual decisions critical to personal autonomy because those decisions are essentially private and

---

[96] *Ibid.* at 192–93.

[97] A recent survey charges that the majority in *Hardwick* chose to emphasize the eighteenth and nineteenth centuries, thus "selectively examin[ing] history to find condemnation of homosexuality. Had the Court explored earlier or later periods, it would have found ambiguity or social tolerance." "Sexual Orientation and the Law," 1524. Cited here are Anne B. Goldstein, "History, Homosexuality, and Political Values: Searching for the Hidden Determinants of Bowers v. Hardwick," *Yale Law Journal* 97 (May 1988): 1081–91, and John Boswell, *Christianity, Social Tolerance, and Homosexuality: Gay People in Western Europe from the Beginnings of the Christian Era to the Fourteenth Century* (Chicago: University of Chicago Press, 1980).

[98] This is especially true given that—to quote Justice Holmes—"[i]t is revolting to have no better reason for a rule of law than that . . . it was laid down in the time of Henry IV. It is still more revolting if the grounds upon which it was laid down have vanished long since, and the rule simply persists from blind imitation of the past." Holmes is quoted by Justice Blackmun in his dissent in *Hardwick*, 478 U.S. at 199, quoting O. W. Holmes, "The Path of the Law," *Harvard Law Review* 10 (1897): 469.

[99] See "Sexual Orientation and the Law," 1523.

beyond the legitimate reach of a civilized society." Michael Hardwick "desires to engage privately in sexual activity with another consenting adult. Although this behavior is not procreative, it does involve important associational interests," and "[t]he Supreme Court has indicated . . . that the intimate associations protected by the Constitution are not limited to those with a procreative purpose."[100] Such activity "is quintessentially private and lies at the heart of an intimate association beyond the proper reach of state regulation. Such a right is protected by the Ninth Amendment . . . and the notion of fundamental fairness embodied in the due process clause of the Fourteenth Amendment."[101]

For the court of appeals, the precedents in question protect not just heterosexual behavior, but intimate behavior between two consenting adults. Such a conclusion would seem to be compelled by at least two precedents, as well as by the equal protection clause: the recognition of *Griswold* that nonreproductive sex is constitutionally protected; and the recognition of *Eisenstadt* that rights of sexual intimacy belong to individuals, and not only to married couples.

Like these precedents concerning intimate behavior, there are cases governing the protection of the "family" that also lend strong support to the assertion that the Constitution protects the rights of people such as Michael Hardwick, for they demonstrate that the "family" is often a matter, not of the traditional nuclear family or of biological ties, but rather of individuals choosing to be intimate with each other.[102]

Moore v. East Cleveland, for example, struck down a municipal housing ordinance that limited occupancy of a dwelling unit to "a single family," defining "family" in a manner that excluded one Inez Moore, who resided with her son and two grandsons; the boys were first cousins rather than brothers. In sustaining Mrs. Moore's claim, the Supreme Court emphasized the long-standing American tradition of extended families, as well as the city's drawing of an arbitrary boundary—"the boundary of the nuclear family."[103] Although relying on "tradition" to say that the due process clause protected the extended family, Justice Powell's plurality opinion contains language going beyond a rationale based solely on tradition; Powell writes that the Supreme Court must not

[100]   760 F.2d at 1211.
[101]   *Ibid.* at 1212.
[102]   For a discussion of the legal and constitutional issues raised by the "family," see Note, "Developments in the Law: The Family," *Harvard Law Review* 93 (April 1980): 1157–1383; see also Martha Minnow, "We the Family: Constitutional Rights and American Families," *Journal of American History* 74 (December 1987): 959–83.
[103]   431 U.S. at 502.

"close [its] eyes to the basic reasons why certain rights associated with the family have been accorded shelter under the Fourteenth Amendment's Due Process Clause. . . ." Moreover, "understanding those reasons requires careful attention to this Court's function under the Due Process Clause."[104] There follows a long quotation from Justice Harlan's opinion in Poe v. Ullman,[105] a pre-*Griswold* birth control case. The passage is worth quoting at length because it is often used to express the Court's rationale for substantive due process:

> Due process has not been reduced to any formula; its content cannot be determined by reference to any code. The best that can be said is that through the course of this Court's decisions it has represented the balance which our Nation, built upon postulates of respect for the liberty of the individual, has struck between that liberty and the demands of organized society. If the supplying of content to this Constitutional concept has of necessity been a rational process, it certainly has not been one where judges have felt free to roam where unguided speculation might take them. The balance of which I speak is the balance struck by this country, having regard to what history teaches are the traditions from which it developed as well as the traditions from which it broke. That tradition is a living thing. . . .
>
> [T]he full scope of the liberty guaranteed by the Due Process Clause cannot be found in or limited by the precise terms of the specific guarantees elsewhere provided in the Constitution. This "liberty" is not a series of isolated points pricked out in terms of the taking of property; the freedom of speech, press, and religion; the right to keep and bear arms; the freedom from unreasonable searches and seizures; and so on. It is a rational continuum which, broadly speaking, *includes a freedom from all substantial arbitrary impositions and purposeless restraints,* . . . and which also recognizes, what a reasonable and sensitive judgment must, that certain interests require particularly careful scrutiny of the state needs asserted to justify their abridgment.[106]

This quotation is notable for a number of reasons. It straightforwardly embraces judicial subjectivity—"due process has not been reduced to

---

[104] *Ibid.* at 501.
[105] 367 U.S. 497 (1961).
[106] 367 U.S. at 542–43, quoted in Moore v. East Cleveland, 431 U.S. at 501–2; emphasis added.

any formula; its content cannot be determined by reference to any code." And it embraces both rationales for substantive due process—the rationale based on tradition (sufficient, in *Moore*, to overturn the statute in question) as well as the rationale based on "ordered liberty," which is here equated with a judgment about arbitrariness—due process "includes a freedom from all substantial arbitrary impositions and purposeless restraints. . . ." Further, it endorses the ideas of strict scrutiny and fundamental rights, for the due process clause "recognizes, what a reasonable and sensitive judgment must, that certain interests require particularly careful scrutiny of the state needs asserted to justify their abridgment."[107]

This passage appears repeatedly when the Court wishes to explain the rationale for substantive due process; it makes explicit the link between due process and liberty understood as the absence of arbitrariness.•Applied to Michael Hardwick, such reasoning could be used to say that it is arbitrary—and therefore a violation of due process—to deny to homosexuals the same right to engage in sexual intimacy as is granted to heterosexuals.[108]

A recent decision of the New York Court of Appeals demonstrates the applicability—and power—of such reasoning when attempting to adjudicate issues governing homosexual relations.[109] The appellant, Miguel Braschi, was served with an eviction notice from his rent-controlled Manhattan apartment after the death of his male lover, Leslie Blanchard, from AIDS. The apartment had been leased in Blanchard's name only. New York law provides for the protection from eviction of occupants of rent-controlled apartments who are the "surviving spouse of the deceased tenant or some other member of the deceased tenant's *family* who had been living with the tenant [of record]."[110] The question of the case is thus whether Braschi can be characterized as "surviving spouse" or "family."

In holding in favor of Braschi, the New York Court of Appeals wrote that "the intended protection against sudden eviction should not

---

[107] For a discussion of strict scrutiny, see pp. 194–97, 224–40.
[108] While the Court extended constitutional protection to the extended family in *Moore*, in other cases it has denied similar protection to nonsexual communal living arrangements. In Village of Belle Terre v. Boraas, 416 U.S. 1 (1974), six university students had rented a house in a neighborhood zoned for groups of no more than two unrelated people. The Court denied the students' challenge to the statute, holding that it did not impinge on any fundamental right. See "Developments in the Law: The Family," 1272.
[109] Braschi v. Stahl Associates, 74 N.Y.2d 201 (1989).
[110] *Ibid.* at 206; emphasis in original.

rest on fictitious legal distinctions or genetic history, but instead should find its foundation in the reality of family life."[111] That reality included the following facts: Braschi and Blanchard "lived together as permanent life partners for more than ten years." They "regarded one another, and were regarded by friends and family, as spouses." Both their "families were aware of the nature of the relationship"; the two men "regularly visited each other's families and attended family functions together as a couple. Even today, appellant continues to maintain a relationship with Blanchard's niece, who considers him an uncle."[112]

Financially, "the two men shared all obligations including a household budget." They "were authorized signatories of three safe-deposit boxes, they maintained joint checking and savings accounts, and joint credit cards." Rent "was often paid with a check from their joint checking account." Blanchard "executed a power of attorney in appellant's favor so that appellant could make necessary decisions—financial, medical, and personal—for him during his illness." Finally, "appellant was the named beneficiary of Blanchard's life insurance policy, as well as the primary legatee and coexecutor of Blanchard's estate."[113]

Given these facts, the court concludes that "the term family as used in [the noneviction statute] should not be rigidly restricted to those people who have formalized their relationship by obtaining, for instance, a marriage certificate or an adoption order." The term *family* should include "two adult lifetime partners whose relationship is long-term and characterized by an emotional and financial commitment and interdependence." This conclusion, the court says, "comports both with our society's traditional concept of 'family' and with the expectations of individuals who live in such nuclear units. . . ."[114] This last conclusion is of major significance, for it demonstrates that traditional *concepts* can be used to protect nontraditional *individuals*. What the New York court has done in this case is to translate the traditional concept "family" into functional terms—individuals who cohabit and share both emotional and financial intimacy and commitment—and applied such a functional definition to the facts of the case.[115]

---

[111] *Ibid.* at 211.
[112] *Ibid.* at 213.
[113] *Ibid.*
[114] *Ibid.* at 211.
[115] There is a sense in which the court's close, detailed examination of the "facts" of these two men's lives is contrary to the notion that, as part of their fundamental liberty, individuals should be able to define for *themselves* whether or not they constitute a "couple." For a discussion of some related questions, see "Sexual Orientation and the Law," 1603–28.

Although the New York court does not venture into explicit constitutional discourse, it would be but a short step to do so, for, once we accept the functional definition of "family," the argument can easily be made that to *deny* that Braschi and Blanchard constitute a "family" would be to deny them due process, for it would be based on an arbitrary exclusion of their kind of relationship from our understanding of the social world. Only by breaking down the category "family" into its functional components can we prevent the arbitrary exclusion of fundamental social facts about how some people live.

Similar reasoning compels the conclusion that Michael Hardwick deserves constitutional protection from Georgia's sodomy law, for to exclude him from the protection of the privacy cases is to ignore fundamental social facts about homosexuality and homosexual relations. In the eyes of science and social science[116]—as opposed to religion—homosexuality is not a perversion or a disease, but a stable, deeply entrenched manifestation of human sexuality. Whether its causes are genetic or psychodynamic, or both, it is today reasonably clear that a homosexual sexual orientation is not in any meaningful sense a rational "choice," but is rather an innate preference determined early in life and not subject to alteration later. What is a choice for the homosexual is the expression of his or her preference in overt behavior. Moreover, it is abundantly clear that forcing people to deny their most intimate feelings does real and substantial harm to them, a harm at least as severe as the stigma of racial discrimination that lies at the heart of the Court's holding in Brown v. Board of Education.[117] As Justice Blackmun states in his dissent in *Hardwick,* "homosexual orientation may well form part of the very fiber of an individual's personality,"[118] and "only the most willful blindness could obscure the fact that sexual intimacy is a 'sensitive, key relationship of human existence, central to family life, community welfare, and the development of

---

[116] See Richards, *Foundations of American Constitutionalism,* 238–39 and the sources cited therein. See also "Sexual Orientation and the Law," esp. 1511–19. Three of the most important sources are: Alan P. Bell and Martin S. Weinberg, *Homosexualities* (New York: Simon and Schuster, 1978); C. A. Tripp, *The Homosexual Matrix* (New York: McGraw-Hill, 1975); Wainwright Churchill, *Homosexual Behavior Among Males* (New York: Hawthorn Books, 1967). See also Richard A. Isay, *Being Homosexual* (New York: Avon Books, 1989). As is well known, neither the American Psychiatric Association nor the American Psychological Association currently define homosexuality as a manifestation of psychological problems. Richards, *Foundations of American Constitutionalism,* 239, n.187.

[117] 347 U.S. 483 (1954). See above, pp. 91–92.

[118] 478 U.S. at 202, n.2.

human personality. . . .' "[119] Blindness to social facts leads to the draw-ing of arbitrary lines, and arbitrary lines deny due process because they restrict liberty. "The fact that individuals define themselves in a significant way through their sexual relations with others suggests, in a Nation as diverse as ours, that there may be many 'right' ways of conducting those relationships and that much of the richness of a relationship will come from the freedom an individual has to choose the form and nature of these intensely personal bonds."[120]

All of this suggests that "freedom of intimate association" must be regarded as a fundamental right for all individuals. Of course, this does not mean that the state can never regulate such association, but rather that, to do so, it must have a compelling justification and must use the least restrictive means available.[121] Under these standards, what could justify the state's criminalization of homosexual relations?

There are only two possible answers. The first is concrete, physical harm to the participants or to third parties; the second is the enforce-ment of the "morality" of society's majority.

The first ground—concrete harm—is a matter of evidence; the state should be required to prove that homosexual relations are harmful, and—under strict scrutiny—that such harm cannot be prevented by any means less drastic than the criminalization of the acts themselves. But, as Justice Blackmun says, "[n]othing in the record before the Court" in *Hardwick* "provides any justification for finding the activity forbidden . . . to be physically dangerous, either to the persons engaged in it or to others."[122]

---

[119] *Ibid.* at 205, quoting Paris Adult Theatre I v. Slaton, 413 U.S. 49, 63 (1973).

[120] 478 U.S. at 205; emphasis in original. Blackmun here cites Karst, "Free-dom of Intimate Association," 637.

[121] See pp. 194–97, 224–40 for a discussion of strict scrutiny.

[122] 478 U.S. at 209. In his opinion Justice Blackmun argues that homosexual-ity, which he views as truly "victimless," might be distinguishable from adultery and incest, "the only two vaguely specific 'sexual crimes' to which the majority points." He writes:

> Marriage, in addition to its spiritual aspects, is a civil contract that entitles the contracting parties to a variety of governmentally provided benefits. A State might define the contractual commitment necessary to become eligible for these benefits to include a commit-ment of fidelity and then punish individuals for breaching that contract. Moreover, a State might conclude that adultery is likely to injure third persons, in particular, spouses and children of per-sons who engage in extramarital affairs. With respect to incest, a court might well agree with respondent that the nature of familial relationships renders true consent to incestuous activity sufficiently

history v. precedent
≠

The second ground—the enforcement of majority morality—is, in and of itself, illegitimate. The "moral" argument against homosexuality usually has one of three sources: religion, history, or simple feelings of disapproval. The religious argument—that "[c]ondemnation of [such] practices is firmly rooted in Judeao-Christian moral and ethical standards," as Chief Justice Burger puts it in his concurrence in *Hardwick*[123]—is barred by the establishment clause of the First Amendment. As Justice Blackmun says, "[t]he theological nature of the origin of Anglo-American antisodomy statutes is patent," and "cannot provide an adequate justification for" the Georgia statute.[124] He goes on: "That certain, but by no means all, religious groups condemn the behavior at issue gives the State no license to impose their judgment on the entire citizenry. The legitimacy of secular legislation depends instead on whether the State can advance some justification for its law beyond its conformity to religious doctrine."[125]

Nor is "history" alone—the fact that, as Justice White says, "proscriptions against [the] conduct have ancient roots"—adequate justifi-

---

problematical that a blanket prohibition of such activity is warranted. *Ibid.* at 209–10, n.4.
Moreover, even if it were argued that reducing the risk of the transmission of AIDS were an important governmental objective, this would still be insufficient grounds for statutes such as Georgia's. As a recent survey of the law in this area reports:

Although the disproportionately high incidence of AIDS among gay men might support a state's argument that an important government health interest is at stake, lesbians as a group have almost no risk of contracting the disease through sexual contact. Even if sodomy statutes were more narrowly tailored to prohibit only same-sex sodomy between males, they would still be grossly overinclusive, as not all prohibited acts carry a high risk of transmission, and the risks depend on the acts themselves rather than the gender of the participants. In addition to being overinclusive and underinclusive, same-sex sodomy statutes are not the least restrictive means of controlling AIDS. "Sexual Orientation and the Law," 1529–30.

The authors here cite Kathleen M. Sullivan and Martha A. Field, "AIDS and the Coercive Power of the State," *Harvard Civil Rights–Civil Liberties Law Review* 23 (Winter 1988): 182–89, who argue that any use of the criminal law to prohibit the transmission of AIDS is overly inclusive, and that "education and tort suits against persons transmitting AIDS through sexual conduct are other viable alternatives for deterring AIDS transmission." "Sexual Orientation and the Law," 1530, n.77, citing Sullivan and Field, "Coercive Power," 192–93.
[123] 478 U.S. at 196.
[124] *Ibid.* at 211, n.6, and at 211.
[125] *Ibid.* at 211.

cation for abridging a fundamental right. Here, the analogy need only be made between sodomy and miscegenation.[126] Many American states had a long history of preventing blacks and whites from marrying each other, but this did not prevent the Supreme Court from declaring such laws unconstitutional in Loving v. Virginia.[127] As Justice Blackmun says, "the parallel between *Loving* and [*Hardwick*] is almost uncanny."[128] He explains that

> there, too, the State relied on a religious justification for its law. . . . There, too, defenders of the challenged statute relied heavily on the fact that when the Fourteenth Amendment was ratified, most of the States had similar prohibitions. . . . There, too, at the time the case came before the Court, many of the States still had criminal statutes concerning the conduct at issue. . . . Yet the Court held, not only that the invidious racism of Virginia's law violated the Equal Protection Clause . . . but also that the law deprived the Lovings of due process by denying them the "freedom of choice to marry" that had "long been recognized as one of the vital personal rights essential to the orderly pursuit of happiness by free men."[129]

Nor are "feelings of disapproval" on the part of society's majority, no matter how strongly held, sufficient to outweigh the fundamental rights of homosexuals. The analogies one can make here are legion—the racial prejudices of vast majorities in many American states both before and after *Brown;* the majority's disapproval of the religious beliefs and practices of any number of sects; the majority's disapproval of pornography; the belief that women are inferior and unfit for many positions of influence or power—none of these prejudices, by themselves, are sufficient to outweigh the fundamental rights of the groups in question.[130] This is not to say that the same argument would necessarily

---

[126] Both Blackmun and Stevens make the analogy in their dissents; see 478 U.S. at 210, n.5, and at 216, n.9.

[127] See note 60.

[128] 478 U.S. at 210, n.5.

[129] *Ibid.*, quoting Loving v. Virginia, 388 U.S. at 12.

[130] As Justice Blackmun points out, it is important to note that laws such as the Georgia sodomy statute do not protect "public sensibilities" but rather regulate private morality. "Statutes banning *public* sexual activity are entirely consistent with protecting the individual's liberty interest in decisions concerning sexual relations: the same recognition that those decisions are intensely private which justifies protecting them from governmental interference can justify protecting individuals from unwilling exposure to the sexual activities of others." 478 U.S. at 212–13; emphasis added.

apply to a *unanimous* moral judgment against homosexuality, embodied in statutes such as Georgia's. If—hypothetically—the sentiment against homosexuality were as strong as the sentiment against murder, the case would be different.[131] But the sentiment against homosexuality is not unanimous in this way, and it is not unanimous in the same way in large part because there is no equivalent physical harm. The sentiments of even large majorities are not enough to abridge the rights of minorities; this is perhaps the most basic tenet of American constitutionalism.[132]

V.

In each of these three cases—*DeShaney, Michael H.,* and *Hardwick*—we have seen that close attention to the social facts of the case reveals important conclusions about the state's abridgment of liberty. This interpretive framework can be extended to the legal controversies surrounding many different minority groups. Controversial cases involving the rights of mental patients, for example—often considered the paradigmatic case of an issue upon which liberal, activist courts illegitimately "legislate" on "policy" matters[133]—demonstrate the utility of this approach.

For example, some of the most vexing constitutional issues presented by civil commitment procedures involve the question of what standard of proof is required before a given individual can be involuntarily committed, and with what sorts of due process requirements attached. The social facts relevant to these cases include the uncertainty and variability of mental illness, the concomitant difficulty of predicting whether a given individual is "dangerous" to herself or others, and the fact that many mental illnesses are untreatable.

Consider, for example, the fate of one "suicidal" and "paranoid" woman in a small Wisconsin town.[134] Alberta Lessard was "picked up by two police officers in front of her residence" and taken to a state mental health center. There, the bureaucracy detained her against her will. The arresting officers "filled out a form entitled 'Emergency Detention for Mental Observation,' following which Miss Lessard was detained on an emergency basis." A few days later, the officers appeared before a judge and "restated the allegations contained in the petition

---

[131] See pp. 99–100.
[132] For a similar argument, see Richards, *Foundations of American Constitutionalism,* 236.
[133] See chapter 1, note 103 and text accompanying.
[134] Lessard v. Schmidt, 349 F. Supp. 1078 (1972).

for emergency detention." Neither Lessard nor anyone representing her was present. On the basis of the officers' testimony, the judge issued an order allowing her confinement for ten additional days. A few days later, a physician at the mental health facility filed an " 'Application for Judicial Inquiry' . . . stating that Miss Lessard was suffering from schizophrenia and recommending permanent commitment." The judge ordered two physicians to examine her and signed a second temporary detention document; this was later extended. "Neither Miss Lessard nor anyone who might act on her behalf was informed of any of these proceedings."[135]

The judge then "held an interview with Miss Lessard at the Mental Health Center." He informed her "that two doctors had been appointed to examine her and that a guardian *ad litem*[136] would be appointed to represent her." She "was not told of this interview in advance and was given no opportunity to prepare for it."[137] She was not told by the judge that these interviews could become the basis for her continued confinement.

Lessard, "on her own initiative," obtained a lawyer through legal services. A commitment hearing was postponed to give this attorney a chance to appear. Lessard's request that "she be allowed to go home during the interim was denied."[138]

At the hearing, "Miss Lessard requested that the judge permit her to go home and agreed that if this was allowed she would seek treatment voluntarily on an out-patient basis."[139] But "testimony was given by one of the [original] police officers and three physicians and Miss Lessard was ordered committed for thirty additional days." The judge "gave no reasons for his order except to state that he found Miss Lessard to be 'mentally ill.' "[140] The judge "made no finding on danger-

---

[135] *Ibid.* at 1081.
[136] See note 40 above.
[137] 349 F. Supp. at 1081; emphasis in original.
[138] *Ibid.* at 1081–82.
[139] *Ibid.* at 1096.
[140] *Ibid.* at 1082. When reviewing the case, the district court writes: "A review of the record indicates that [the original judge] thought that he need only find 'probable cause' for believing Miss Lessard to be mentally ill. . . ." Examining the evidence available, the district court writes that "the judge apparently based his decision on a belief that she had been previously convicted" of a minor, non-violent crime, "making telephone calls to Marquette University . . . ," and that this judge was guilty of "an overwhelming reliance on medical opinion. . . ." The "only other evidence," the district court writes, "related to Miss Lessard's belief that the National Education Association is infiltrated by Communists, a belief which, whether or not valid, is shared by

ousness despite the fact that all of the evidence that she had attempted 'suicide' . . . was of a hearsay character and the fact that Dr. Kennedy, staff psychiatrist at the mental hospital, testified that in his opinion she had no present suicidal tendencies."[141] In committing her, the judge did not consider "alternative methods of treatment. . . ."[142] The judge's thirty-day commitment order was extended each month, until Lessard filed a class-action suit in federal court.

Lessard alleged in her suit that the Wisconsin procedure for involuntary civil commitment violated her due process rights in a number of ways:

[I]n permitting involuntary detention for a possible maximum period of 145 days without benefit of hearing on the necessity of detention; in failing to make notice of all hearings mandatory; in failing to give adequate and timely notice where notice is given; in failing to provide for mandatory notice of right to trial by jury; in failing to give a right to counsel or appointment of counsel at a meaningful time; in failing to permit counsel to be present at psychiatric interviews; in failing to provide for exclusion of hearsay evidence and for the privilege against self-incrimination; in failing to provide access to an independent psychiatric examination by a physician of the allegedly mentally ill person's choice; in permitting commitment of a person without a determination that the person is in need of commitment beyond a reasonable doubt; and in failing to describe the standard for commitment so that persons may be able to ascertain the standard of conduct under which they may be detained with reasonable certainty.[143]

In examining and agreeing with most of Lessard's due process claims, the federal district court judge examines the justifications that

others whom no one appears to have accused of being mentally ill." *Ibid.* at 1096–97, n.27.
[141] *Ibid.* at 1096–97. "His testimony was as follows:
[Q] . . . Do you think, or are you of the opinion that Miss Lessard presently has suicidal tendencies?
[A] I am of the opinion that Alberta Lessard presently does not have suicidal tendencies today.
[Q] And do you know of any present tendency on the part of Miss Lessard to harm other members of society?
[A] I know of no plans on the part of Miss Alberta Lessard to harm any other members of society. . . ." *Ibid.* at 1097, n.8.
[142] *Ibid.* at 1097.
[143] *Ibid.* at 1082.

are traditionally put forward for the absence of due process protections in the treatment of the mentally ill. Broadly speaking, there are two *mental* such justifications: first, that commitment constitutes "treatment," *illness* rather than punishment; second, that society has a right, under the police power, to protect itself from mentally ill individuals who pose a threat of violence.

The "treatment" rationale for the absence of due process is put forward as part of the doctrine of *parens patriae* (literally, "father of the country"), a common law doctrine under which the sovereign had responsibility for acting on behalf of "persons under disability."[144] But this "treatment" rationale—the idea that the state is acting as a "parent" toward the individual—is belied by a number of cold facts. First, "many mental illnesses are untreatable."[145] Here, the court in *Lessard* quotes "psychiatric findings that recovery rates from long-term paranoid schizophrenia—the diagnosis given Miss Lessard's condition—are very low."[146] Second, there is "substantial evidence" that "any lengthy hospitalization, particularly when it is involuntary, may greatly *increase* the symptoms of mental illness and make adjustment to society *more difficult*."[147]

Third, there is overwhelming evidence that, due to overcrowding,

---

[144] *Black's Law Dictionary*, 4th ed. rev. (St. Paul: West, 1968), 1269. As the district court points out, the common law doctrine originated in England at a time in which there were no asylums. The King "was appointed the guardian of the person and goods of a lunatic" under a statute passed in the thirteenth century. The person so affected "was committed to the care of a friend who received an allowance with which to care for the unfortunate person." The individual was "entitled to an accounting from the King." In the United States, few mental institutions were built until the middle of the nineteenth century. "As a result of the lack of facilities and limited medical knowledge of methods of treatment, those confined were generally clearly deranged and violent." But "gradually, as more asylums were built, the number of persons committed increased, and confinement was not limited to the obviously dangerous." Thus "there was . . . a very real difference between the English practice, which could only be for the benefit and protection of the incompetent, and which was only effective during periods of insanity, and the American innovation, which resulted in total, and perhaps permanent, loss of liberty." 349 F. Supp. at 1085.

[145] 349 F. Supp. at 1087.

[146] *Ibid.*, quoting J. M. Livermore, C. P. Malmquist, and P. E. Meehl, "On the Justifications for Civil Commitment," *University of Pennsylvania Law Review* 117 (November 1968): 93.

[147] 349 F. Supp. at 1087; emphasis added. Here the court quotes U.S. Congress, Senate Subcommittee on Constitutional Rights, *Hearings*, 91st Cong., 1st and 2nd sess., 1969 and 1970, 214–15, 319, 409. Hereafter referred to as *1970 Hearings*.

lack of funds, and lack of qualified personnel, state mental institutions provide no real "treatment" but only minimal custodial care, custodial care that is often degrading and inhumane. Here, the district court judge in *Lessard* makes an analogy to juvenile justice, another field in which the *parens patriae* rationale had long been put forward to justify the absence of due process protections. He quotes the Supreme Court in Kent v. U.S.[148]:

> . . . the admonition to function in a "parental" relationship is not an invitation to procedural arbitrariness. . . . While there can be no doubt of the original laudable purpose of juvenile courts, studies and critiques in recent years raise serious questions as to whether actual performance measures well enough against theoretical purpose to make tolerable the immunity of the process from the reach of constitutional guarantees applicable to adults. There is much evidence that some juvenile courts, . . . lack the personnel, facilities, and techniques to perform adequately as representatives of the State in a *parens patriae* capacity. . . . There is evidence, in fact, that there may be grounds for concern that the child receives the worst of both worlds: that he gets neither the protections accorded to adults nor the solicitous care and regenerative treatment postulated for children.[149]

The court then concludes that "few persons familiar with the mental health field will question the applicability of much of the above to persons subjected to involuntary commitment in state institutions."[150]

---

[148] In Kent v. United States, 383 U.S. 541 (1966), the Supreme Court construed the District of Columbia Juvenile Court Act in light of the Constitution, and required juvenile courts to abide by a number of due process requirements; this included holding hearings and according counsel. See Donald L. Horowitz, *The Courts and Social Policy* (Washington: Brookings Institution, 1970), 171.

[149] 349 F. Supp. at 1087, quoting Kent v. United States, 383 U.S. 541, 554–56 (1966); emphasis omitted.

[150] 349 F. Supp. at 1087. The validity of this conclusion is reinforced by any number of cases. Consider, for example, the facts recited in Wyatt v. Stickney, 334 F. Supp. 1341 (1971), concerning Bryce Hospital in Tuscaloosa, Alabama:

> . . . the dormitories are barn-like structures with no privacy for patients. For most patients there is not even a space provided which he can think of as his own. The toilets in rest rooms seldom have partitions between them. These are dehumanizing factors which

Not only may the supposed "treatment" consist of no more than minimal custodial care, but this form of institutionalization may do actual harm to the individual involved. The court quotes the testimony of one expert about the "iatrogenic" effects of hospitalization:

Although 7 days may not appear to some to be a very long time, experience has indicated that any kind of forcible detention of a person in an alien environment may seriously affect him in the first few days of detention, leading to all sorts of acute traumatic and iatrogenic symptoms and troubles. By "iatrogenic" I mean things that are caused by the very act of hospitalization which is supposed to be therapeutic; in other words, the hospitalization process itself causes the disturbance rather than the disturbance requiring hospitalization.[151]

Similarly, drugs administered to the institutionalized patient may *create* "incapacity";[152] "often it is the drugs themselves which are responsible for 'crazy' behavior. Tranquilizers often give people a blank starey look and make them slow in responding to questions" at commitment hearings.[153] Furthermore, affording the mentally ill patient the protections of due process may itself have beneficial psychological results; the court cites "medical evidence that indicates that patients respond more favorably to treatment when they feel they are being treated fairly and are treated as intelligent, aware, human beings."[154]

Finally, there is the simple fact that commitment for mental illness constitutes a "total involuntary loss of freedom,"[155] carrying great stigma,[156] and that "less drastic means" are available for treating the

degenerate the patients' self-esteem. Also contributing to the poor psychological environment are the shoddy wearing apparel furnished the patients, the non-therapeutic work assigned to patients (mostly compulsory, uncompensated housekeeping chores), and the degrading and humiliating admissions procedure. . . . Other conditions which render the physical environment at Bryce critically substandard are extreme ventilation problems, fire and other emergency hazards, and overcrowding. . . . In addition, the quality of the food served the patients is inferior. . . . *Ibid.* at 1343.

[151] 349 F. Supp. at 1091, n.18, quoting testimony of Arthur Cohen, *1970 Hearings,* 210.

[152] 349 F. Supp. at 1092.

[153] *Ibid.* at 1092, n.19, quoting *1970 Hearings,* 426.

[154] 349 F. Supp. at 1101–02.

[155] *Ibid.* at 1100.

[156] *Ibid.* at 1091. See also Donaldson v. O'Connor, 493 F.2d 507, 520 (1974). At the court in *Donaldson* says, the infliction of stigma may constitute

mentally ill.[157] A severe deprivation of liberty should not be imposed unless "the person recommending full-time involuntary hospitalization" bears the burden "of proving (1) what alternatives are available; (2) what alternatives were investigated; and (3) why the investigated alternatives were not deemed suitable."[158]

All of these facts concerning "treatment" undermine the first of the two rationales heretofore offered to justify the absence of due process protections for involuntary commitment. As for the second rationale—society's right to protect itself from "dangerous" individuals—the factual evidence is overwhelming in demonstrating that it is notoriously difficult to accurately predict if a given individual is, in fact, dangerous.[159] This leads the court in *Lessard* to examine the standard of proof upon which a "finding" of "dangerousness" is made, and to require "a finding of a recent overt act, attempt or threat to do substantial harm to oneself or another."[160] Because there is a "*massive curtailment of liberty*" in civil commitment, "the state must bear the burden of proving that there is an extreme likelihood that if the person is not

---

a constitutionally significant deprivation of liberty; this was recognized in Board of Regents v. Roth, 408 U.S. 564 (1972).

[157] 349 F. Supp. at 1096.

[158] *Ibid.* "These alternatives include voluntary or court-ordered out-patient treatment, day treatment in a hospital, placement in the custody of a friend or relative, placement in a nursing home, referral to a community mental health clinic, and home health aide services." *Ibid.*

[159] For a discussion of the empirical evidence concerning the prediction of dangerousness, see Stephen J. Pfohl, "Predicting Dangerousness: A Social Deconstruction of Psychiatric Reality," in Linda A. Teplin (ed.), *Mental Health and Criminal Justice* (Beverly Hills: Sage Publications, 1984), 201–225. Pfohl writes:

> Despite an increasing demand for their use, methodologies for predicting dangerousness find very little empirical support. One recent review article has gone so far as to characterize the assessment process as nothing more than "flipping coins in the courtroom. . . ." As inaccurate as predictions may be, equally troubling is the manner in which they consistently err through overprediction. In one study after another, the same conclusion emerges: For every one correct prediction of violence, there are numerous incorrect predictions. *Ibid.*, 203.

Rates of "false positives" (i.e., a prediction of dangerousness belied by the subject's later behavior) run as high as 54 to 99 percent, *despite* the fact that the populations of such studies are "systematically biased in the direction of positive results," in that the research subjects are "primarily convicted offenders, sexual psychopaths, and adjudicated delinquents." *Ibid.*, 205–06.

[160] 349 F. Supp. at 1093.

confined he will do immediate harm to himself or others."[161] Thus a statute that is interpreted to allow a judge or jury to commit a person based on a "preponderance of the evidence"[162] violates due process; "the state must prove beyond a reasonable doubt all facts necessary to show that an individual is mentally ill and dangerous."[163]

[161] *Ibid.*; emphasis in original. The court is here quoting and interpreting *dicta* of the United States Supreme Court in Humphrey v. Cady, 405 U.S. 504 (1972). The district court in *Lessard* holds that "even an overt attempt to substantially harm oneself cannot be the basis for commitment unless the person is found to be (1) mentally ill and (2) an immediate danger at the time of the hearing of doing *further* harm to oneself. The considerations which permit society to detain those who because of mental illness are likely to harm others do not necessarily apply to potential harm to oneself." 349 F. Supp. at 1093, n.24; emphasis added.

[162] "Preponderance of the evidence" is the standard in many civil cases involving a monetary dispute between private parties. As the Supreme Court explains in Addington v. Texas, 441 U.S. 418, 423 (1979), "since society has a minimal concern with the outcome of such private suits, plaintiff's burden of proof is a mere preponderance of the evidence. The litigants thus share the risk of error in roughly equal fashion."

[163] 349 F. Supp. at 1095. In Addington v. Texas the United States Supreme Court declined to require such a stringent standard. Although rejecting Texas's use of the "preponderance of the evidence" standard, the Court found that "within the medical discipline, the traditional standard for 'factfinding' is a 'reasonable medical certainty,' " 441 U.S. at 430, and noted that "the 'beyond a reasonable doubt' standard historically has been reserved for criminal cases." *Ibid.* at 428. Thus the Court required the use of the standard of "clear and convincing evidence," noting that many states already used this or a similar standard by statute. *Ibid.* at 431–32. The Court noted that "the subtleties and nuances of psychiatric diagnosis render certainties virtually beyond reach in most situations." *Ibid.* at 430.

Although conceding that it was important to avoid an "erroneous confinement," the Court said that "the layers of professional review and observation of the patient's condition, and the concern of family and friends generally will provide continuous opportunities for an erroneous commitment to be corrected." *Ibid.* at 428–29. These assumptions can so easily be challenged that the Court's reasoning borders on the ludicrous. The "layers of professional review and observation" may be completely nonexistent or totally inadequate, see above, p. 147 and below, pp. 181–82, and family members may sometimes *want* a "difficult" individual confined. See below, pp. 183–89.

The Court also reasons that "it is not true that the release of a genuinely mentally ill person is no worse for the individual than the failure to convict the [criminally] guilty," because "one who is suffering from a debilitating mental illness and in need of treatment is neither wholly at liberty nor free of stigma." *Ibid.* at 429. The key word here, of course, is *genuinely;* the Court is carelessly assuming that most individuals who are committed really do need institutionalization. An equivalent assumption in a criminal case would be,

The difficulty of predicting dangerousness is, for the court, related to a more general factual problem, the difficulty and imprecision of defining when a given individual is "mentally ill." The court quotes one group of experts to the effect that "the definition of mental illness is left largely to the user [of the term]. . . ." Calling someone mentally ill

> effectively masks the actual norms being applied. And, because of the unavoidably ambiguous generalities in which the American Psychiatric Association describes its diagnostic categories, the diagnostician has the ability to shoehorn into the mentally diseased class almost any person he wishes, for whatever reason, to put there.[164]

On the basis of this and all the other facts concerning mental illness and institutionalization, the district court in *Lessard* puts forward a number of due process requirements for civil commitment. The maximum allowable detention of an individual without a preliminary hearing is forty-eight hours; a full hearing on the necessity of continued confinement is required within ten to fourteen days. Such a hearing must conform to constitutional requirement of adequate notice.[165] The involuntarily detained individual has a right to counsel (including a state-appointed attorney if he is indigent)[166] and a right to be free from self-incrimination, interpreted to mean that the individual must be

---

"we can't let guilty people off on technicalities, because after all, most people accused of a crime do need to be punished."

[164] 349 F. Supp. at 1094, quoting Livermore, Malmquist, Meehl, "On the Justification for Civil Commitment," 80.

[165] Such notice must include informing the patient "of the basis for his detention, his right to a jury trial, the standard upon which he may be detained, the names of examining physicians and all other persons who may testify in favor of his continued detention, and the substance of their proposed testimony." 349 F. Supp. at 1092.

[166] The court cites empirical studies demonstrating "overwhelmingly the importance of representative counsel for those who wish to contest commitment." *Ibid.* at 1099, citing Raj Gupta, "New York's Mental Health Information Service: An Experiment in Due Process," *Rutgers Law Review* 25 (Spring 1971): 438. A guardian *ad litem* does not function the same way as an attorney; another empirical study demonstrates that "in almost all cases where a guardian is appointed he sees his role not as an advocate for the prospective patient. . . ." 349 F. Supp. at 1099, citing George Dix, "Hospitalization of the Mentally Ill in Wisconsin: A Need for Reexamination," *Marquette Law Review* 51 (Summer 1967): 33.

informed that he is not obliged to speak to state-appointed psychiatrists, and that such interviews may be the basis for commitment.[167]

VI.

The social and scientific facts governing the institutionalization of the mentally ill, outlined above, raise an even more basic constitutional issue than the due process questions raised by *Lessard*. Is there a constitutional right to treatment, or to treatment of any particular type, for example, treatment in the "least restrictive environment" available?

Consider first the case of Kenneth Donaldson.[168] Donaldson was civilly committed to the Florida State Hospital at Chattahootchee in January 1957. The commitment was initiated by his father, "who thought that his son was suffering from 'delusions.' "[169] under a Florida statute that did not require a finding of "dangerousness."[170] After a "brief hearing before a county judge," Donaldson was diagnosed as suffering from "paranoid schizophrenia"; "the committing judge told Donaldson that he was being sent to the hospital for 'a few weeks' to 'take some of this new medication,' after which the judge said that he was certain that Donaldson would be 'all right' and would 'come back here.' "[171]

It didn't work out that way. Donaldson—in the words of the Supreme Court—was "kept in custody . . . against his will for nearly fifteen years."[172] During those fifteen years, Donaldson "received little

[167] The court does not require the presence of counsel during the psychiatric interview itself. See 349 F. Supp. at 1101. The district court opinion in *Lessard* was twice vacated on procedural grounds by the Supreme Court and later reinstated. See 414 U.S. 473 (1975), 379 F. Supp. 1376 (1974), 421 U.S. 957 (1975), and 413 F. Supp. 1318 (E.D. Wis. 1976).

[168] O'Connor v. Donaldson, 422 U.S. 563 (1975).

[169] *Ibid.* at 565.

[170] See *ibid.* at 566–67, n.2. Justice Stewart writes: ". . . it is noteworthy that Donaldson's 'Order for Delivery of Mentally Incompetent' to the Florida State Hospital provided that he required 'confinement or restraint to prevent self-injury or violence to others, *or* to insure proper treatment.' . . . [T]he Florida commitment statute provided no judicial procedure whereby one still incompetent could secure his release on the ground that he was no longer dangerous to himself or others." *Ibid.*; emphasis in original.

[171] Donaldson v. O'Connor, 493 F.2d 507, 510 (1974).

[172] 422 U.S. at 563.

or no psychiatric care or treatment."[173] Indeed, "there is little dispute about the general nature of the conditions under which [he] was confined. . . ."[174] Donaldson simply rotted.[175] When his case eventually came to trial, one of the hospital's physicians "mentioned 'recreational' and 'religious' therapy as forms of therapy given Donaldson"; but, in the words of the court of appeals, "this amounted to allowing Donaldson to attend church and to engage in recreational activities, privileges he probably would have been allowed in a prison."[176] The hospital "made much of what they called 'milieu therapy,' " but, in the eyes of the skeptical court, "this was nothing more than keeping [him] in a sheltered hospital 'milieu' with other mental patients; the defendants did not refer to anything specific about the 'milieu' that was in any special way therapeutic."[177]

Donaldson was "usually confined in a locked room," in which "there were about sixty beds, with little more room between beds than was necessary for a chair; his possessions were kept under the bed."[178] While trying to sleep he was often awakened by "some patients who had fits" and by some—in Donaldson's words—"who would torment other patients, screaming and hollering." There was, too, "the fear, always the fear you have in your mind . . . when you go to sleep that maybe somebody will jump on you during the night."[179] Roughly a third of the patients in Donaldson's ward were criminals, and Donaldson testified that "the entire operation of the ward was geared to criminal patients."[180]

Q. Now, did you sleep in the same rooms as the criminal patients?

---

[173] 493 F.2d at 509.

[174] 493 F.2d at 511.

[175] As a Christian Scientist, Donaldson refused to take drugs or submit to electroshock, and "no other therapy was offered." *Ibid.*

[176] *Ibid.*

[177] *Ibid.* In a footnote, the court of appeals writes that " 'milieu therapy' is a frequent response by doctors and hospitals to claims by patients that they are receiving inadequate treatment," and cites Charles R. Halpern, "A Practicing Lawyer Views the Right to Treatment," *Georgetown Law Journal* 57 (March 1969): 787, n.19, who writes that "milieu therapy" is an "amorphous and intangible" idea, "the easiest therapeutic claim for an institution to assert and the most difficult for a patient to refute." 493 F.2d at 551, n.4.

[178] 493 F.2d at 511.

[179] *Ibid.* at 512, n.5.

[180] *Ibid.* at 511.

A. Yes.
Q. Did you get up at the same time?
A. Yes.
Q. Did you eat the same food?
A. Yes.
Q. In the same dining room?
A. Yes.
Q. Did you wear the same clothes?
A. Yes. The entire operation of the wards I was on was geared to the criminal patients.
Q. Let me ask you, were you treated any differently from the criminal patients?
A. I was treated worse than the criminal patients.
Q. In what sense were you treated worse?
A. The criminal patients got the attention of the doctors. Generally a doctor makes a report to the court every month.
Q. For the criminal?
A. On the criminal patients, and that would be a pretty heavy case load. It didn't give them time to see the ones who weren't criminal patients.[181]

The court of appeals notes that "[d]uring his first ten years at the hospital, progress reports on Donaldson's condition were irregularly entered at intervals averaging about one every two and a half months."[182] He was denied grounds privileges and occupational therapy despite the fact that he requested both.[183] "In short," the court of appeals concludes, Donaldson "received only the kind of subsistence level custodial care he would have received in a prison, and perhaps less psychiatric treatment than a criminally committed inmate would have received."[184]

After obtaining his release, Donaldson sued the hospital and his attending physicians for damages, charging them with "bad faith . . . and with intentional, malicious, and reckless disregard for his constitutional rights." The heart of his complaint was that the physicians "acted intentionally and maliciously in 'confining Donaldson against

[181] *Ibid.* at 511–12, n.5.
[182] *Ibid.* at 512.
[183] *Ibid.*
[184] *Ibid.*

his will, knowing that [he] was not physically dangerous to himself or others,' " and that they confined him " 'knowing that [he] was not receiving adequate treatment, and knowing that absent such treatment the period of his hospitalization would be prolonged.' " A jury awarded Donaldson modest sums in compensatory and punitive damages against the two physicians in charge of his case at different points in his hospitalization.[185] In sustaining these awards against the physicians' appeal, the court of appeals notes that "there was ample evidence to support the jury's reaching any or all" of its conclusions. The evidence, the court says, "establishes that there were at least three forms of treatment . . . withheld from Donaldson"—grounds privileges, occupational therapy, and psychiatric consultation.[186]

The physicians "could not give a convincing explanation" for the refusal of grounds privileges. "Since the purpose of hospitalization is to restore the capacity for independent living, one of the most basic modes of treatment is giving a patient an increasing degree of independence and personal responsibility."[187] Independent expert witnesses testified that Donaldson was "ideally suited" for grounds privileges as well as for occupational therapy. According to Donaldson, at least one of the physicians "did not want him to go into occupational therapy" because he "feared he would learn touch-typing and would use this skill . . . to 'write writs'. . . ." The physician "gave no reason why he denied Donaldson occupational therapy."[188]

As for psychiatric consultation, Donaldson testified "that the total time he spent talking to O'Connor"—one of the two physicians in charge of his case—"did not consume more than one hour" in eighteen months. In the eight and one half years he spent under the supervision of the other physician, he received a *total* of two hours of therapy— "an average of about fourteen minutes a year." He testified that neither physician "ever heeded his requests to discuss his case."[189]

Together with this almost laughably inadequate "treatment," "[t]he jury could have concluded that Donaldson should have been marked, at his entrance to the hospital, as a prime candidate for an early release. . . ."[190] Especially relevant here is Donaldson's history. "Fourteen years before he was hospitalized in Florida, Donaldson had been hospitalized

---

[185] *Ibid.* at 513. Donaldson was awarded $22,000 against one physician and $16,500 against the other.

[186] *Ibid.*

[187] *Ibid.*

[188] *Ibid.* at 514.

[189] *Ibid.*

[190] *Ibid.*

. . . in New York, with the same diagnosis. . . . On that occasion, [he] was released after three months."[191] Also particularly troubling to the court of appeals was a "progress note" made by one of the physicians "after his first diagnostic interview with Donaldson," recording that the patient " 'appeared' to be 'in remission.' "[192] This physician "testified that Donaldson was not released because he wanted to 'observe [him] further,' " but "after that interview the first progress note entered in Donaldson's hospital record is dated four months later; and the next report five months after that." Questioned about this the physician replied that " 'when you have 900 patients you do that' "; "later, he insisted that he had seen Donaldson frequently, but had not recorded progress notes after each observation."[193] The court of appeals says that "the jury . . . could have discounted this testimony and concluded that [the physician] acted wantonly in giving a patient who had appeared to be 'in remission' the same treatment he gave his 900 other patients."[194]

Especially chilling is the undisputed fact that "two efforts" were "made to secure Donaldson's release"; one by "Helping Hands, Inc., a Minneapolis organization which runs halfway houses for mental patients," and one by "John H. Lembcke, a college friend of Donaldson."[195]

Helping Hands wrote the hospital that it was interested in taking Donaldson into one of its homes where "a maximum of six people" lived. Included was a letter "from the Minneapolis Clinic of Psychiatry and Neurology, stating that 'it would be impossible in any of our State Hospitals for a patient to receive the type of attention and care' provided at Helping Hands."[196] The hospital refused; the doctors responded to the inquiry by saying that Donaldson, if released from the hospital, would " 'require very strict supervision, which he would not tolerate. Such a release would be to the parents.' " The court of appeals writes that "the jury could have decided" that the physicians in charge of the hospital "acted wantonly and maliciously in issuing this response, and that this conduct foreclosed an opportunity for Donaldson to win back at least a part of his freedom, and to gain access to a level of psychiatric treatment unavailable to him at the Florida Hospital."[197]

---

[191] *Ibid.* at 514, n.7.
[192] *Ibid.* at 514.
[193] *Ibid.* at 515.
[194] *Ibid.*
[195] *Ibid.*
[196] *Ibid.*
[197] *Ibid.*

The hospital responded similarly to Lembcke, who repeatedly sought to take responsibility for Donaldson. Lembcke went so far as to obtain a notarized letter of consent from Donaldson's parents, but, after a prolonged struggle, Lembcke "gave up; whenever he met the conditions imposed by the hospital officials, new conditions were imposed."[198]

Thus, officials at Florida Hospital "continued to confine Donaldson knowing he was not dangerous. . . ." Lembcke "testified that in his half century of knowing Donaldson, he had never known [him] to be 'violent,' 'aggressive,' or 'belligerent'; that, on the contrary, he knew Donaldson to be a 'gentle' man." Various expert witnesses testified that they did not believe that Donaldson was dangerous. The court of appeals noted that "[t]here was *no evidence* in the record of Donaldson's *ever* having been violent *in any way*."[199] Thus "the jury would have been justified in finding that Donaldson was non-dangerous, and in inferring that the defendants knew him to be so."[200]

As for the two physicians' claim that they did "the best they could with available resources,"[201] the court of appeals notes that after his eventual transfer to the care of a third physician, Donaldson was allowed both ground privileges and occupational therapy. This third physician "spoke with him frequently, and within a year of taking charge of his case arranged a staff conference that recommended his release."[202]

It is worth reviewing the outrageous details of Donaldson's case so thoroughly because they so clearly support the court of appeals in its legal reasoning—that Donaldson's liberty was abridged; that the due process clause provides a patient such as Donaldson a right to "receive such individual treatment as will give him a realistic opportunity to be cured or to improve his mental condition," and that "[t]he purpose of involuntary hospitalization is treatment and not mere custodial care or punishment if a patient is not dangerous to himself or others."[203]

The court of appeals begins its constitutional reasoning by noting

---

[198] *Ibid.* at 517. For example, the hospital told Lembcke at one point that the notarized letter from Donaldson's parents was not sufficiently "recent." *Ibid.* One of the physicians attached a note to one of Lembcke's many letters saying that "this man must not be well himself to want to get involved with someone like this patient. . . ." *Ibid.* at 516.

[199] *Ibid.* at 517; emphasis added.

[200] *Ibid.*

[201] *Ibid.* at 518.

[202] *Ibid.*

[203] This is the language of the trial judge's instructions to the jury. *Ibid.*

"the indisputable fact that civil commitment entails a 'massive cur-tailment of liberty' in the constitutional sense. . . ."[204] The confinement of involuntary commitment involves "[t]he destruction of an individu-al's personal freedoms . . . scarcely less total than that affected by confinement in a penitentiary." The comparison is unavoidable, given the brute facts of Donaldson's confinement. "Indeed, civil commit-ment, because it is for an indefinite term, may in some ways involve a more serious abridgement of personal freedom than imprisonment for commission of a crime usually does."[205] Moreover, "[c]ivil commit-ment involves stigmatizing the affected individuals, and the stigma attached, though in theory less severe than the stigma attached to criminal conviction, may in reality be as severe, or more so."[206] Thus the conclusion follows that "[s]ince civil commitment involves depriva-tions of liberty of the kind with which the due process clause is fre-quently concerned, that clause has the major role in regulating govern-ment actions in this area."[207]

The court of appeals here is saying the following: Civil commitment deprives an individual of his liberty as much, if not more, than impris-onment. Due process governs any such deprivations of liberty by the state; therefore, due process governs civil commitment. It can argue this not merely in the abstract, but based on the manner in which Donaldson was actually treated. Donaldson *was* confined by the state in a locked room, indefinitely. He was given no more than custodial care.

The next step is to declare the "fundamental, and all but universally accepted proposition that 'any nontrivial governmental abridgement of [any] freedom . . .' " recognized as part of the liberty of the Fourteenth Amendment "must be justified in terms of some 'permissible govern-mental goal.' "[208] Once this step is taken, "the next step is to ask precisely what governmental interests justify the massive abridgement of liberty civil commitment entails."[209]

If Donaldson had been dangerous to himself or to others, a police power rationale could be said to justify his confinement. But absent

[204] *Ibid.* at 520, quoting Humphrey v. Cady, 405 U.S. 504, 509 (1972).
[205] 493 F.2d at 520.
[206] *Ibid.*
[207] *Ibid.* at 520.
[208] *Ibid.* The court of appeals is here quoting Laurence H. Tribe, "Foreward: Toward a Model of Roles in the Due Process of Life and Law," *Harvard Law Review* 87 (November 1973): 17.
[209] 493 F. Supp. at 520.

such evidence, the only available rationale is under the doctrine of *parens patriae*, that is, Donaldson's need for treatment.[210] "[W]here, as in Donaldson's case, the rationale for confinement is the 'parens patriae' rationale that the person is in need of treatment, the due process clause requires that minimally adequate treatment be in fact provided."[211] Why? Because otherwise the involuntary commitment "amount[s] to an *arbitrary* exercise of government power proscribed by the due process clause."[212] The court of appeals here quotes district court judge Frank M. Johnson, Jr. in the well-known case of Wyatt v. Stickney:[213] "To deprive any citizen of his or her liberty upon the altruistic theory that the confinement is for humane therapeutic reasons and then fail to provide adequate treatment violates the very fundamentals of due process."[214] This conclusion, the court in *Donaldson* says, "draws considerable support from, if indeed it is not compelled by,"[215] the Supreme Court's decision in Jackson v. Indiana.[216] In *Jackson*, the Supreme Court had held that the state could not indefinitely commit a mentally defective individual solely because he was incompetent to stand trial. Jackson was a deaf mute accused of purse snatching. His condition was highly unlikely to improve and thus it was highly unlikely that he would ever become competent to stand trial. Under these circumstances, the Supreme Court ruled that the state could confine him "only for 'the reasonable period of time necessary to determine whether there is a substantial probability that he will attain that capacity [to stand trial] in the foreseeable future.' "[217] In announcing this holding, the Supreme Court announced the general principle that "[a]t the least, due process requires that the nature and duration of commitment bear some reasonable relation to the purposes for which the individual is committed."[218] That the state needs good reasons for curtailing someone's liberty is the very essence of due process.

As the court of appeals in *Donaldson* interprets this principle, it requires them to say that "[i]f the 'purpose' of commitment is treatment, and treatment is not provided, then the 'nature' of the commit-

---

[210] *Ibid.* at 520–21.
[211] *Ibid.* at 521.
[212] *Ibid.*; emphasis added.
[213] 325 F. Supp. 781 (1971). *Wyatt* concerned conditions at Bryce Hospital; see above, p. 150, n.50.
[214] *Ibid.* at 785.
[215] 493 F.2d at 521.
[216] 406 U.S. 715 (1972).
[217] 493 F.2d at 521, n.20, quoting 406 U.S. at 738.
[218] 493 U.S. F.2d at 521, quoting 406 U.S. at 738.

ment bears no 'reasonable relationship' to its 'purpose,' and the constitutional rule of *Jackson* is violated."[219] If the state says it will do something, and then doesn't, it is acting arbitrarily.

In a very real sense, the court of appeal's holding that Kenneth Donaldson possessed a due process right to treatment is related to the Constitution's most basic commitment, the commitment to liberty unrestricted except for agreed, limited purposes.[220] The "purpose" of restricting Donaldson's liberty was treatment—but he was not treated. Implicit here is the recognition that the government is capable of acting arbitrarily—that is, outside the scope of the Constitution's understanding of liberty—in a variety of institutional and social settings.

The court of appeals recognizes that in announcing a general right to treatment, there is still the difficulty of finding "judicially manageable or ascertainable standards."[221] The appellants—the two physicians—"argue strenuously" that judges cannot say exactly what "treatment" the Constitution requires. The physicians point out, for example, that "there are as many as forty different methods of psychotherapy," and that "professional judgment" in the field of mental health is often tentative and uncertain.[222]

But, the court says, this argument "can be answered on two levels." First, even if the courts are incapable of formulating abstract standards of treatment, "[t]here will be cases—and the case at bar is one— where it will be possible to make determination [sic] whether *a given individual* has been denied his right to treatment" without using such abstract standards.[223] In Donaldson's case, "the jury properly could have concluded that Donaldson had been denied his rights" by comparing his treatment at the hands of the first two physicians with the treatment he received at the hands of the third. Or, the jury "could have concluded that Donaldson's rights had been violated on the basis of the evidence that the defendants obstructed his release even though they knew he was receiving no treatment."[224] "Neither judgment," the court points out, "required any *a priori* determination of what constitutes or would have constituted adequate treatment. . . ."[225]

On another level, the court refuses to "concede that determining what constitutes adequate treatment is beyond the competence of the

[219] 493 F.2d at 521.
[220] See chapter 2.
[221] 493 F.2d at 525.
[222] *Ibid.*
[223] *Ibid.* at 525–26; emphasis added.
[224] *Ibid.* at 526.
[225] *Ibid.*

judiciary."[226] Courts can rely on expert testimony and "pertinent data concerning standards for mental care," provided by counsel for both sides.[227] Data can also be taken, the court notes, from professional associations such as the American Psychiatric Association. The "lack of finality" of professional judgment "cannot relieve the court of its duty to render an informed decision."[228] Precedent is also useful; "[t]here are by now many cases where courts have undertaken to determine whether treatment in an individual case is adequate or have ordered that determination to be made by a trial court."[229] Again, the court cites Wyatt v. Stickney, where "agreement was reached among the parties on almost all of the minimum standards for adequate treatment ordered by the district court, and the defendants [i.e., the state hospital] joined in submitting the standards to the district court." These standards "were supported and supplemented by testimony from numerous expert witnesses," and "there was a striking degree of consensus among the experts, including the experts presented by the defendants. . . ."[230]

An argument the court did not make, but might well have, would be to compare the field of mental health to other areas where complex standards must be developed to implement constitutional principles, such as school desegregation. School attendance boundaries and neighborhood residential patterns are complicated and various; it is impossible to formulate a single national standard for desegregation. Does this mean (the court might well have asked) that there is no Fourteenth Amendment right to be free of discriminatory state action in assigning pupils to schools? Judges are not experts on education any more than they are on mental health, but this does not mean that the Constitution is silent as to how people are treated by state-run institutions such as schools or mental hospitals.

The two physicians who lost before the court of appeals in *Donaldson* appealed to the Supreme Court. The Supreme Court, following its tradition of deciding cases on the narrowest possible grounds, shifted the focus of the case away from a right to treatment and instead focused on the question of whether Donaldson should have been con-

---

[226] *Ibid.*

[227] *Ibid.* The court is here quoting Judge Bazelon discussing the implementation of a *statutory* right to treatment in the District of Columbia in a landmark case, Rouse v. Cameron, 373 F.2d 451, 457 (1966).

[228] 493 F.2d at 526; the court is again quoting Judge Bazelon in *Rouse*, 373 F.2d at 457.

[229] 493 F.2d at 526.

[230] *Ibid.* Of course, conflict among the experts is possible; see below, pp. 189–93.

fined in the first place.[231] "In its present posture," Justice Stewart writes, "this case involves not involuntary treatment but simply custodial confinement."[232] Justice Stewart can reach this conclusion because he characterizes the evidence as showing "that Donaldson's confinement was a simple regime of enforced custodial care, not a program designed to alleviate or cure his supposed illness."[233] Given that Donaldson was not dangerous, "what was left as justification for keeping Donaldson in continued confinement? . . . A finding of 'mental illness' alone cannot justify a state's locking a person up against his will and keeping him indefinitely in simple custodial confinement." Justice Stewart asks whether a state may "confine the mentally ill merely to ensure them a living standard superior to that they enjoy in the private community." The answer is no; "the mere presence of mental illness does not disqualify a person from preferring his home to the comforts of an institution." Similarly, "[m]ay the State fence in the harmless mentally ill solely to save its citizens from exposure to those whose ways are different? One might as well ask if the State, to avoid public unease, could incarcerate all who are physically unattractive or socially eccentric. Mere public intolerance or animosity cannot constitutionally justify the deprivation of a person's physical liberty."[234]

The Supreme Court is saying that the physicians should have let Donaldson leave the hospital, while the court of appeals had said that they should have treated him while he was there. It is worth noting that the Supreme Court can avoid the question of treatment only because of the fact that the physicians acted unconstitutionally toward Donaldson. Justice Stewart characterizes the state's behavior toward Donaldson as merely "enforced custodial care," and thereby says that the issues surrounding "treatment" are irrelevant to the case. But this ignores the physicians' own claim that they were, in fact, treating Donaldson as best they could, with "milieu" therapy and so forth. The court of appeals accepted the state's claim that it was at least trying to treat Donaldson, and found the treatment insufficient. The physicians

---

[231] Although it declined to announce a right to treatment, the Court did not say that the adequacy of treatment was a nonjusticiable question "that must be left to the discretion of the psychiatric profession," as the two physicians maintained. "That argument," Justice Stewart wrote, "is unpersuasive. Where 'treatment' is the sole asserted ground for depriving a person of liberty, it is plainly unacceptable to suggest that the courts are powerless to determine whether the asserted ground is present." 422 U.S. at 574, n.10. Stewart here cites Jackson v. Indiana. See below, p. 170.

[232] 422 U.S. at 574, n.10.

[233] *Ibid.* at 569.

[234] *Ibid.* at 574–75.

said, "we were treating Donaldson, to the best of our ability." The court of appeals sustained the jury's decision that this treatment was not, in fact, sufficient. The Supreme Court says, in effect, "No, you weren't treating him, and since you weren't, let's forget about treatment; you had no right to keep him."

Although both approaches to the case announce important constitutional principles governing the mentally ill, the Supreme Court could not for long continue to avoid the constitutional issues surrounding adequacy of treatment.

VII.

Like the mentally ill, the mentally retarded—individuals with impairments in learning capacity and adaptive behavior[235]—are often institutionalized. Such individuals are in need of "habilitation"—education and training—rather than treatment.[236] When they are institutionalized, the mentally retarded are often neglected and mistreated in many of the same ways as the mentally ill, raising the question of whether there is a right to habilitation for them parallel to the right to treatment for the mentally ill.[237]

This issue arose in dramatic fashion in the case of Pennhurst State School and Hospital in Pennsylvania. In a trial in federal district court, it was found that "[s]ince its founding in 1908, the institution has been overcrowded and understaffed."[238] The hospital and its staff as well as state officials readily admitted that "Pennhurst as an institution is inappropriate and inadequate for the habilitation of the retarded."[239]

---

[235] Halderman v. Pennhurst State School and Hospital, 446 F. Supp. 1295, 1298 (1977).

[236] According to one authority,

[t]he use of the concept "habilitation" instead of "treatment" in the context of mental retardation reflects an awareness that "mental illness" is not synonymous with "mental retardation." Mental illness concerns an inability to cope with one's environment regardless of intellectual level. Mental illness can occur at any stage of life while mental retardation is considered to be a developmental disability beginning in the early years. *Ibid.* at 1314, quoting Bruce G. Mason and Frank J. Menolascino, "The Right to Treatment for Mentally Retarded Citizens: An Evolving Legal and Scientific Interface," *Creighton Law Review* 10 (October 1976): 147, n.72.

[237] Legal discussions often blur the distinction and speak of a single right to "treatment" for both the mentally ill and the mentally retarded.

[238] 446 F. Supp. at 1302.

[239] *Ibid.* at 1304.

The records of residents, the district court notes, "commonly contain a notation that they would benefit from specific types of programming. However, such programming has, for the most part, been unavailable to the individual because of staff shortages. . . ."[240] Without adequate staff, "restraints are used as control measures." Such restraints on patients "can be either physical or chemical." Physical restraints "range from placing the individual into a seclusion room to binding the person's hands or ankles . . . and binding the individual to a bed or chair. Chemical restraints are usually psychotropic . . . drugs."[241] Such drugs "are often used for control and not for treatment, and the rate of drug use on some of the units is extraordinarily high. . . ."[242] It was also found that "residents on drugs were inadequately monitored."[243]

Conditions within the hospital were found to be almost unspeakably horrible. "The physical environment at Pennhurst is hazardous to the residents, both physically and psychologically. . . . There is often excrement and urine on ward floors . . . and the living areas do not meet minimum professional standards for cleanliness. . . . Outbreaks of pinworms and infectious disease are common. . . ."[244] Bathrooms "do not have towels, soap or toilet paper, and the bathroom facilities are often filthy and in a state of disrepair. Obnoxious odors and excessive noise permeate the atmosphere at Pennhurst."[245] The noise is so bad "that many residents simply stop speaking. . . ."[246]

Residents not only fail to learn; they regress. "The environment at Pennhurst is not only not conducive to learning new skills, but it is so poor that it contributes to losing skills already learned."[247] A survey conducted by a physician "revealed that 34% of the individuals . . . had some notation of regression in their records."[248] At meals, "[s]taff supervision is at a minimum, and residents are often free to steal food from other residents—which results in some residents not getting enough to eat. . . ."[249]

In such an environment, physical injuries abound. "Injuries to resi-

---

[240] *Ibid.*
[241] *Ibid.* at 1306 and 1306, n.33.
[242] *Ibid.* at 1307.
[243] *Ibid.*
[244] *Ibid.* at 1308.
[245] *Ibid.*
[246] *Ibid.*
[247] *Ibid.*
[248] *Ibid.* at 1308, n.40.
[249] *Ibid.* at 1308.

dents by other residents, and through self-abuse, are common."[250] Residents have caused the deaths of other residents. In one typical month, there were "833 minor and 25 major injuries reported" among 1,230 residents.[251]

The district court's ultimate fact-finding conclusion is that "[m]any of the residents have suffered physical deterioration and intellectual and behavioral regression during their residency at Pennhurst." Terri Lee Halderman, the original plaintiff, had been admitted to Pennhurst in 1966 when she was twelve years old.[252] "During her eleven years at Pennhurst, as a result of attacks and accidents, she has lost several teeth and suffered a fractured jaw, fractured fingers, a fractured toe and numerous lacerations, cuts, scratches and bites." Before entering the hospital she could say a few words, but "[s]he no longer speaks."[253] The fate of other residents has been similar.[254]

All of these facts about conditions at Pennhurst are considered by

[250] *Ibid.*
[251] *Ibid.* at 1309.
[252] *Ibid.*
[253] *Ibid.* at 1309.
[254] The court recites a numbing list of injuries to the named plaintiffs, including:

> Plaintiff Charles DiNolfi was admitted to Pennhurst when he was nine years old; he is now forty-five. . . . [H]is sister [has] testified that whenever she or her family visited him, Mr. DiNolfi had some type of bandage on. . . . Twenty-six years ago, while at Pennhurst, Mr. DiNolfi lost an eye. . . . The sight in his remaining eye has been impaired due to injury. . . . He has only a few teeth remaining and his nose has been battered.
>
> Plaintiff Robert Hight . . . was placed on a ward with forty-five other residents. His parents visited him two and one-half weeks after his admission and found that he was badly bruised, his mouth was cut, he was heavily drugged and did not recognize his mother. On this visit, the Hights observed twenty-five residents walking the ward naked, others were only partially dressed. During this short period of time, Robert lost skills that he had possessed prior to his admission. . . .
>
> Plaintiff Nancy Beth Bowman entered Pennhurst at the age of ten in 1961. She was placed on a large ward which had sixty-five residents and often only two child-care aides in attendance. . . . During her residency at Pennhurst she developed maladaptive behavior, i.e., biting and pushing. . . . As a result of this maladaptive behavior she has been placed in seclusion for days at a time. . . . While at Pennhurst, she has lost teeth, been badly bruised and has been abused by the staff. . . . When asked about her present physical condition, Nancy Beth's mother replied, "Nancy Beth will be scarred for the rest of her life. . . ." *Ibid.* at 1309–10.

the district court in the context of the current state of professional knowledge concerning treatment of the mentally ill. "Since the early 1960s," the court notes, the professional literature is "replete with the acceptance of the theory of normalization for the habilitation of the retarded."[255] The theory of normalization is "an outgrowth of studies showing that those in large institutions suffered from apathy, stunted growth and loss in I.Q., and that the smaller the living unit on which the retarded individual lived, the higher the level of behavioral functioning shown by the individual. . . ."[256] Under normalization, "the retarded individual is treated as much like the non-retarded person as possible."[257] The basic principle of normalization "is that a person responds according to the way he or she is treated. . . ."[258] Habilitation through normalization seeks "the remediation of the delayed learning process so as to develop the maximum growth potential by the acquisition of self-help, language, personal, social, educational, vocational and recreation skills. . . ." This new theory of normalization contrasts with "the older theories of habilitating the retarded," which "stressed [merely] protecting the individual, and were characterized by little expectation of growth. Given this lack of expectation, the individual rarely exhibited growth."[259] But, "once removed from depressing, restrictive routines, the retarded have been able to accomplish a great deal. . . ."[260]

Adding together the findings of fact and these new theories, the district court concludes that "[t]he environment at Pennhurst is not conducive to normalization."[261] Although the *principles* of normalization "have been accepted by the administration of Pennhurst and by the Department of Public Welfare," they are stymied by the absence of smaller, community-based facilities and, of course, by a lack of funds. "Many individuals now living at Pennhurst could be moved

[255] *Ibid.* at 1311. The court here cites Mason and Menolascino, "Right to Treatment," 136.

[256] 446 F. Supp. at 1311.

[257] *Ibid.*

[258] *Ibid.*

[259] *Ibid.*

[260] *Ibid.* In a footnote, the court quotes one mother's testimony "concerning the changes she has observed in her son . . . since his transfer from Pennhurst into a community home. . . . While at Pennhurst, he was subdued and never talked; now, she testified, you cannot stop him. He is now able to cook, work, and keep his own bank account." The mother testified that the child "had learned more in the last 3 and 1/2 years while in the community than he had in the 38 years that he had resided at Pennhurst. . . ." *Ibid.* at 1311, n.47.

[261] *Ibid.* at 1311.

immediately into the community and would be able to cope with little or no supervision. . . . All the parties in this litigation are in agreement that given appropriate community facilities, all the residents at Pennhurst, even the most profoundly retarded with multiple handicaps, should be living in the community. . . ."[262]

Given all of this, the district court finds that there is a constitutional right to "minimally adequate habilitation" similar to the right to treatment for the mentally ill. Moreover, "once admitted to a state facility, the residents have a constitutional right to be provided with minimally adequate habilitation under the least restrictive conditions consistent with the purpose of commitment. . . ."[263] The court's reasoning is exactly analogous to the reasoning of the court of appeals in *Donaldson*. The retarded have committed no crime, and are not dangerous to society; thus, "the only possible justification for committing the retarded to an institution such as Pennhurst is to provide them with habilitation, i.e., education, training and care."[264] If the state fails to provide habilitation, there is no justification for institutionalization and the state is acting arbitrarily and in violation of due process. "Failure to provide adequate habilitation may well mean commitment for life. . . ."[265] The court holds that when a state institutionalizes retarded persons, "it must provide them with such habilitation as will afford them a reasonable opportunity to acquire and maintain those life skills necessary to cope as effectively as their capacities permit. . . ."[266]

Like the court of appeals in *Donaldson*, the district court in Pennhurst cites the U.S. Supreme Court opinion in Jackson v. Indiana: "[a]t the least, due process requires that the nature and duration of commitment bear some reasonable relationship to the purposes for which the individual is committed."[267] Once again, the state is being forced to declare its reasons for curtailing an individual's liberty, and is being held to its reasons. Unlike the court of appeals in *Donaldson*, the district court in *Pennhurst* also relies on the Eighth Amendment— the right to be free from cruel and unusual punishment. This argument rests principally on Robinson v. California,[268] in which the Supreme

---

[262] *Ibid.* at 1311–12.
[263] *Ibid.* at 1319.
[264] *Ibid.* at 1315.
[265] *Ibid.* The court reports that the average resident stays twenty-one years. *Ibid.*
[266] *Ibid.* at 1317–18.
[267] *Ibid.* at 1315, quoting Jackson v. Indiana, 406 U.S. at 738.
[268] 370 U.S. 660 (1962).

Court held that "incarceration solely on the basis of an individual's *status* constitutes cruel and unusual punishment. . . ."[269] If they are not receiving minimally adequate habilitation, the residents of Pennhurst are being incarcerated solely on the basis of their status—that is, solely because they are mentally retarded.

The court concedes that the state is not constitutionally required to undertake any program for the mentally retarded in the first place. "However, whenever a state accepts retarded individuals into its facilities, it cannot create or maintain those facilities in a manner which deprives those individuals of the basic necessities of life."[270] This is a familiar constitutional principle—the state is not obliged to provide a service at all, but if it does choose to provide it, it must do so in a manner consistent with the Constitution.

The district court in *Pennhurst* not only declares a right to minimally adequate habilitation; it also finds that such habilitation "cannot be provided in an institution such as Pennhurst."[271] Accordingly, it orders the hospital closed. The court approvingly quotes authorities who claim that "full implementation of habilitation can only be achieved in a non-institutional setting."[272] Institutions such as Pennhurst—even were conditions improved—provide "a closed and segregated society founded on obsolete custodial models. . . ." Large institutions "can rarely normalize and habilitate the mentally retarded citizen to the extent of community programs. . . ." Any large institution leaves in place "the two . . . characteristics most antithetical to the application of the normalization principle . . . : segregation from the community and the total sheltering of retarded citizens in all spheres of their lives."[273]

Together with the right to minimally adequate habilitation, the district court declares the existence of a constitutional right "to be free from harm," under both the Eighth and Fourteenth Amendments. The court cites an opinion by another district court judge concerning Willowbrook, an institution in New York state; once again, an analogy to confinement in prison is relevant:

> Since Willowbrook . . . residents are for the most part confined behind locked gates, and are held without the possibility of a meaningful waiver of their right to freedom, they must be

[269] 446 F. Supp. at 1316; emphasis added. Robinson was a narcotics addict.
[270] *Ibid.* at 1318.
[271] *Ibid.*
[272] *Ibid.*
[273] *Ibid.*, quoting Mason and Menolascino, "Right to Treatment," 156–57.

entitled to at least the same living conditions as prisoners. . . .
One of the basic rights of a person in confinement is protection
from assaults by fellow inmates or by staff. . . . Another is the
correction of conditions which violate "basic standards of
human decency."[274]

The court also notes that, although the Supreme Court in Ingraham v.
Wright[275] held that the Eighth Amendment did not apply to the use
of corporal punishment in public schools, the retarded residents at
Pennhurst "have none of [the] safeguards" which led the Supreme
Court to deny schoolchildren the protection of the Eighth Amendment:

Due to their own handicaps, few of the retarded are in a
position to aid or protect their fellow residents, or to complain
about their own treatment. Pennhurst is isolated and segregated from the community. The residents are not free to leave
at the end of the day. In addition, few, if any, of the physically
abusive incidents at Pennhurst were committed as disciplinary
measures.[276]

The district court also declares that mentally retarded citizens at institutions such as Pennhurst have a constitutional right to "nondiscrimina-
tory habilitation," that is, the retarded have "a constitutional right
pursuant to the Equal Protection Clause of the Fourteenth Amendment
to receive at least as much education and training as [is] being afforded
by the [state] to others."[277] On the basis of the evidence the court finds
"that the confinement and isolation of the retarded in the institution
called Pennhurst is segregation in a facility that clearly is separate and
not equal."[278]

[274] 446 F. Supp. at 1321, quoting New York Association for Retarded
Children v. Rockefeller, 357 F. Supp. 752, 764–65 (E.D.N.Y. 1973).
[275] 430 U.S. 651 (1977).
[276] 446 F. Supp. at 1320–21.
[277] *Ibid.* at 1321. The court is here quoting and applying the logic of a
separate case, Pennsylvania Association for Retarded Children v. Common-
wealth of Pennsylvania, 343 F. Supp. 279 (E.D. Pa. 1972).
[278] 446 F. Supp. at 1321–22; emphasis in original. The court quotes one
authority who claims that the holding of *Pa. Ass'n for Retarded Children*
can and should mean that any state program that segregates mentally retarded citizens as such from others is highly suspect and
. . . courts will require states to treat mentally retarded persons
indistinguishably from others, except in ways that are both very
limited and very clearly beneficial to the individual. By this test,
segregation of the mentally retarded in a remote large-scale institution could never pass constitutional muster. . . .
[E]xisting large-scale geographically remote institutions cannot

On the basis of these constitutional rights, the district court orders the state and the county "to provide suitable community living arrangements" for residents (including individuals on the hospital waiting list), "together with such community services as are necessary to provide them with minimally adequate habilitation until such time as the retarded individual is no longer in need of such living arrangement and/or community service." State and county officials are also ordered "to develop and to provide a written individualized program plan, formulated in accordance with professional standards" for each resident, to provide annual review of such program plans, and to provide each resident or his or her guardian the opportunity to comment on the plan.[279] A special master[280] is appointed and various review mechanisms are set up. This master is ordered to formulate and implement a plan that will include "the recruitment, hiring and training of a sufficient number of qualified community staff" in each of the community-based living units.[281]

The master is instructed by the court to limit strictly the use of mechanical and chemical restraints. Drugs can be administered only by a physician, and mechanical restraints "shall be used to control acute or episodic, aggressive behavior only when a resident is acting in such a manner as to be a clear and present danger to self or others and only when less restrictive measures and techniques have been proven to be less effective." Such restraints "may be used only upon the order of a qualified mental retardation professional for a period not to exceed two hours. . . ." The resident "must be checked every fifteen minutes

by their nature provide adequate programs to remedy the intellectual and emotional shortcomings and the galling social stigma that led the retarded residents to these institutions. If this evidence is fully marshalled in litigation, courts can . . . rule that present patterns of state segregation of retarded persons for "habilitation" or "educational" purposes are impermissible. Courts can . . . force states to close the . . . Willowbrooks and, even more important, to require alternative programs for mentally retarded persons which treat them as indistinguishably as possible from other persons. . . . A powerful case can thus be mounted that courts should command states to use extraordinary effort to avoid institutionalizing retarded citizens. . . . 446 F. Supp. at 1321, quoting Robert A. Burt, "Beyond the Right to Habilitation," in Michael Kindred, et al., (eds.), *The Mentally Retarded Citizen and the Law* (New York: Free Press, 1976), 425–32.

[279] 446 F. Supp. at 1326.

[280] That is, a qualified professional to oversee the implementation of the Court's orders.

[281] 446 F. Supp. at 1327.

and must be examined by a physician before the initial order is renewed."[282]

The Third Circuit Court of Appeals affirmed most of the district court's remedial order, although it did not agree that Pennhurst needed to be closed immediately.[283] However, it based its holding on statutory rather than on constitutional grounds.[284] In 1975 Congress had passed the Developmentally Disabled Assistance and Bill of Rights Act, providing money to states for the treatment of the disabled. Although none of the litigants mentioned this act when the district court opinion was appealed to the third circuit,[285] the court of appeals "itself suggested the applicability of the Act and requested supplemental briefs on the issue. . . ."[286]

The court of appeals held that Congress intended in this act to condition the receipt of federal money on a state's actions to protect the rights of the disabled, and that certain sections of the act created *statutory* rights to " 'appropriate treatment, services and habilitation' in 'the setting that is least restrictive of . . . personal liberty.' "[287]

The United States Supreme Court reversed the court of appeals. In an opinion written by Justice Rehnquist, it held that the act did not create any substantive rights to treatment, and that Congress did not place any conditions on the receipt of money by the states concerning such "new" statutory rights. In addition to reversing the court of

---

[282] *Ibid.* at 1328.

[283] 612 F.2d 84, 113–14 (1979), The court of appeals refused to order the close of the hospital because of the adverse effect this would have on some patients, writing that

> [i]t is probably true, as the trial court found, that in general institutions are less effective than community living arrangements in facilitating the right to habilitation in the least restrictive setting. . . . But in making this wholesale judgment, the trial court did not adequately canvass the discrete needs of *individual* patients. For some patients a transfer from Pennhurst might be too unsettling a move. Long-term patients, for example, may have suffered such degeneration in the minimum skills needed for community living that habilitation outside an institution is a practical impossibility.

Ibid. at 114; emphasis in original.

[284] See *ibid.* at 94, 104. "The federal courts have long been directed to decide whether causes of action can be supported on statutory ground before they adjudicate constitutional law issues." *Ibid.* at 104.

[285] It can be hypothesized that constitutional grounds were viewed by the litigants as a firmer basis for any holding.

[286] Pennhurst State School and Hospital v. Halderman, 451 U.S. 1, 8, n.3 (1981).

[287] *Ibid.* at 8, quoting 612 F.2d at 97.

appeals on this matter of statutory construction, the Supreme Court in *Pennhurst* completely ignored the constitutional argument of the district court. However, in a second case decided a year later, focusing more narrowly on the question of the residents' safety within the institution, the Supreme Court did declare that an individual involuntarily committed to a state institution for the mentally retarded had constitutionally protected "liberty interests" under the due process clause to "safety" and "freedom from unreasonable restraints," as well as such "minimally adequate training" as may be "reasonable" in light of such liberty interests.[288]

Justice Rehnquist's reversal of the court of appeals on the questions of statutory construction in *Pennhurst* is based on the most extraordinarily tortured logic, and is a remarkably clear example of renegade judicial activism in the service of conservative political goals. Not only does a conservatively inclined Supreme Court sometimes ignore clearly relevant facts; it also misreads statutes.

The act in question speaks clearly about the rights of the disabled. It begins with a statement of purpose, declaring that Congress means

> [t]o assist the states to assure that persons with developmental disabilities receive the care, treatment, and other services necessary to enable them to achieve their maximum potential through a system which coordinates, monitors, plans and evaluates those services and which ensures *the protection of the legal and human rights* of persons with developmental disabilities.[289]

Section 6010 of the act is the "Bill of Rights" provision:

> Congress makes the following findings respecting the rights of persons with developmental disabilities:
> (1) Persons with developmental disabilities *have a right* to appropriate treatment, services, and habilitation for such disabilities.
> (2) The treatment, services, and habilitation for a person with developmental disabilities should be designed to maximize the developmental potential of the person and *should be provided in the setting that is least restrictive of the person's liberty.*

---

[288] Youngberg v. Romeo, 457 U.S. 307, 321–22 (1982). See below, pp. 178–83.
[289] 42 U.S.C. sec. 6000(b)(1) (1976 ed., Supp. III), as quoted in 451 U.S. at 11–12; emphasis added.

(3) The Federal Government and the States both have an *obligation* to assure that public funds are not provided to any institutio[n] . . . that—(*a*) does not provide treatment, services, and habilitation which is appropriate to the needs of such person; or (*b*) does not meet the following minimum standards. . . .[290]

The act then places a number of conditions on the states receiving federal funds. For example, the Secretary of Health and Human Services is told to require "that 'each recipient of . . . assistance take affirmative action' to hire qualified handicapped individuals."[291] And section 6012(a) of the Act, as Justice Rehnquist ·dutifully reports, "conditions aid on a State's promise to 'have in effect *a system to protect and advocate* the rights of persons with developmental disabilities.' "[292]

This language seems straightforward; section 6012(a) says the states must protect and advocate certain rights; section 6010 lists what those rights are. But Rehnquist reads these two provisions *separately:* "Noticeably absent *from section 6010* is any language suggesting that *section 6010* is a 'condition' for the receipt of federal funding under the Act. . . . Sec. 6010," Rehnquist says, "stands in sharp contrast" to sec. 6012 and the other "conditional" provisions.[293]

Rehnquist here is almost beyond belief. Section 6012 says with great clarity that the states receiving money must protect and advocate "rights"; other sections spell out what those rights are. But because section 6012 does not say in so many words, "states must protect those rights *listed in section 6010,*" Rehnquist refuses to link the two sections of the Act.[294]

Not only does he read section 6010 in isolation from the rest of the act; Rehnquist also interprets section 6010—the "Bill of Rights" provision—as creating "no rights whatsoever."[295] He finds that section 6010 is enacted under the congressional spending power rather than under the Fourteenth Amendment,[296] and hence "if Congress intends

---

[290] Quoted in 451 U.S. at 13; emphasis added.
[291] Section 6005, quoted in 451 U.S. at 12.
[292] 451 U.S. at 13; emphasis added.
[293] *Ibid.*; emphasis added.
[294] For a different evaluation of this case, see Cass R. Sunstein, *After the Rights Revolution: Reconceiving the Regulatory State* (Cambridge, Mass.: Harvard University Press, 1990), 199–201.
[295] 451 U.S. at 16, n.12.
[296] Any Fourteenth Amendment right would, of course, exist independent of any argument about money.

to impose a condition on the grant of federal moneys, it must do so unambiguously. . . ."[297] The states must "voluntarily" and "knowingly" accept the terms of the "contract" being offered.[298]

Using these standards, he finds section 6010 unclear. The fact that it speaks in general terms of "rights" is irrelevant;[299] "the specific language and the legislative history of section 6010 are ambiguous."[300] Rehnquist is "persuaded" that section 6010 "does no more than express a congressional *preference* for certain kinds of treatment. It is simply a general statement of 'findings' and, as such, is too thin a reed to support the rights and obligations read into it by the court below."[301] Here, Congress was intending to "encourage, rather than mandate, the provision of better services to the developmentally disabled."[302]

Rehnquist here is simply wrong; section 6010 speaks of congressional "findings" concerning "rights" *and* spells out what those rights are; that's a lot less thin a reed than even many of the clauses of the Constitution. Section 6012 places conditions on the receipt of money related to those rights. Nothing is left to the imagination or to innuendo.

The lengths to which Rehnquist is willing to go to eviscerate section 6010 is revealed by his interpretation of paragraph 3, which states that both the federal and state governments have an "obligation to assure that public funds are not provided" to any institution that does not "provide treatment, services, and habilitation. . . ." Rehnquist says that "by its terms," this paragraph "states that both the Federal Government and the States should not spend public money for substandard *institutions.* Nothing reveals an intent to condition the grant of federal funds under the Act on the State's promise to provide appropriate habilitation to *individuals.*"[303] Completely missing here is any recognition of the elementary truth that institutions act on individuals. Institutions do not provide "treatment, services, and habilitation" to themselves. Institutions—school boards, state agencies, police departments—are subject to the Constitution only because they act—in the name of the state—on individuals who have rights.

There is still more nonsense in Rehnquist's opinion, but the point is clear: he is going out of his way to destroy the statute to avoid "bur-

---

[297] 451 U.S. at 17.
[298] *Ibid.*
[299] *Ibid.* at 18.
[300] *Ibid.* at 19.
[301] *Ibid.*; emphasis added.
[302] 451 U.S. at 20.
[303] *Ibid.* at 24, n.18; emphasis in original.

dening" the states, and to avoid the conclusion reached by the court of appeals: that Congress created statutory rights in this act. As Justice White—no wild-eyed judicial liberal—says in his partially dissenting opinion, "as clearly as words can" section 6010 declares the existence of real, substantive rights to "appropriate treatment, services and habilitation."[304] What is unfortunate, perhaps, is that the court of appeals chose to ignore the *constitutional* argument of the district court, thus leaving the door open to the kind of narrow opinion Rehnquist delivers.

VIII.

A year later, however, Rehnquist joined a unanimous court in—for the first time—deciding that the involuntarily committed do, in fact, have some substantive rights under the due process clause of the Fourteenth Amendment.[305]

Nicholas Romeo, thirty-three and "profoundly retarded," was sent to Pennhurst Hospital by his mother after the death of his father; Nicholas was twenty-six at the time.[306] Mrs. Romeo's petition to the local court stated that "[s]ince my husband's death I am unable to handle him. He becomes violent—kicks, punches, breaks glass; he can't speak—wants to express himself but can't."[307] At Pennhurst, Romeo "was injured on numerous occasions, both by his own violence and by the reactions of other residents to him." His mother "became concerned about these injuries." She complained to the hospital, and eventually filed a legal complaint, alleging that during a two-year period Nicholas had " 'suffered injuries on at least sixty-three occasions.' "[308] The complaint alleged that Pennhurst's director and

---

[304] *Ibid.* at 39. As Justice White recounts, this conclusion is amply supported by legislative history. See *ibid.* at 42–47. White's opinion is only a partial dissent because he agrees that the case "does not involve the exercise of congressional power to enforce the Fourteenth Amendment as the court of appeal held, but is an exercise of the spending power." *Ibid.* at 53. As such, he would vacate the judgment of the court of appeals and remand the case for further proceedings. The court of appeals "should have announced what it thought was necessary to comply with the act and then permitted an appropriate period for the State to decide whether it preferred to give up federal funds and go its own route." *Ibid.* at 54. In White's view, the court of appeal's appointment of a special master was also inappropriate. See *ibid.*

[305] Youngberg v. Romeo, 457 U.S. 307 (1982).

[306] *Ibid.* at 309.

[307] *Ibid.* at 309, n.2.

[308] *Ibid.* at 310.

two supervisors "knew, or should have known, that Romeo was suffering injuries and that they failed to institute appropriate preventive procedures. . . ."[309]

After the complaint was filed, "Romeo was transferred from his ward to the hospital for treatment of a broken arm. While in the infirmary, and by order of a doctor, he was physically restrained during portions of each day."[310] An amended complaint was filed alleging that the hospital staff was "restraining [Romeo] for prolonged periods on a routine basis."[311] This second complaint "added a claim for damages to compensate Romeo for the defendants' failure to provide him with appropriate 'treatment or programs for his mental retardation. . . .'"[312]

When the case reached the Third Circuit Court of Appeals, the court ruled that, under the Fourteenth Amendment, "the involuntarily committed retain liberty interests in freedom of movement and in personal security"; it also found, more generally, that "the involuntarily committed have a liberty interest in habilitation designed to 'treat' their mental retardation. . . ."[313]

On appeal, the Supreme Court sustains the first, narrower constitutional claim, but leaves open the second, broader claim. In sustaining Romeo's first constitutional argument, Justice Powell begins with the recognition that "[t]he mere fact that Romeo has been committed under proper procedures does not deprive him of all substantive liberty interests under the Fourteenth Amendment. . . ."[314] The Court's previous decisions recognize a liberty interest both in safety and in freedom from bodily restraint.[315] On the question of safety, the Court takes note of several decisions protecting the safety of prisoners, and reasons that if it is unconstitutional "to hold convicted criminals in unsafe conditions, it must be unconstitutional to confine the involuntarily committed—who may not be punished at all—in unsafe conditions."[316]

---

[309] *Ibid.*

[310] *Ibid.*

[311] *Ibid.* at 311.

[312] *Ibid.* Romeo's complaint "uses 'treatment' as synonymous with 'habilitation' or 'training.'" *Ibid.* at 311, n.5.

[313] *Ibid.* at 313.

[314] *Ibid.* at 315.

[315] *Ibid.* Here the Court cites Ingraham v. Wright, 430 U.S. 651 (1977); Hutto v. Finney, 437 U.S. 678 (1978); and Greenholtz v. Nebraska Penal Inmates, 442 U.S. 1 (1979) (Powell, J., concurring).

[316] 457 U.S. at 315–16.

And, further, "[l]iberty from bodily restraint always has been recognized as the core of the liberty protected by the Due Process Clause from arbitrary governmental action."[317] Since "this interest survives criminal conviction and incarceration . . . it must also survive involuntary commitment."[318]

This established, the key step in Powell's argument is to recognize the fact that "training may be necessary to avoid unconstitutional infringement" of these two rights.[319] Romeo seeks a "self-care" program, which is "needed to reduce his aggressive behavior."[320] At the original trial, Romeo "repeatedly indicated that, if allowed to testify, his experts would show that additional training programs . . . were needed to reduce his aggressive behavior. . . ."[321] What Powell is saying here is that because of Romeo's aggressive behavior, he cannot remain safe and free from restraint *unless* his aggression is dealt with through training. Thus Romeo's constitutional rights—to safety and freedom from restraint—are being construed in the light of two facts: the fact that he *is* aggressive, and the fact that "training" programs do, in fact, exist that could reduce such aggression. Powell sees no need "to define or identify the type of training that may be required in every case. A court may properly start with the generalization that there is a right to minimally adequate training . . . [that] is reasonable in light of identifiable liberty interests and the circumstances of the case."[322]

Powell next turns to the all-important question of what standard should be applied to determine "whether a State adequately has protected the rights of the involuntarily committed mentally retarded."[323] At the original trial, the jury had been instructed that "only if they

[317] *Ibid.* at 316, quoting Greenholtz v. Nebraska Penal Inmates, 442 U.S. at 18.
[318] 457 U.S. at 316.
[319] *Ibid.* at 318.
[320] *Ibid.*
[321] *Ibid.*
[322] *Ibid.* at 319, n.24. Powell avoids the second, broader constitutional question—whether there is any right to training or habilitation per se, not tied specifically to any question of safety or restraint—by noting that "on the basis of the record before us, it is quite uncertain whether respondent seeks any 'habilitation' or training unrelated to safety and freedom from bodily restraints." *Ibid.* at 318. In other words, all the training Romeo seeks can be explained as being related to his safety or to the question of bodily restraint, thus allowing the Court to skirt the broader question. Justice Blackmun addresses the broader question in his concurrence, see *ibid.* at 327–29.
[323] *Ibid.* at 321.

found the defendants 'deliberate[ly] indifferen[t] to the serious medical
. . . needs' of Romeo could they find that his . . . rights had been
violated."[324] In contrast, the court of appeals held that physical restraint can only be justified on a showing of "compelling necessity."[325]
It held further that any failure to provide for a resident's safety could
be justified only by a showing of "substantial necessity."[326] There is,
of course, a world of difference here; "deliberate indifference" is very
difficult for a complaining patient to demonstrate, while "compelling"
or "substantial" necessity places the burden of proof on the hospital,
and requires it to utilize any less restrictive available means.

The Supreme Court holds that the appropriate standard is for the
courts to "make certain that professional judgment in fact was exercised."[327] Thus, physical restraint may be one of several choices available to the professional, but " '[i]t is not appropriate for the courts to
specify which of several professionally acceptable choices should have
been made.' "[328] Powell reasons that "[p]ersons who have been involuntarily committed are entitled to more considerate treatment and
conditions of confinement than criminals," and thus the "deliberate
indifference" standard is inappropriate.[329] "At the same time," Powell
reasons, "compelling" or "substantial" necessity "would place an un-
due burden on the administration of institutions such as Pennhurst and
also would restrict unnecessarily the exercise of professional judgment
as to the needs of residents."[330] A decision, "if made by a professional,
is presumptively valid. . . ."[331]

Powell further holds that "[i]n an action for damages against a
professional in his independent capacity . . . the professional will not
be liable if he was unable to satisfy his normal professional standards
because of budgetary constraints. . . ."[332] He also acknowledges—in a
footnote—that "day-to-day decisions regarding care—including deci-

---

[324] *Ibid.* at 312. The district court judge was here adopting the standard of
Estelle v. Gamble, 429 U.S. 97 (1976), a prisoners' rights case. See 457 U.S. at
312, n.11.
[325] 457 U.S. at 313. The Court reasoned that such restraint "raises a presumption of punitive sanction. . . ." *Ibid.*
[326] *Ibid.*
[327] *Ibid.* at 321.
[328] *Ibid.* Powell here is quoting from the dissenting opinion of Chief Judge
Seitz of the court of appeals, 644 F.2d 147, 178 (1980).
[329] 457 U.S. at 321–22.
[330] *Ibid.*
[331] *Ibid.* at 323.
[332] *Ibid.*

sions that must be made without delay–necessarily will be made in many instances by employees *without formal training* but who are subject to the *supervision* of qualified persons."[333]

Powell here, and in his discussion of standards generally, is making enormous concessions that go far toward vitiating the importance of his substantive holding concerning Romeo's rights under the due process clause. For the fact is that gross understaffing and stingy budgets are the rule, rather than the exception, in such facilities, making it highly unlikely that patients such as Nicholas Romeo will get the kind of close supervision directly from a professional that Powell apparently envisions. In such a setting the patient in a state hospital comes into contact with staff—orderlies, assistants—who are often not trained at all and who are "supervised" only in the loosest possible manner.

Powell attempts to justify his application of these loose standards by saying that "it is necessary to balance 'the liberty of the individual' and 'the demands of an organized society.' "[334] In effect—as Powell admits[335]—he is applying a "rationality" test (the state can act so long as it has some rational reason for doing so) rather than strict scrutiny, the test usually applied when a fundamental right is abridged.[336] The court of appeal's use of the test of "compelling" or "substantial" necessity is an example of strict scrutiny, completely appropriate for a case involving the abridgment of liberty under due process.

Powell explains this deviation from the court of appeals, and from the Court's usual practice when dealing with fundamental rights, by pointing out that Romeo's "liberty interests in safety and freedom from bodily restraint . . . are not absolute; indeed to some extent they are in conflict."[337] That is, to the extent that Romeo is free from restraint, he may harm himself (or engage in behavior that causes others to harm him), thus jeopardizing his own safety. But Powell has engaged in a trick here, for he is using the fact that Romeo's two separate liberty interests must be balanced against *each other* to justify the balancing of Romeo's rights against the *interests of the state*. The fact that Romeo has two separate liberty interests—safety and freedom from restraint— does prove that his interest in *either one*, separately, is not overriding. But this does not justify allowing Romeo's liberty *in general* to be

---

[333] *Ibid.* at 323, n.30; emphasis added.
[334] *Ibid.* at 320, quoting Poe v. Ullman, 367 U.S. 497, 542 (1961) (Harlan, J., dissenting).
[335] See 457 U.S. at 320.
[336] See pp. 224–27.
[337] 457 U.S. at 319–20.

compromised by assuming that professionals in these institutional settings do what is best. The Supreme Court does not defer to professionals in the field of education when deciding issues concerning racial
discrimination or the abridgment of students' First Amendment rights;
why should it defer here? Powell has not provided a satisfactory
answer.

IX.

In discussing whether there is a constitutional right to treatment for
the mentally ill and a right to habilitation for the mentally retarded,
we have been dealing with the social and medical facts surrounding
these conditions, as well as with the "fact" of the government's behavior when it actually institutionalizes given individuals. It has been
argued that the commitment of adults is unconstitutional without due
process protections, and unless the government does, in fact, provide
the care that underlies the theory of *parens patriae*. Such holdings
flow directly from our earlier arguments concerning the nature of the
Constitution's liberty, especially the proposition that liberty can be
restricted only for agreed, limited purposes.

Other kinds of social facts further complicate the picture when we
are dealing with children who are committed at the behest of their
parents. In these cases—as in many others[338]—the law assumes an
identity of interest between parent and child; that is, the law assumes
that parents act in the child's best interest. But what if a given parent
"dumps" a child—that is, has him or her committed to an institution
for the mentally ill because of the child's unruly or "difficult" behavior?
Should the law assume the parent is acting in good faith? And what
implications do such questions have for the question of what type of
due process protections the Constitution requires when a parent has a
child committed?

The answer one gives to this constitutional question will depend on
how one views the underlying social reality of parent-child relations.
Thus, as in Bowers v. Hardwick, how the Supreme Court construes

---

[338] For example, Wisconsin v. Yoder, 406 U.S. 205 (1972), in which the
Court holds that Amish parents may withdraw their children from public
school after the eighth grade. The Court's decision is based upon the right of
the *parents* to the free exercise of their religion, and does not consider whether
the parents' wishes conform to the wishes or best interests of their children; it
simply assumes that they do. Only Justice Douglas raises the possibility of
conflict between parents and children in his separate opinion.

the social reality of a "family" is highly relevant to a constitutional decision. For a five-member majority of the Supreme Court in Parham v. JR,[339] that social reality is construed as one in which, most of the time, parents do act in their child's best interest. Such assumptions lie at the heart of age-old common law doctrines, in which "[o]ur jurisprudence historically has reflected Western civilization concepts [sic] of the family as a unit with broad parental authority over minor children."[340] Citing Blackstone, Chief Justice Burger tells us that the law historically "has recognized that natural bonds of affection lead parents to act in the best interest of their children."[341]

Chief Justice Burger adds to these historical assumptions a medical analogy; that is, when a parent decides that his or her child requires institutionalization for mental illness, this is no different from a decision concerning "a tonsillectomy, appendectomy, or other medical procedure."[342] Justice Stewart, in his concurrence, also analogizes the decision to have a child committed to a decision to undertake major surgery. "[S]urely the Fourteenth Amendment is not invoked when an informed parent decides upon major surgery for his child, even in a state hospital. I can perceive no basic constitutional differences. . . ."[343]

Combining the historical commitment to parental autonomy with this medical analogy, five members of the Court are able to conclude that no due process hearing is required at any point when a child is committed by a parent. In effect, they are deciding that such a commitment is voluntary, equivalent to an adult voluntarily committing himself.[344] The majority thus finds no constitutional defect in Georgia's procedures, which provide for medical review of the child's case during institutionalization, but no formal or quasi-formal due process hear-

---

[339] 442 U.S. 584 (1979). The case involved the constitutionality of Georgia's scheme for the commitment of children. Under Georgia's statute, a child could be admitted to a state hospital for "observation and diagnosis" based upon a statement signed by a parent or guardian. *Ibid.* at 590–91. "If, after observation, the superintendent [of the state hospital found] 'evidence of mental illness' and that the child [was] 'suitable for treatment' in the hospital, then the child [could] be admitted 'for such period and under such conditions as may be authorized by law.' " *Ibid.* at 591.

[340] *Ibid.* at 602.

[341] *Ibid.*, citing William Blackstone, *Commentaries on the Laws of England*, vol. 1 (London: Dawsons of Pall Mall, 1966), Book I, chapter 16, 434–47; James Kent, *Commentaries on American Law*, Vol. 2 (New York: DeCapo Press, 1971), 159–79.

[342] 442 U.S. at 603.

[343] *Ibid.* at 624.

[344] See especially Justice Stewart's comments, *ibid.* at 622–23.

ings either before or after the decision to commit.[345] Indeed, the majority fears that setting up any administrative procedures might discourage parents from seeking the care their child needs.[346]

Three members of the Court disagree. In his partially dissenting opinion Justice Brennan first points out—correctly—that, in general, "parental rights are limited by the legitimate rights and interests of their children."[347] He also argues that "[t]he consequences of an erroneous commitment decision are more tragic where children are involved."[348] Brennan cites a government report indicating that children are generally committed for longer periods of time than adults,[349] and argues that "childhood is a particularly vulnerable time of life and children erroneously institutionalized during their formative years may bear the scars for the rest of their lives."[350] Moreover, "[d]ecisions of the lower courts have chronicled the inadequacies of existing mental health facilities for children. . . ."[351]

All of this is put by Brennan into the general context of psychiatric institutionalization, in which "[e]ven under the best of circumstances

[345] *Ibid.* at 605–06.

[346] *Ibid.* at 605. Burger writes: "The *parens patriae* interest in helping parents care for the mental health of their children cannot be fulfilled if the parents are unwilling to take advantage of the opportunities because the administrative process is too onerous, too embarrassing, or too contentious." *Ibid.*

[347] *Ibid.* at 630. Brennan quotes Prince v. Massachusetts, 321 U.S. 158, 170 (1944): "Parents may be free to become martyrs themselves. But it does not follow they are free, in identical circumstances, to make martyrs of their children before they have reached the age of full and legal discretion when they can make that choice for themselves." (In *Prince,* the Court upheld a statute forbidding a minor from selling newspapers or merchandise in public places, despite the fact that the child in question believed it was her religious duty as a Jehovah's Witness to distribute religious literature.) Brennan points out that

> [t]his principle is reflected in the variety of statutes and cases that authorize state intervention on behalf of neglected or abused children, and that . . . curtail parental authority to alienate their children's property, to withhold necessary medical treatment, and to deny children exposure to ideas and experiences they may later need as independent and autonomous adults. 442 U.S. at 630–31; citations omitted.

It is worth noting that this principle casts considerable doubt on the legitimacy of the Court's holding in Wisconsin v. Yoder; see note 338 above.

[348] 442 U.S. at 627–28.

[349] *Ibid.* at 628; see also *ibid.* at 634, n.21.

[350] *Ibid.* at 628. Brennan here cites several academic sources; see *ibid.* at 628, n.7, 8.

[351] *Ibid.* at 628.

... diagnosis and therapy decisions are fraught with uncertainties. ..."[352] Such uncertainties are particularly aggravated with children, "when, as [here], the psychiatrist interviews the child during a period of abnormal stress in connection with the commitment, and without adequate time or opportunity to become acquainted with the patient."[353] This problem can "be further aggravated when economic and social class separate doctor and child. ..."[354] Brennan also cites statistics that demonstrate that "psychiatrists tend to err on the side of medical caution and therefore hospitalize patients for whom other dispositions would be more beneficial."[355] One study, conducted by the National Institute of Mental Health, "recently found that only 36% of patients below age 20 who were confined" at one hospital in the District of Columbia "actually required such hospitalization."[356] And a Georgia study "concluded that more than half of the State's institutionalized children were not in need of confinement if other forms of care were made available or used. ..."[357]

Brennan goes on to argue that both the majority's "medical" analogy and their assumption that parents always act in their children's best interests are false in this context. As in a minor's decision to abort a pregnancy, "the parent-child dispute at issue here cannot be characterized as involving only a *routine* child-rearing decision made within the context of an ongoing family relationship."[358] When parents decide to institutionalize a child, the child has been "ousted from his family" and the assumptions of family autonomy do not apply; such a child "has even greater need for an independent advocate" than a minor seeking an abortion.[359]

[352] *Ibid.* at 629. Brennan here cites O'Connor v. Donaldson; see above, pp. 155–66.
[353] *Ibid.* Brennan here cites several authorities; see *ibid.* at 629, n.12.
[354] *Ibid.* at 629. Again, Brennan here cites authorities; see *ibid.* at 629, n.13.
[355] *Ibid.* at 629; see also *ibid.* at 629, n.14.
[356] *Ibid.* at 629; see also *ibid.* at 629, n.15.
[357] *Ibid.* at 629. Brennan here cites the district court opinion in *Parham*, 412 F. Supp. 112, 122 (M.D.Ga. 1976).
[358] *Ibid.* at 631; emphasis added.
[359] *Ibid.* The Court's holdings concerning parental control of a minor seeking an abortion have been complex. In general, the Court has distinguished between laws granting a parental veto over the minor's decision to abort a pregnancy and laws requiring notice to the parents before the abortion is performed; it has struck down the former but sometimes sustained the latter. See Gerald Gunther, *Constitutional Law*, 11th ed. (Mineola, N.Y.: Foundation Press, 1985), 537; see also Planned Parenthood of Missouri v. Danforth, 428 U.S. 52 (1976); Bellotti v. Baird, 443 U.S. 622 (1979); H.L. v. Matheson, 450 U.S. 398 (1981). In Hodgson v. Minnesota, 497 U.S.__(1990), a majority of

Brennan states flatly that "[t]he presumption that parents act in their children's best interests, while applicable to most child-rearing decisions, is not applicable in the commitment context."[360] He cites "[n]umerous studies" that "reveal that parental decisions to institutionalize their children *often* are the results of dislocation in the family *unrelated* to the children's mental condition."[361] Even if parents are "well-meaning," they "lack the expertise necessary to evaluate the relative advantages . . . of inpatient as opposed to outpatient psychiatric treatment."[362] Thus "[p]arental decisions to waive hearings in which such questions could be explored . . . cannot be conclusively deemed either informed or intelligent."[363] Given these facts, "it ignores reality to assume blindly that parents act in their children's best interests when making commitment decisions and when waiving their children's due process rights."[364]

All of this for Justice Brennan does not mean that states must give children *precommitment* hearings.[365] He accepts that such "adversary hearings prior to admission might deter parents from seeking needed medical attention for their children," and that such hearings "might delay treatment of children whose home life has become impossible and who require some form of immediate state care." An adversary hearing prior to commitment "would necessarily involve direct challenges to parental authority, judgment, or veracity" and could "result in pitting the child and his advocate against the parents. This . . . might traumatize both parent and child and make the child's eventual return to his family more difficult."[366]

---

the Court struck down a Minnesota requirement that both parents of any minor be notified forty-eight hours before an abortion was performed, but a different majority upheld the same notification requirement so long as a judicial "bypass" procedure was available.

[360] 442 U.S. at 632.

[361] *Ibid.*; emphasis added. Brennan here cites Charles W. Murdock, "Civil Rights of the Mentally Retarded: Some Critical Issues," *Notre Dame Law Review* 48 (October 1972): 138; and Ezra Vogel and Norman Bell, "The Emotionally Disturbed Child as the Family Scapegoat," in Ezra Vogel and Norman Bell (eds.), *A Modern Introduction to the Family*, Rev. ed. (New York: Free Press, 1968), 412.

[362] 442 U.S. at 632.

[363] *Ibid.*

[364] *Ibid.*

[365] This is why Brennan's opinion is only a partial dissent. The federal district court had ordered *pre*commitment proceedings, and Brennan agrees with the Supreme Court majority that this is not required by due process.

[366] *Ibid.* at 632–33.

Such concerns, however, do not apply to *post*-admission hearings.[367] At the same time, the current Georgia procedures for admission are "informal" and "simply not enough to qualify as hearings—let alone reasonably prompt hearings."[368] The procedures "lack all the traditional due process safeguards." Commitment decisions "are made *ex parte*."[369] Children are not informed of the reasons for commitment, "nor do they enjoy the right to be present at the commitment determination, the right to representation, the right to be heard, the right to be confronted with adverse witnesses, the right to cross-examine, or the right to offer evidence of their own."[370] Brennan concludes that "[b]y any standard of due process, these procedures are deficient. . . ."[371]

In the case of children who are wards of the state, Brennan would require *pre*-admission hearings. The majority had concluded that wards of the state present no special difficulty, because "[n]o one has questioned the validity of the statutory presumption that the State acts in the child's best interest."[372] Justice Brennan "find[s] this reasoning particularly unpersuasive. With equal logic, it could be argued that criminal trials are unnecessary since prosecutors are not supposed to prosecute innocent persons."[373] The factors that lead Brennan to reject the argument for pre-admission hearings of children committed by their natural parents do not apply when children are "committed by their social workers. . . ."[374] Such social workers will not be deterred from seeking medical attention where it is needed, and "hearings in which the decisions of state social workers are reviewed by other state

---

[367] Brennan points out that post-admission hearings "would not delay the commencement of needed treatment"; he also argues that "the interest in avoiding family discord would be less significant at this stage since the family autonomy already will have been fractured by the institutionalization of the child." *Ibid.* at 635. And, of course, post-admission hearings would be "unlikely to deter parents from seeking medical attention for their children." *Ibid.* At post-admission hearings, "the case for and against commitment would be based upon the observations of the hospital staff and the judgments of the staff psychiatrists, rather than upon parental observations and recommendations. The doctors urging commitment, and not the parents, would stand as the child's adversaries." *Ibid.* Thus post-admission hearings "are unlikely to involve direct challenges to parental authority, judgment, or veracity." *Ibid.*

[368] *Ibid.* at 634.

[369] "On one side only"; that is, without the presence of anyone representing the interests of the child.

[370] 442 U.S. at 634.

[371] *Ibid.*

[372] *Ibid.* at 618.

[373] *Ibid.* at 637.

[374] *Ibid.*

officials are not likely to traumatize the children or to hinder their eventual recovery."[375]

The decision in *Parham*—like many others in this chapter—demonstrates why it is pointless to seek the sources of constitutional decision making solely in the text of the Constitution or based solely on "neutral" principles. What due process requires in *Parham* depends on how social facts are interpreted, what analogies are made, what context is applied. Is the decision to commit a child equivalent to a simple "medical" decision, or is it like a minor's decision to have an abortion, where the child and the parents may have interests that diverge? What would result from unnecessary institutionalization? How often does this occur? Are there negative consequences of pre-admission hearings? Of post-admission hearings? *Parham* cannot be decided without first answering these questions. Although Chief Justice Burger's opinion at first glance may seem as though it is based solely on proper legal principles—principles stretching back to Blackstone—such a decision is possible only if certain "factual" questions are answered in a particular way. For Burger, the decision to institutionalize a child is no different from any other routine parental decision, and thus it can be assumed that the parents act in the child's best interest. Without that assumption, the opinion begins to collapse, for the commitment of the minor can no longer be characterized as essentially voluntary.

X.

Of course, in many cases the social or medical facts relevant to a constitutional decision will come in the form of complex or difficult-to-interpret data; the opinion of experts may well vary. This concluding section looks briefly at some examples of the sometimes difficult process of basing decisions on accurate "facts."

Consider Washington v. Harper,[376] in which the mentally ill inmate of a state prison challenged a prison policy that authorized his treatment with an antipsychotic drug without a judicial hearing. The drug, prolixin, is known to sometimes produce serious side effects, including tardive dyskinesia (T.D.), "a neurological disorder, irreversible in some cases, that is characterized by involuntary, uncontrollable movements of various muscles, especially around the face. . . ."[377] The parties to the suit as well as several professional associations filing *amicus* briefs

---

[375] *Ibid.* at 638.
[376] 110 S.Ct. 1028 (1990).
[377] *Ibid.* at 1041.

"sharply disagree about the frequency with which tardive dyskinesia occurs, its severity, and the medical profession's ability to treat, arrest, or reverse the condition."[378]

A majority of the Supreme Court, however, relies on the brief of the American Psychiatric Association to conclude that "[a] fair reading of the evidence . . . suggests that the proportion of patients treated with antipsychotic drugs who exhibit the symptoms of [T.D.] ranges from 10% to 25%."[379] Further, 60 percent of such cases are "mild or minimal in effect," while only 10 percent of such cases "may be characterized as severe."[380]

Within the context of this data, the majority of the Court decides that the prison procedures of Washington State are constitutionally adequate; these procedures allow the decision to administer the drug to be made by medical professionals within the prison without a judicial hearing. At first blush this seems eminently reasonable; if the data is complex, let trained doctors make the decision.

But the case merits a closer look. As Justice Blackmun notes in his concurrence, the brief filed by the American Psychiatric Association is contradicted by a brief filed by the American Psychological Association.[381] And as Justice Stevens points out in his opinion dissenting on the merits, there are good reasons to be suspicious of the psychiatrists' data. First, the psychiatrists' brief relies on old data, collected from 1950 to 1970. The psychologists point this out and, further, present data that the rate of T.D. has been increasing "at an alarming rate" since 1970.[382] Using more current data, the psychologists argue that "the chance of suffering this potentially devastating disorder is greater than one in four."[383]

Secondly, "psychiatrists also may not be entirely disinterested experts."[384] Litigation against psychiatrists ordering the administration of drugs causing T.D. "is expected to explode within the next five years. Some psychiatrists and other physicians continue to minimize the seriousness of T.D. . . . [despite] continual warnings."[385] The reliance on the psychiatrists' brief is therefore problematic. Stevens also

---

[378] *Ibid.*
[379] *Ibid.*
[380] *Ibid.*
[381] *Ibid.* at 1044. Psychiatrists are physicians who can prescribe drugs; psychologists generally are not.
[382] *Ibid.* at 1046, n.5.
[383] *Ibid.*
[384] *Ibid.*
[385] *Ibid.* Stevens is quoting from the psychologists' brief, which is itself quoting a dissenting psychiatrist.

notes that "the risk of side effects increases over time"[386] and that, during the time in which he agreed to take some other psychotropic drugs, Harper had already exhibited some serious side effects.[387] Given *these* facts, Justice Stevens concludes that Harper's "right to refuse such medication is a fundamental liberty interest deserving the highest order of protection."[388]

This case suggests that courts must be careful when handling complex data; they cannot passively accept the first statistic that comes their way, especially when there is good reason to be on the alert to the presentation of biased or unreliable data. Similarly, courts must be careful when citing any broad behavioral propositions. This is illustrated by *In re Gault*, the landmark case establishing formal due process protections for juvenile courts.[389]

In *Gault*, the Supreme Court relied on social science in a number of ways. It relied on figures concerning recidivism to argue that the system of informal, non-judicial juvenile proceedings was inadequate, as it was not doing the job of rehabilitating a sufficient number of juvenile offenders. "Neither sentiment nor folklore should cause us to shut our eyes . . . to such startling findings" as the recidivism data, Justice Fortas wrote.[390] But, as Donald Horowitz cogently argues, "[t]here were . . . alternative ways of interpreting the recidivism figures."[391] An alternative hypothesis would be that "[r]ecidivism rates might be even higher, were it not for the informal procedures of the juvenile court."[392] Or, as is "[m]ore likely," juvenile offenders "may recidivate despite the guidance they receive in juvenile court or, for that matter, despite any disposition they might receive in any court."[393] Thus "[t]he judicial process may simply have no bearing on recidivism one way or another." Even though "high recidivism rates often 'have been interpreted as an indication of the inefficiency of the juvenile court as a delinquency prevention and treatment agency,' they might 'equally be used to indicate the stubbornness of the social pressures that determine delinquent conduct despite efforts at treatment and control.' "[394]

---

[386] *Ibid.* at 1046, quoting the *Physician's Desk Reference*, 43rd ed. (Oradell, N.J.: Medical Economics, 1989), 1639.

[387] 110 S.Ct. at 1046, n.4.

[388] *Ibid.* at 1047.

[389] 387 U.S. 1 (1967). My discussion of *Gault* is based on Horowitz, *The Courts and Social Policy*, chapter 5.

[390] 387 U.S. at 21, quoted in Horowitz, *The Courts and Social Policy*, 174.

[391] Horowitz, *The Courts and Social Policy*, 178.

[392] *Ibid.*

[393] *Ibid.*

[394] *Ibid.* Horowitz is here quoting Harry Manuel Shulman, *Juvenile Delinquency in American Society* (New York: Harper, 1961), 82, n.40.

Similarly, Horowitz challenges the Court's endorsement of the hypothesis that affording juveniles the protections of due process through full adversary hearings would have a beneficial impact on them, convincing them they had been dealt with fairly.[395] "The expert authority to which the Court recurs," Horowitz writes, "reinforces its view that formal procedure is not only legally essential but may actually have marginally therapeutic effects on the delinquency problem itself."[396] But an alternative hypothesis is available;

> [i]t could surely be argued that the atmosphere of adversariness typical of the full-fledged criminal trial does not generally convince the defendant that he has been dealt with fairly, for he may possess strong psychological defense mechanisms to help him avoid confronting his own guilt. Instead, the combative trial atmosphere, with its emphasis on challenge and rebuttal and on denial of responsibility, may reinforce the defendant's hostility toward the community's agents, thereby retarding rather than fostering rehabilitation.[397]

Horowitz finds that the Court relied largely on two sources for all of its behavioral propositions. Looking closely at them, he finds that one source was offering mostly "offhand speculations"; its authors "were far more modest than the Court about what they did not know."[398] The second source was the report of the National Crime Commission; "the stronger, more positive statements" of this commission "were accepted as if they were supported by evidence, though the Crime Commission cited none."[399] Reports by government commissions are often unreliable; "there is good reason to regard commission reports on social problems with at least as much skepticism as the Court lavishes on juvenile courts."[400]

Having blasted the Court's handling of empirical data, Horowitz concedes that "[i]t would be wrong to overemphasize the role of these behavioral findings in moving the Court to action. They were not decisive."[401] Horowitz is quite right; the opinion in *Gault* could easily

---

[395] Horowitz, *The Courts and Social Policy*, 176–77.
[396] *Ibid.*
[397] *Ibid.*, 179–80; citations omitted.
[398] *Ibid.*, 178.
[399] *Ibid.*
[400] *Ibid.*, 179. Horowitz here cites Martha Derthick, "On Commissionship—Presidential Variety," *Public Policy* 19 (Fall 1971): 623–38.
[401] Horowitz, *The Courts and Social Policy*, 176.

have been written without any of these "findings."[402] But Horowitz does pose for us an important warning. Judges cannot passively cite the conclusions of experts without examining the data upon which they rely, and without surveying the field in question to determine if contradictory findings exist. In this task, as in any type of judicial fact finding, judges are aided by the briefs of both parties to a dispute (which can usually be relied upon to present contradictory data) as well as by the availability of *amici*. If necessary, they can direct the parties to reargue a case concentrating on a particular question or questions. The task of finding relevant and accurate data may sometimes be difficult, but it is not impossible. And there is no a priori reason for believing that it will be more difficult in civil liberties cases than in (for example) complex antitrust litigation. And many cases—such as several of those discussed in this chapter—may well turn on facts that are indisputable.

[402] Such an opinion would have stuck more closely to the manner in which juvenile proceedings were wantonly arbitrary, as well as to the extent to which juvenile institutions—such as mental institutions—do not "treat" but merely provide minimal custodial care. The arbitrariness of juvenile proceedings is clear from the facts of the *Gault* case itself. Fifteen-year-old Gerald Gault was taken into police custody because of a complaint from a neighbor concerning an offensive phone call. No notice was given to Gerald's parents that he was being taken into custody; when they arrived home on that particular day, they found him gone. A petition was filed but never served on the Gaults. The petition made no reference to any specific facts but said simply that Gerald needed the "protection" of the Court.

When the petition was heard before a juvenile judge, the complaining neighbor was not there. "No one was sworn at this hearing. No transcript or record was made. No memorandum or record of the substance of the proceeding was prepared." 387 U.S. at 5. At this hearing "there was conflict as to what" Gerald had said in the telephone call. At the conclusion of the hearing the judge said he would "think about it." *Ibid.* at 6. Gerald was returned to a detention home.

A few days later, after having been in custody for several days, Gerald was released. On that day, Gerald's mother received a note, "on plain paper, not letterhead," concerning a further hearing. At this second hearing, no transcript was made. (Throughout, no lawyer for Gerald was present.) Again the complainant was not present; "the judge did not speak to [her] or communicate with her at any time." *Ibid.* at 7. Again, there was later conflict concerning what Gerald did and did not admit to at this hearing. At this hearing, the judge committed Gerald to a state institution as a juvenile delinquent until his twenty-first birthday.

No appeal was permitted under Arizona law. When later questioned about the precise legal basis for his commitment of Gerald, the judge, in the words of the Supreme Court, was "somewhat vague[ ]." *Ibid.* at 9.

As an adult, the maximum penalty Gerald could have suffered for his offense would have been a fine of $5 to $50 or two months in prison.

CHAPTER 5

DEMOCRACY, EMPATHY, AND SUSPECT CLASSES

I.

Previous chapters have argued that social and scientific "facts" are essential to constitutional decision making in a number of different ways. Such "facts," in the form of overwhelming public opinion, may underlie a judicial determination of what is "reasonable" under the Fourteenth Amendment.[1] Or, a political crisis may force the Supreme Court to suddenly recognize crucial "new" facts, as it did during the New Deal.[2] The Court's *construction* of facts may be crucial to the outcome of a case, as in *DeShaney*, where the majority of the Supreme Court ignored the extent to which the state had acted effectively to confine a young boy to the home of his violent father.[3] The Court may sometimes ignore facts crucial to a decision, as in *Michael H.*, where the majority ignores unequivocal medical evidence, as well as social reality;[4] or the Court may ignore the importance of facts when weighing individual interests against the interests of the state, as in Bowers v. Hardwick, where the Court's majority ignores both the nature and the importance to the individual of a homosexual sexual orientation.[5]

There is one type of social fact to which the Supreme Court has paid particular attention, at least with reference to certain groups: the existence of societal prejudice. The modern Court's treatment of race as a "suspect" classification begins with the simple observation that

[1] See pp. 63–66.
[2] See pp. 85–87.
[3] See pp. 116–23.
[4] See pp. 123–33.
[5] See pp. 134–46.

prejudice exists, making decisions by legislative majorities "suspect" and therefore deserving of special judicial scrutiny.

Implicit in the Court's application of strict scrutiny to suspect classifications is the idea that, to operate fairly, the democratic process demands a certain degree of empathy among social groups, thus guaranteeing that no group becomes a permanent and total "loser" in the political process.[6] So long as this empathy can be presumed, so long as no group is permanently ignored or cheated or legislated against, the Court lets legislation pass muster without a searching inquiry into the legislature's motives or evidence. The Court allows "normal" legislation to pass so long as there is some "rational" relationship between the legislature's chosen means and the ends it pursues, and so long as those ends are "legitimate." The legislature, and the democratic process, have the benefit of the doubt.

But in the late 1930s the Supreme Court began to recognize that there are special circumstances in which these normal assumptions of the democratic process do not apply. One such circumstance, according to the famous footnote four of the *Carolene Products* case, is when statutes are directed "at particular religious . . . or national . . . or racial minorities"; that is, when "prejudice against discrete and insular minorities" poses a "special condition," a condition "which tends seriously to curtail the operation of those political processes ordinarily to be relied upon to protect minorities." Such a situation "may call for a correspondingly more searching judicial inquiry," in which "there may be narrower scope for operation of the presumption of constitutionality."[7]

It is crucial to recognize that this sensitivity to minority rights, as Robert Cover has pointed out, was "spawned in the context of both the New Deal at home and totalitarianism abroad. . . ."[8] Both the Court's abdication of review over economic legislation and its heightened awareness of the vulnerability of minorities grew out of a larger political and ideological context. In the fight over the New Deal, the

---

[6] The concept of empathy was first suggested as lying behind Supreme Court doctrine in this area by Louis Lusky; see *By What Right: A Commentary on the Supreme Court's Power to Revise the Constitution* (Charlottesville, Va.: Michie, 1975), 12. Lusky is quoted in Robert M. Cover, "The Origins of Judicial Activism in the Protection of Minorities," *Yale Law Journal* 91 (June 1982): 1296, n.26. Lusky was law clerk to Justice Stone at the time of the *Carolene Products* case; see his article, "Footnote Redux: A *Carolene Products* Reminiscence," *Columbia Law Review* 82 (October 1982): 1093–1105.

[7] United States v. Carolene Products Co., 304 U.S. 144, 154, n.4 (1938).

[8] Cover, "Origins of Judicial Activism," 1289.

Court surrendered the supervision of the economy to the political process, thus making majoritarianism the "dominant constitutional perspective."[9] At the same time, the 1930s revealed events and circumstances in the world at large—particularly the appearance of mass-based totalitarian movements—that made majoritarianism highly problematic.[10]

The solution for the Supreme Court was to divide judicial review in two; that is, the Court's solution was to commit itself "to the now familiar dichotomy between the scope of review for economic legislation—a nearly absolute majoritarianism—and that afforded legislation affecting"[11] either civil liberties,[12] the democratic process itself,[13] or the rights of "discrete and insular" minorities.

Footnote four thus argues for the protection of minorities "in terms of their *vulnerability* to perversions by the majoritarian process."[14] It is important to note that this is a relatively new argument in American constitutional discourse; the very meaning of the term *minority* is being subtly transformed. Although "[m]any constitutional sources from before 1938 speak of judicial protection of minorities," such sources

---

[9] *Ibid.*, 1294.

[10] Indeed, Cover writes,

> by the 1930s popular government and the institutions of mass democracy had themselves become so problematic that they could not, in and of themselves, serve to justify outcomes that appeared *intrinsically unjust.* The manipulation of mass politics had become for the twentieth century what "special interest" politics had been for the age of the Robber Barons: a practical and theoretical challenge to the sufficiency of popular government as the governing constitutional principle.
>
> If all or most substantive interests were to be subordinated to the process principle of popular government, to majoritarianism, the Court would have to explain how the virtues of popular government were to triumph in the age that had seen the rise of bolshevism and fascism, the orchestration of mass oppression of minorities, the cynical manipulation of elections, and the ascendancy of apparatus and party over state and society. . . . *Ibid.*, 1289; emphasis added.

Cover's accurate use of the term *intrinsically unjust* points out that the philosophy of footnote four has nothing whatever to do with the "text" of the Constitution, thus once again rendering the argument over interpretivism quite pointless. See pp. 3–9; Chapter 2.

[11] *Ibid.*

[12] See paragraph one of footnote four in the *Carolene Products* case, 304 U.S. at 154, n.4.

[13] See paragraph two, *ibid.*

[14] Cover, "Origins of Judicial Activism," 1292; emphasis in original.

"use the phrase in an obviously different sense: to refer to losing factions in political struggles or, more importantly, to broad sectional or economic interests that may be at a majoritarian disadvantage."[15] Implicit in the ideology of the *Federalist* is the hope that no single faction will be a *permanent* loser; shifting coalitions and the large size and diversity of the republic will make such a condition unlikely. At the same time, the "sympathy" between social classes, and thus between a representative and his constituents, will help guarantee adequate representation.[16] Usages of the term *minority* in the *Federalist* or in judicial sources before the 1930s "present no theory that it is this characteristic of the group—its 'minority-ness'—that requires special judicial solicitude."[17] Moreover, such older usages "justify constitutional protection by the substantive character of the rights involved rather than by the nature of the groups protected."[18] Thus, for example, Pierce v. Society of Sisters in 1922 argues that a parent—any parent— has a right to send her child to private school; the fact that the state law in question was directed at a religious minority was not crucial. Strictly speaking, that fact was irrelevant.[19]

For footnote four and for the modern Supreme Court, however, it is precisely a group's "minority-ness" that is most important. In the 1930s the Supreme Court recognizes that some minority groups "are not simply losers in the political arena, they are perpetual losers."[20] Because they are "insular," these groups "may be characteristically helpless, passive victims of the political process."[21] Thus strict scrutiny by the Supreme Court becomes an innovation in basic American constitutional theory; this "more searching judicial scrutiny" into legislative action is "superimposed upon the structural protections against 'factions' relied on by the original Constitution—the diffusion of political power and checks and balances."[22]

The manner in which the philosophy of footnote four carried the Supreme Court into many of its holdings on racial questions—engendering a revolution in American politics—is a familiar story. This

---

[15] *Ibid.*, 1294.
[16] See chapter 2, pp. 45–50; see especially the discussion of representation in *Federalist 35*.
[17] Cover, "Origins of Judicial Activism," 1295.
[18] *Ibid.*
[19] 268 U.S. 510 (1925). See also Cover, "Origins of Judicial Activism," 1295, n.22.
[20] Cover, "Origins of Judicial Activism," 1296.
[21] *Ibid.*
[22] *Ibid.*

chapter will consider two topics: the extent to which the Rehnquist Court is attempting to neutralize the philosophy of footnote four through a series of "technical" maneuvers; and, secondly, the extent to which the philosophy of footnote four can, and should, be used to protect a larger category of groups than heretofore chosen by the Court as deserving special protection. After presenting these arguments, the relationship between democracy and empathy will be much clearer.

II.

Between late January and mid-June of 1989, a bare majority of the Supreme Court handed down five conservative decisions dealing with questions of discrimination:

*In City of Richmond v. Croson,[23] the Court ruled that that city's minority "business utilization plan" violated the equal protection clause because it discriminated against whites. Applying strict scrutiny to the city's affirmative action plan, it found that the city failed to demonstrate a "compelling governmental interest" in the plan and that it was not "narrowly tailored" to remedy the effects of prior discrimination.

*In a case dealing with discrimination under Title 7 of the Civil Rights Act of 1964, the Court made it more difficult for a minority to prove discrimination. In Wards Cove v. Atonio,[24] it ruled that statistical evidence did not establish "disparate impact" in Title 7 cases. In effect, this decision shifted the burden of proof from employers to employees who say they are victims of discrimination.

*In Lorance v. AT & T,[25] the Court ruled that women and minorities must challenge a change in an employer's seniority policy within 300 days of that policy's implementation, even if they had no way of knowing then that they would be hurt by it.

*At the same time, in Martin v. Wilks,[26] the Court ruled that white fire fighters could challenge a court-approved affirmative action plan years after it was adopted.

*In Patterson v. McLean Credit Union,[27] the Court ruled that black employees who are victims of racial harassment in the course of their employment may not sue for damages under the Civil Rights Act

[23] 109 S.Ct. 706 (1989).
[24] 109 S.Ct. 2115 (1989).
[25] 109 S.Ct. 2261 (1989).
[26] 109 S.Ct. 2180 (1989).
[27] 109 S.Ct. 2363 (1989).

of 1866, thus sharply limiting the previous decision of Runyon v. McCrary.[28]

In none of these decisions, of course, did the Rehnquist Court say that the state could freely discriminate on the basis of gender or race; in all of these decisions the Court's five-person majority pays rhetorical heed to the lofty goals of equal protection. Yet in all of these decisions there is on the part of this majority a blindness to social reality, and a corresponding overreliance on the formal mechanics of the law. Coming, as they did, so close together, it is difficult to consider these decisions as anything but the expression of an ideology. There is in these majority opinions a rush to find some available detail by which affirmative action can be thwarted or discrimination can be made more difficult to prove.

Thus, in Patterson v. McLean, the Court is faced with a question concerning the meaning of section 1981 of the United States Code, a question that can be interpreted—wrongly—as a narrow, technical matter. Section 1981, passed after the Civil War, holds that "[a]ll persons within the jurisdiction of the United States shall have the same right . . . to make and enforce contracts . . . as is enjoyed by white citizens. . . ."[29] In Runyon v. McCrary, in 1976, the Court had ruled (over the dissents of Justices White and Rehnquist) that section 1981 prohibited racial discrimination in the making and enforcement of private contracts, that is, contracts between two private parties. In *Runyon*, black children had been held entitled to relief under section 1981 against a private school to which they were refused admission because of their race. Justice Stewart wrote for the Court in *Runyon* that section 1981 had been passed by the reconstruction Congress as part of its power to enforce the Thirteenth Amendment's ban on slavery; the school's refusal to accept blacks was thus a "badge" of slavery that Congress could constitutionally outlaw. The schools there in question had made a *public* offer: "[t]he schools extended a public offer open, on its face, to any child meeting certain minimum qualifications who chose to accept."[30] The schools in question "advertised . . . and engaged extensively in general mail solicitations to attract students." These schools "are operated strictly on a commercial basis, and *one fairly could construe* their open-end invitations as offers *that matured into binding contracts* when accepted by those who met the academic, financial, and other racially neutral specified conditions as

---

[28] 427. U.S. 160 (1976).
[29] Quoted in 109 S.Ct. at 2372.
[30] 427 U.S. at 188.

to qualifications for entrance."[31] Further, there was "no reason to assume that the schools had any special reason for exercising an option of personal choice among those who responded to their public offers." This is not the same case as would be involved in "[a] small kindergarten or music class, operated on the basis of personal invitations extended to a limited number of preidentified students. . . ."[32] There is here a recognition of an important social reality: some "private" institutions—schools, businesses—engage in quasi-public functions. A school seeking pupils or a business seeking employees is not the social equivalent of an individual seeking a baby-sitter, as Justice White disingenuously claims in his dissent.[33] Justice White's argument borders on the absurd; by his logic, General Motors dealing with its employees after they are hired is as much engaged in a private matter as Joe and Mary Smith hiring Suzy White—or Suzy Black—to baby-sit. To accept Justice White's analogy is to fail to recognize any gray area between government action and private behavior.[34]

In *Patterson*, in 1989, the petitioner was a black woman employed by a credit union as a teller and file coordinator. After ten years she was laid off. She alleged that her supervisors "had harassed her, failed to promote her to an intermediate accounting clerk position, and then discharged her, all because of her race."[35] Patterson testified that her supervisor "gave her too many tasks, causing her to complain that she was under too much pressure; that among the tasks given her were sweeping and dusting, jobs not given to white employees. On one occasion, she testified, [her supervisor] told [her] that blacks were known to work slower than whites." The supervisor "also criticized her in staff meetings while not similarly criticizing white employees."[36] Patterson claimed that she was "not offered training for higher level jobs, and denied wage increases, all because of her race."[37]

After the case was first argued before them, the Supreme Court asked the parties in *Patterson* to reargue an "additional question"[38] not originally raised: whether *Runyon* should be overruled. This request for reargument was widely reported in the press as a signal that the Court was considering a major retreat on civil rights, and was made

---

[31] *Ibid.*; emphasis added.
[32] *Ibid.*
[33] *Ibid.* at 211.
[34] See pp. 116–23.
[35] 109 S.Ct. at 2369.
[36] *Ibid.* at 2373, quoting court of appeals, 805 F.2d 1143, 1145 (1986).
[37] 109 S.Ct. at 2373.
[38] *Ibid.* at 2369.

over the vigorous dissent of Justices Blackmun, Brennan, Marshall, and Stevens. On the reargument question Justice Blackmun wrote that the Court was "reach[ing] out to reconsider" a "question not presented," in a manner "neither restrained, nor judicious, nor consistent with the accepted doctrine of *stare decisis*."[39] Blackmun pointed out that many lower court opinions, as well as Congress, relied on *Runyon*; he wrote that he was "at a loss to understand the motivation of five Members of this Court to reconsider an interpretation of a civil rights statute that so clearly reflects our society's earnest commitment to ending racial discrimination, and in which Congress so evidently has acquiesced."[40] Justice Stevens, for his part, wrote that even the decision to reconsider *Runyon* "will, by itself, have a deleterious effect on the faith reposed by racial minorities in the continuing stability of a rule of law that guarantees them the 'same right' as 'white citizens.' "[41] Stevens further complained that "[t]o recognize an equality right—a right that 12 years ago we thought 'well-established'—and then to declare unceremoniously that perhaps we were wrong and had better reconsider our prior judgment, is to replace what is ideally a sense of guaranteed right with the uneasiness of unsecured privilege." Stevens feared that some of "the harm that will flow" from the order to reconsider *Runyon* "may never be completely undone."[42]

As it turned out, the Court in *Patterson* did not overrule *Runyon*; instead, it sharply limited its force, holding that racial harassment in the *course* of employment was not actionable under Section 1981. Seizing upon the words "to make and enforce contracts," Justice Kennedy for the majority writes that "[s]ection 1981 cannot be construed as a general proscription of racial discrimination in *all aspects* of contract relations. . . ."[43] By its "plain terms," section 1981 protects only "two rights: 'the same right . . . to make . . . contracts' and 'the same right . . . to . . . enforce contracts.' "[44] And the right to "make" a contract "extends only to the *formation* of a contract, but not to problems that may rise later from the conditions of continuing employment."[45] Thus for Justice Kennedy there is a clear and sharp line between the single moment when a contract is formed and what hap-

---

[39] 108 S.Ct. 1419, 1421 (1988); emphasis in original.
[40] *Ibid.* at 1422. Congress, of course, could have modified section 1981 at any time.
[41] *Ibid.* at 1423.
[42] *Ibid.*
[43] 109 S.Ct. at 2372; emphasis added.
[44] *Ibid.*
[45] *Ibid.*; emphasis added.

pens later. And the employer's conduct in this case, "reprehensible though it be if true,"[46] falls on the wrong side of the line—it occurred after the contract was formed. The Court is merely acting judiciously in limiting section 1981 "to the enumerated rights within its express protection. . . ."[47] *Runyon* is preserved, and, although its interpretation of section 1981 may be "right or wrong as an original matter, it is certain that it is not inconsistent with the prevailing sense of justice in this country. To the contrary, *Runyon* is entirely consistent with our society's deep commitment to the eradication of discrimination. . . ."[48]

But, as the four dissenters note, "[w]hat the Court declines to snatch away with one hand, it takes away with the other."[49] Justice Kennedy's bright line between the formation of a contract and what happens after is untenable, and flies in the face of too much reality. What of an employer who engages in "severe or pervasive" discrimination after a contract is formed: did that employer *really* enter into the contract in a racially neutral manner, as the statute requires? Such discriminatory conduct might "demonstrate[] that the contract was not really made on equal terms at all."[50] An employer might simply conceal his discriminatory intent when the contract is entered into, and "it is difficult to discern why an employer who makes his intentions known has discriminated in the 'making' of a contract, while the employer who conceals his discriminatory intent until after the applicant has accepted the job, only later to reveal that black employees are intentionally harassed and insulted, has not."[51] Thus "[t]he question in a case in which an employee makes a section 1981 claim alleging racial harassment should be whether the acts constituting harassment were sufficiently severe or pervasive *as effectively to belie* any claim that the contract was entered into in a racially neutral manner."[52] Moreover, "[w]here a black employee demonstrates that she has worked in conditions *substantially different* from those enjoyed by similarly situated white employees, and can show the necessary racial animus, a jury may infer that the black employee has not been afforded the same right to

[46] *Ibid.* at 2374.
[47] *Ibid.* at 2375.
[48] *Ibid.* at 2371.
[49] *Ibid.* at 2379 (Brennan, J., concurring in the judgment in part and dissenting in part). The four dissenters concur only on a relatively minor matter pertaining to the jury instructions at the original trial; on the major questions they dissent.
[50] *Ibid.* at 2389.
[51] *Ibid.* at 2396.
[52] *Ibid.* at 2389; emphasis added.

make an employment contract as white employees."[53] If an employer intends to discriminate, "the employer's different contractual expectations are unspoken. . . ."[54] Further, "a company's imposition of discriminatory working conditions on black employees will tend to deter other black persons from seeking employment."[55]

Justice Kennedy's bright line thus disappears when a dose of reality is introduced. Kennedy has engaged in formalism denuded of any real-life content; for him, a "contract" is completely formed in a discrete instant and is unaffected by what comes later. This ignores that people conceal their intent, and it ignores that "[a] contract is not just a piece of paper. Just as a single word is the skin of a living thought, so is a contract evidence of a vital, ongoing *relationship* between human beings."[56] An employee such as Brenda Patterson, who works "at will," "is not merely performing an existing contract; she is constantly remaking that contract."[57] As Justice Stevens persuasively argues,

> [w]henever significant new duties are assigned to the employee—whether they better or worsen the relationship—the contract is amended and *a new contract is made.* Thus, if after the employment relationship is formed, the employer deliberately implements a policy of harassment of black employees, he has imposed a contractual term on them that is not the "same" as the contractual provisions that are "enjoyed by white citizens." Moreover, whether employed at-will or for a fixed term, employees typically strive to achieve a more rewarding relationship with their employers. By requiring black employees to work in a hostile environment, the employer has denied them *the same opportunity for advancement* that is available to white citizens. A deliberate policy of harassment of black employees who are competing with white citizens is, I submit, manifest discrimination in the making of contracts in the sense in which that concept was interpreted in *Runyon.* . . .[58]

Stevens says that he "cannot believe that the decision in" *Runyon* "would have been different if the school had agreed to allow the black

---

[53] *Ibid.*; emphasis added.
[54] *Ibid.*
[55] *Ibid.* at 2389, n.13.
[56] *Ibid.* at 2396; emphasis added.
[57] *Ibid.*
[58] *Ibid.*; emphasis added.

students to attend, but subjected them to segregated classes and other racial abuse"—which is the clear implication of the majority holding in *Patterson*.[59] The majority's limited and formal definition of "making a contract" is simply untenable. Though it preserves *Runyon*, the majority's decision is deeply contrary to the spirit of equal protection.

III.

A similar legal formalism divorced from social reality underlies the majority decision in Lorance v. AT & T, in which the Court was faced with an interpretive question involving the time limitations attached to Title 7 challenges to employment practices. The Court's ruling made it impossible for women who claim they were demoted in violation of equal protection principles to have their claim heard by the Equal Employment Opportunity Commission (EEOC). On the very same day, however, the majority abandons formalism to rule in favor of white fire fighters who challenge a city's affirmative action plan. The law is an ambiguous science, indeed.

In *Lorance*, female employees at an AT & T factory challenged a complicated seniority system.[60] That system, until 1979, gave "all hourly wage earners accrued competitive seniority exclusively on the basis of years spent in the plant . . ."; workers promoted to the position of "tester"—as the women in question had been—kept their seniority when promoted. A new rule, however, adopted in 1979, "altered the manner of calculating tester seniority." Under this new agreement "a tester's seniority was to be determined not by length of plantwide service, but by time actually spent as a tester. . . ."[61] The women in question became testers between 1978 and 1980. During the 1982 recession, their low seniority under the new, 1979 rule "caused them to be selected for demotion."[62] It is conceded that "they would not have been demoted had the former plantwide seniority system remained in place." They claimed that the new seniority system "was the product of an intent to discriminate on the basis of sex," and filed a complaint with the EEOC in 1983.[63]

The case turns on the fact that the women did not file their complaint

[59] *Ibid.*
[60] The women were covered by collective-bargaining agreements between AT & T and a union of electrical workers.
[61] 109 S.Ct. at 2263.
[62] *Ibid.* at 2264.
[63] *Ibid.*

within the time limit supposedly set by the rules of Title 7. The relevant rule states that "a charge must be filed with the EEOC within 180 days *of the alleged unfair employment practice* unless the complainant has first instituted proceedings with a state or local agency, in which case the period is extended to a maximum of 300 days."[64] The majority of the Court interprets this rule to require the filing of the complaint within the correct number of days from the date the change in question was actually *made*, rather than from the date the new rule was *applied* to the women in question. As such, they rule against the women's right to file their claim.

Justice Scalia for the majority concedes that "of course . . . it is possible to establish a different theoretical construct: to regard the employers as having been guilty of a *continuing violation* which 'occurred,' for purposes of [the rule in question], not only when the contractual right was eliminated but also when each of the concrete effects of the elimination were felt."[65] Such a theory would seem to comport with the words of the rule, which speak in a general way about "unfair employment *practices*," not unfair contracts or decisions. But Scalia rejects this and any other interpretation helpful to the women because, he says, such a "continuing violation" theory is rejected by the relevant precedents.

Justice Marshall, in his dissent, calls Justice Scalia's interpretation of the rule "severe," "bizarre," and "impractical."[66] Such an interpretation, Marshall says, "will come as a surprise to Congress, whose goals in enacting Title VII surely never included conferring absolute immunity on discriminatorily adopted seniority systems that survive their first 300 days."[67] The practical consequences of the majority's decision are "austere," for "[o]n the day AT & T's seniority system was adopted, there was no reason to believe that a woman who exercised her plantwide seniority would *ever* be demoted as a result of the new system."[68] If not for the recession, the women in question "might never have been affected." Thus the Court's holding penalizes the women for failing to *anticipate* "that these contingencies would one day place them among the new system's casualties."[69]

Marshall finds the majority's result compelled by neither the text

---

[64] *Ibid.* at 2264, n.2; emphasis added.
[65] *Ibid.* at 2265–66; emphasis added.
[66] *Ibid.* at 2270 and 2271.
[67] *Ibid.* at 2270.
[68] *Ibid.*; emphasis in original.
[69] *Ibid.*

nor the legislative history of Title 7, and he is able to distinguish the precedents in question. Even though he finds these precedents "ill-advised," the decision of the majority "giv[es] them unnecessarily broad scope."[70] The Court has "[n]ever . . . held or even intimated that, in the context of a statute of limitations inquiry, one must evaluate challenges to a seniority system born of discriminatory intent as of the moment of its adoption."[71] Marshall finds the majority decision "the latest example of how this Court, flouting the intent of Congress, has gradually diminished the application of Title VII to seniority systems."[72] Such a decision "serves only to reward those employers ingenious enough to cloak their acts of discrimination in a facially neutral guise, identical though the effects of this system may be to those of a facially discriminatory one."[73]

The majority in *Lorance*, however, is not as enamored of technical rules when they are challenged by whites claiming that an affirmative action agreement violates *their* rights.[74] The city of Birmingham, Alabama, under the threat of a lawsuit, entered into an agreement with the NAACP concerning the hiring and promotion of fire fighters. White fire fighters could have become a party to the suit and the eventual consent decree, but chose not to; later, they attacked the adopted plan. Their attack was thrown out by the district court under the doctrine of "impermissible collateral attack," which—given their failure to become a party to the suit—would have allowed them to attack the outcome only if it were "collusive, fraudulent, or transparently invalid."[75]

---

[70] *Ibid.* at 2271.

[71] *Ibid.* In one precedent applied by the majority—United Airlines v. Evans, 431 U.S. 533 (1977)—"the plaintiff never alleged that the seniority system itself was set up in order to discriminate." 109 S.Ct. at 2271. The case concerned an employee who was discharged and then returned to work; the plaintiff alleged that the *discharge* was discriminatory and therefore had an impact upon her seniority when she returned to work. Another precedent cited by the majority—Machinists v. NLRB, 362 U.S. 411 (1960)—was brought under a different statute and did not involve a seniority system. 109 S.Ct. at 2272. In a third case, involving the denial of tenure and dismissal of a college instructor, "there was no mystery about . . . the impact" the denial of tenure would have; it would clearly result in dismissal a year later. *Ibid.* Therefore the instructor in question could easily have filed his suit within the necessary time period. See Delaware State College v. Ricks, 449 U.S. 250 (1980).

[72] 109 S.Ct. at 2271.

[73] *Ibid.*

[74] The majority in *Lorance* was composed of Justice Scalia, Rehnquist, White, Stevens, and Kennedy. Justice O'Connor did not participate. The five-member majority in Martin v. Wilks includes O'Connor but not Stevens.

[75] 109 S.Ct. at 2198.

Although the rules in question are quite different, the case is essentially analogous to *Lorance*. There, the women could have challenged the seniority system within the specified time frame, but did not. Here, the white fire fighters could have joined the original suit, but chose not to. Yet Justice Rehnquist for the majority in *Martin* is suddenly less interested in the relevant technical rule (the doctrine of "impermissible collateral attack") than in general principles, such as "our 'deep-rooted historic tradition that everyone should have his own day in court.' "[76] Conceding that "the great majority of the federal courts of appeals" have had no difficulty applying the doctrine of "impermissible collateral attack," Justice Rehnquist nevertheless rules the other way, finding the doctrine inconsistent with the general federal rules of civil procedure.[77] Because the judgment was—in Rehnquist's opinion—*binding* on the white fire fighters, they should have been "joined"—that is, *forced* to become a party to the agreement. The NAACP's argument— that a requirement to "join" every party affected by its litigation would be burdensome and would discourage civil rights litigation—is not persuasive to Rehnquist. Even though the difficulties the NAACP foresees "are undoubtedly present," such problems "arise from the nature of the relief sought. . . ."[78] You ask for a lot, you pay the price.

Justice Stevens, in dissent, argues that the white fire fighters were not *bound* by the decision, but were *affected* by it; the only people legally bound by the decision were city officials. "As a matter of law," he writes, "there is a vast difference between persons who are actual parties to litigation and persons who merely have the kind of interest that may as a practical matter be impaired by the outcome of a case."[79] The consent decree in question did not bind the white fire fighters "in any legal sense"; that is, it did not require them to do anything or to cease from doing anything. Hence the rules of civil procedure cited by Justice Rehnquist are inapplicable. Rather, the consent decree "produce[d] changes in *conditions* at the white fire fighters' place of employment that, as a practical matter, may have a serious *effect* on their opportunities for employment or promotion. . . ."[80] Because they were in this second category of "practically effected" parties, the fire fighters had a right to intervene if they so chose, but, as "bystanders," they

---

[76] *Ibid.* at 2184, quoting C. Wright, A. Miller, and E. Cooper, *Federal Practice and Procedure*, Vol. 18 (St. Paul, Minn.: West, 1981), section 4449, 417.

[77] 109 S.Ct. at 2185.

[78] *Ibid.* at 2187.

[79] *Ibid.* at 2188.

[80] *Ibid.* at 2189; emphasis added.

have "no right to appeal from a judgment no matter how harmful it may be."[81] The consent decree did not deprive the white fire fighters "of any *contractual* rights, such as seniority . . . or accrued vacation pay. . . ."[82] They knew they might be affected by the consent decree, yet still chose not to join the legal action; "a person who can foresee that a lawsuit is likely to have a practical impact on his interests may pay a heavy price if he elects to sit on the sidelines. . . ."[83]

Moreover, the white fire fighters' arguments do not fit any of the limited circumstances under which collateral attack is permitted. There is no basis for claiming that the consent decree was collusive, or fraudulent,[84] nor was it "so out of line with settled legal doctrine" as to be "transparently invalid."[85] Rather, "[t]o the contrary, the type of race-conscious relief ordered in the consent decree is entirely consistent with this Court's approach to affirmative action."[86] The white fire fighters "are not responsible for" the "history of discrimination" in Birmingham, but were "nevertheless beneficiaries of the discriminatory practices that the litigation was designed to correct." Thus "[a]ny remedy that seeks to create employment conditions that would have obtained if there had been no violations of law will necessarily have an adverse impact on whites, who must now share their jobs and promotion opportunities with blacks."[87] Justice Stevens finds it "inevitable that nonminority employees or applicants will be less well off under an affirmative action plan than without it, no matter what form it takes."[88]

Given these statements, it is difficult to avoid the conclusion that the different positions of Justices Rehnquist and Stevens on the rather narrow, technical question of "impermissible collateral attack" are a function of their differing perceptions of the substantive validity of the white fire fighters' claim. Justice Rehnquist has considerable sympathy with the claim that their rights were violated; he thus finds the narrow technicality less important than general principle. Justice Stevens sees no merit in the white fire fighters' claim; he thus sees no reason *not* to follow the technical rule, amply supported by precedent as it is. However, even if one is sympathetic to the white fire fighters, it must be

[81] *Ibid.* at 2188.
[82] *Ibid.* at 2189; emphasis added.
[83] *Ibid.* at 2190.
[84] *Ibid.* at 2198.
[85] *Ibid.* at 2196.
[86] *Ibid.* at 2197.
[87] *Ibid.* at 2200.
[88] *Ibid.* at 2200, n.31.

remembered that they could have entered the lawsuit and the negotiation of the consent decree; they knew that *any* affirmative action plan would seriously affect them. It is precisely such a circumstance that the rule of "impermissible collateral attack" is designed to cover. The women in *Lorance*, on the other hand, were victims of economic trends; they had much less reason to expect negative consequences to flow from the adoption of the new seniority rule.

IV.

In a case handed down a week before *Lorance* and *Martin*, the Court faces the question of whether statistical evidence of a certain kind establishes "disparate impact" and thereby triggers the protections of Title 7. Here, too, it is difficult to avoid the conclusion that the differing analyses of the statistical question between the majority and the dissenters is a function of their differing views of what justice in the case demands.

The case concerned employment practices in the Alaskan salmon canneries. There are two kinds of jobs in the canneries: the lower-paid, manual labor of the cannery jobs, which are filled mostly by nonwhite workers, and "noncannery" positions, including administrative positions, filled mostly by whites. The two groups eat and sleep separately.[89]

The court of appeals had allowed a certain statistical comparison—between the percentage of cannery workers who are nonwhite and the percentage of *non*cannery workers who are nonwhite—to be used to establish a "prima facie" case of "disparate impact." Once such impact was established, the court of appeals ruled—on the basis of Supreme Court precedent[90]—the burden of proof shifts to the employer to demonstrate the "business necessity" of the employment practices in question. It is important to remember that the issue here is how much of a burden of proof is put on the employers, not whether they were in fact guilty of discrimination.

---

[89] Because the labor is intense and limited to a few months of the year, and because of the remoteness of the factories, most workers live on the premises during canning season.

[90] The most important precedent is Griggs v. Duke Power Company, 401 U.S. 424 (1971). *Griggs* interpreted Title 7 of the Civil Rights Act of 1964 as preventing an employer from requiring high school diplomas of job applicants and from subjecting them to an I.Q. test. The effect of these practices had been shown to disadvantage black applicants but had not been shown to relate to job performance. Paul Brest and Sanford Levinson, *Processes of Constitutional Decisionmaking*, 2nd ed. (Boston: Little, Brown, 1983), 503–04.

The majority of the Supreme Court rules that the court of appeals accepted the wrong statistical comparison; the relevant statistic is the number of *qualified* nonwhites in the area compared to the actual number of nonwhites hired for noncannery positions.[91] "If the absence of minorities holding such skilled positions is due to a dearth of qualified nonwhite applicants (for reasons that are not [the employers'] fault), [their] selection methods or employment practices cannot be said to have had a 'disparate impact' on nonwhites."[92] If the Court were to accept the court of appeal's statistical comparison, "the only practicable option for many employers will be to adopt racial quotas, insuring that no portion of his work force deviates in racial composition. . . ."[93]

But Justice White's opinion for the majority goes beyond the statistical question to hold—on a question of wide applicability—that *any* statistical evidence, alone, is not sufficient to shift the burden of proof to the employer under Title 7. "[E]ven if on remand" the minorities use the right statistic, "this alone will *not* suffice to make out a prima facie case of disparate impact."[94] The minorities "will also have to demonstrate that the disparity they complain of is the result of one or more of the employment practices they are attacking here, *specifically* showing that *each* challenged practice has a significantly disparate impact on employment opportunities for whites and nonwhites."[95] The minority plaintiffs had "alleged that a *variety* of petitioners' hiring/promotion practices—e.g., nepotism, a rehire preference, a lack of objective hiring criteria, separate hiring channels, a practice of not promoting from within—were responsible for the racial stratification of the work force. . . ."[96] They had not untangled these separate practices and presented evidence concerning each one. Only if they do untangle them, White rules, will the burden of proof shift to the employers.[97]

[91] 109 S.Ct. at 2122.
[92] *Ibid.*
[93] *Ibid.*
[94] *Ibid.* at 2125; emphasis in original.
[95] *Ibid.*; emphasis added. White is here relying on the Court's decision during the previous term in Watson v. Fort Worth Bank and Trust, 108 S.Ct. 2777 (1988). *Watson* was decided by a plurality; the current case turns that plurality into a majority.
[96] 109 S.Ct. at 2120; emphasis added.
[97] At that point, Justice White says, the Court would not apply strict scrutiny—that is, it would not demand that the challenged practice be "essential" or "indispensable," but rather would apply a kind of intermediate scrutiny; it would ask "whether a challenged practice serves, in a *significant* way, the

Once again, Justices Stevens, Brennan, Marshall, and Blackmun dissent; both Stevens and Blackmun write opinions.

Justice Stevens takes issue with the majority's analysis of the statistical question. He points out that the salmon industry is unique, and thus that the general *population* of the area may not constitute the available *labor supply*;[98] moreover, even the definition of the "area" in question is ambiguous:

> Canneries often are located in remote, sparsely populated areas of Alaska. . . . Most jobs are seasonal, with the season's length and the canneries' personnel needs varying not just year-to-year but day-to-day. . . . To fill their employment requirements, [the canneries] must recruit and transport many cannery workers and noncannery workers from States in the Pacific Northwest. . . .[99]

Examining the number of minority candidates *qualified* for noncannery positions—as the majority advocates—would fail to separate those *available* for the intense, live-in work from those unavailable for such work. On the other hand, the statistical evidence the minorities do offer, which the majority rejects, does "identif[y] a pool of workers willing to work during the relevant times and familiar with the workings of the industry."[100] Such evidence "[s]urely" is more useful "than the untailored, general population statistics on which" the employers, and the Court majority, rely.[101] The majority thus "underestimates the probative value of evidence of a racially stratified work force."[102] To put it another way, the majority ignores the unique social reality of the industry in question when deciding what statistic is required.

Moreover, the evidence is strong that the employers *do* discriminate. "[The canneries] recruit employees for at-issue jobs from outside the work force rather than from lower-paying, overwhelmingly nonwhite, cannery worker positions. . . ." Because such jobs usually are not posted or advertised and are made known only by word of mouth, "the maintenance of housing and mess halls that separate the largely white noncanning work force from the cannery workers . . . *coupled*

---

legitimate employment goals of the employer." *Ibid.* at 2125–26; emphasis added.
[98] *Ibid.* at 2134.
[99] *Ibid.* at 2133.
[100] *Ibid.* at 2134.
[101] *Ibid.* at 2134–35.
[102] *Ibid.* at 2127.

with the tendency toward nepotistic hiring, are obvious barriers to employment opportunities for nonwhites."[103] The employers engage in a series of *related* actions that *together* constitute discrimination; the majority's call for each practice to be examined separately is nonsensical. The segregated dining facilities take on special relevance when it is noted that jobs are not advertised, and so on.

Justice Blackmun, in his brief dissent, thus argues that the "practice-by-practice statistical proof of causation" required by the majority "would be impossible." He agrees with Justice Stevens that the "structure of the industry" makes "internal workforce comparisons" the only meaningful statistic.[104] Most revealingly, both Blackmun and Stevens reveal their view of the social realities of the case by comparing the salmon industry to a plantation economy.[105] As Justice Blackmun writes,

> [t]he salmon industry as described [here] takes us back to a kind of overt and institutionalized discrimination we have not dealt with in years: a total residential and work environment organized on principles of racial stratification and segregation, which . . . resembles a plantation economy. . . . This industry long has been characterized by a taste for discrimination of the old-fashioned sort: a preference for hiring nonwhites to fill its lowest-level positions, on the condition that they stay there. The majority's legal rulings essentially immunize these practices from attack under a Title VII disparate impact analysis.[106]

V.

At the end of his dissent in *Wards Cove*, Justice Blackmun laments that the majority's blindness to the realities of racial discrimination "comes as no surprise." He "wonders whether the majority still believes that race discrimination—or, more accurately, race discrimination against non-whites—is a problem in our society, or even remem-

[103] *Ibid.* at 2135; emphasis added.
[104] *Ibid.* at 2136.
[105] Justice Stevens does so in a footnote; see *ibid.* at 2128, n.4.
[106] *Ibid.* at 2136. For an analysis of *Wards Cove* relating it to more general questions concerning statutory interpretation, see Cass R. Sunstein, *After the Rights Revolution: Reconceiving the Regulatory State* (Cambridge, Mass.: Harvard University Press, 1990), 205–07.

bers that it ever was. . . ."[107] He then cites the last of the current cases, City of Richmond v. Croson.

In *Croson*, the Court declares that Richmond's affirmative action plan for minority businesses in the awarding of city contracts is a violation of the equal protection clause, because it discriminates against whites. More importantly, for the first time a clear majority of the Supreme Court declares that affirmative action plans in the states must be subjected to strict scrutiny.

The "right" violated by the city's plan was, Justice O'Connor declares in her opinion for the Court, the right of white citizens "to compete for a fixed percentage of public contracts based solely upon their race."[108] The plan had required prime contractors awarded city construction contracts to subcontract at least 30 percent of the dollar amount of each contract to minority businesses in a type of plan commonly known as a "set-aside."[109] The plan defined a "minority business enterprise" as including a business from anywhere in the country, at least 51 percent of which was owned by black, Spanish-speaking, Oriental, Indian, Eskimo, or Aleut citizens.[110] The plan ran for five years; it declared that it was "remedial" in nature and enacted "for the purpose of promoting wider participation by minority business enterprises in the construction of public projects."[111] The plan was adopted after fact finding and a public hearing by the Richmond City Council. "Proponents of the set-aside provision relied on a study which indicated that, while the general population of Richmond was 50% black, only .67% of the city's prime construction contracts had been awarded to minority businesses in the five-year period from 1978 to 1983."[112] Evidence was also presented "that a variety of contractors' associations, whose representatives appeared in opposition to the ordinance, had virtually no minority businesses within their membership."[113] The city argued that the plan was constitutional under the Supreme Court's decision in Fullilove v. Klutznick,[114] where a 10 percent minority set-aside enacted by Congress was upheld; there was "evidence before Congress that a nationwide history of past discrimina-

[107] 109 S.Ct. at 2136.
[108] 109 S.Ct. at 721.
[109] *Ibid.* at 712–13.
[110] *Ibid.* at 713.
[111] *Ibid.*
[112] *Ibid.* at 714.
[113] *Ibid.*
[114] 448 U.S. 448 (1980).

tion had reduced minority participation in federal construction grants.
.»115
. . .

The Supreme Court had not applied strict scrutiny in *Fullilove*, and
that case's approval of a minority set-aside would seem to be a powerful
precedent in favor of the Richmond plan. But Justice O'Connor has
no difficulty distinguishing the two. What the city "ignores," she says,
"is that Congress, unlike any State or political subdivision, has a
specific constitutional mandate to enforce the dictates of the Fourteenth
Amendment."[116] Simply because "Congress may identify and redress
the effects of society-wide discrimination does not mean that . . . the
States and their political subdivisions are free to decide that such
remedies are appropriate."[117] O'Connor interprets *Fullilove*'s failure
to apply strict scrutiny to be a result of its appropriate deference to "a
co-equal branch" of the federal government,[118] and, further, emphasizes that the minority set-aside there was "flexible."[119] Under the plan
in *Fullilove*, "a waiver could be sought where minority businesses were
not available to fill the 10% requirement or, more importantly, where
[a minority business enterprise] attempted 'to exploit the remedial
aspects of the program by charging an unreasonable price, i.e., a price
not attributable to the present effects of prior discrimination.'"[120]
O'Connor quotes Chief Justice Burger's opinion for the Court in *Fullilove* to the effect that "without this fine tuning to remedial purpose,
the statute would not have 'pass[ed] muster.'"[121]

Having disposed of *Fullilove*, O'Connor next proceeds to declare
that the Richmond plan must be subjected to strict scrutiny, because
it classifies on the basis of race; the fact that it "discriminates" against
whites in an attempt to remedy a history of discrimination against
blacks is irrelevant. It is one of the truisms of constitutional law that
the application of strict scrutiny makes it virtually impossible for any
statute to pass muster;[122] indeed, strict scrutiny was developed as a

---

[115] 109 S.Ct. at 718.
[116] *Ibid.* at 719. O'Connor emphasizes section 5 of that amendment, "[t]he
Congress shall have power to enforce, by appropriate legislation, the provisions
of this Article."
[117] *Ibid.*
[118] *Ibid.* at 717.
[119] *Ibid.* at 718.
[120] *Ibid.*, quoting *Fullilove*, 448 U.S. at 488.
[121] 109 S.Ct. at 718, quoting *Fullilove*, 448 U.S. at 487.
[122] As Gerald Gunther comments, strict scrutiny is " 'strict' in theory but
fatal in fact." "The Supreme Court, 1971 Term—Foreward: In Search of
Evolving Doctrine on a Changing Court: A Model for a Newer Equal Protection," *Harvard Law Review* 86 (November 1972): 1–306.

means of invalidating laws that discriminated *against minorities.* It should also be noted that O'Connor's argument that the level of scrutiny should vary with the level of government in question is an innovation in American constitutional theory; previously, it had always been the nature of the classification, and not the level of government, that determined the level of scrutiny, the assumption being that prejudice was prejudice, whether reflected in Congress or in a state or local ordinance.

But O'Connor, undoubtedly aided by President Reagan's other appointees to the Court,[123] has no difficulty sweeping all of this away. Noting that the text of the Fourteenth Amendment speaks only of discrimination against "persons," she declares that "to whatever racial group" the complainants in an affirmative action case belong, "their 'personal rights' to be treated with equal dignity and respect are implicated by a rigid rule erecting race as the sole criterion in an aspect of public decisionmaking."[124] The Court, she says, has "no way of determining what classifications are 'benign' or 'remedial' and what classifications are in fact motivated by illegitimate notions of racial inferiority or simple racial politics." *All* "[c]lassifications based on race carry a danger of stigmatic harm."[125]

O'Connor's assumptions in these statements, however, are highly questionable. First, as a purely factual matter, race is not the "sole" criterion in the awarding of contracts under the Richmond plan; 70 percent of the contracts are open to whites. If it were the "sole" criterion, no business would receive any contract for any reason other than the race of its owners.

More importantly, O'Connor's understanding of stigma and prejudice is preposterous. She is saying that because the city sets aside 30 percent of its contracts for racial minorities, whites are insulted in their basic dignity. This assumes that the "stigma" of being excluded from these specific contracts is an insult equivalent to assigning black schoolchildren to separate schools, or assigning black passengers to separate railroad cars.

But the insults aren't even remotely similar; not every *exclusion* is an insult to basic dignity. When, before Brown v. Board of Education, black children were assigned to separate schools, it was clearly because

[123] On the Republican party's agenda for the courts, see Herman Schwartz, *Packing the Courts: The Conservative Campaign to Rewrite the Constitution* (New York: Charles Scribner's Sons, 1988).
[124] 109 S.Ct. at 721.
[125] *Ibid.* On "stigmatic" harm, see pp. 91–92.

they were a despised minority, defined as inferior by the white majority. Moreover, every aspect of society in the South was segregated. The Richmond plan does not even vaguely resemble this situation. Is there a white person in America who doesn't know that whites are a majority? When a white contractor fails to receive a job under the Richmond plan, does he go home and wish—for more than a few moments—that he were black? Is he damaged in his self-esteem, in his image of himself, in the same way as the black children in *Brown*? His business interests may suffer—but does his whole sense of self-worth suffer in the same way? That, in effect, is what Justice O'Connor is claiming.

There is even a deeper flaw in O'Connor's reasoning than her misrepresentation of the facts and her questionable social psychology. Strict scrutiny turns on the assumption that certain minority groups deserve special judicial protection because they have long been excluded from the political process; they have been permanent political losers. It is simply impossible to make that claim about whites anywhere in the United States, but particularly not in Richmond, Virginia, which, as Justice Marshall notes in his dissent, is the former capital of the Confederacy.[126] Marshall is surely correct in seeing deep irony in the Supreme Court's application of strict scrutiny to protect whites in Richmond.[127] "As much as any municipality in the United States, Richmond knows what racial discrimination is; a century of decisions by this and other federal courts has richly documented the city's disgraceful history of public and private discrimination."[128] History has always been crucial in designating a suspect class, and whites have no history of being discriminated against in Richmond or anywhere else. As John Ely has argued, "[t]here is no danger that the coalition that makes up the white majority in our society is going to deny to whites generally their right to equal concern and respect."[129]

O'Connor attempts to turn this argument to her advantage by pointing out that, today, Richmond's population is approximately 50 percent black, and blacks hold a slim majority on the city council.[130] But this is too easy; that blacks are not politically excluded today in this one locality does not change the fact that they *were* systematically and

---

[126] *Ibid.* at 739.
[127] *Ibid.* at 740.
[128] *Ibid.*
[129] John Hart Ely, *Democracy and Distrust: A Theory of Judicial Review* (Cambridge, Mass.: Harvard University Press, 1980), 170.
[130] 109 S.Ct. at 722.

violently excluded for decades; nor does it change the fact that that history of discrimination has produced glaring disparities between the number of black and white contractors receiving city business in Richmond. A long history of racial discrimination does not disappear overnight. Moreover, O'Connor's argument is not merely that whites *in Richmond* deserve special protection, but rather that all affirmative action plans—unless enacted by Congress—must be subjected to strict scrutiny.

In the simplest terms, the Supreme Court majority in this case is ignoring the reality of race in America. When O'Connor says there is no way of knowing which racial classifications are remedial and which are discriminatory, she is living in a dreamworld, a world divorced from the simplest facts and the most elementary history. Justice Scalia, in his concurrence, concedes that "[i]t is plainly true that in our society blacks have suffered discrimination immeasurably greater than any directed at other racial groups."[131] But then he states, as a general matter, that "[t]he relevant proposition is not that it was blacks, or Jews, or Irish who were discriminated against, but that it was individual men and women . . . who were discriminated-against."[132] But "individual men and women" weren't discriminated against at random; they were discriminated against because they were perceived only as members of a detested minority group, a group detested by a white, Protestant majority. State governments didn't send "individual men and women" (or boys and girls) to separate schools, they sent niggers there. Restrictive covenants weren't formed against "individual men and women," but against niggers and kikes. If the discrimination suffered by blacks is, as Scalia says, "immeasurably greater than any directed at other racial groups," why is it so hard for him or for Justice O'Connor to figure out which racial classifications are benign and which are remedial?[133]

---

[131] *Ibid.* at 739.

[132] *Ibid.*

[133] There is one objection to affirmative action that is, at least potentially, constitutionally valid, and that might help argue in favor of strict scrutiny. This objection is raised by Justice Stevens in his concurrence: that affirmative action plans stigmatize the racial minorities they are meant to help, by creating the impression that they are less qualified than whites. Stevens quotes his own opinion in *Fullilove*: "[A] statute of this kind inevitably is perceived by many as resting on an assumption that those who are granted this special preference are less qualified in some respect that is identified purely by their race." *Ibid.* at 733, quoting *Fullilove*, 448 U.S. at 454. Given that the concept of stigmatic injury lies at the heart of equal protection jurisprudence, this objection must

Once the Richmond plan is subjected to strict scrutiny, the game is essentially over. The majority proceeds to find that the plan does not serve a "compelling" government goal, and that it is not "narrowly tailored" to the achievement of such a goal. "[A] generalized assertion that there has been past discrimination in an entire industry provides no guidance for a legislative body to determine the precise scope of the injury it seeks to remedy."[134] Such a "generalized assertion" contains "no logical stopping point."[135] Thus "[t]he 30% quota cannot in any realistic sense be tied to any injury suffered by anyone." The district court, in upholding the Richmond plan, had relied on five "facts"; as summarized by Justice O'Connor, they were:

> (1) the ordinance declares itself to be remedial; (2) several proponents of the measure stated their views that there had been past discrimination in the construction industry; (3) minority businesses received .67% of prime contracts from the city while minorities constituted 50% of the city's population; (4) there were very few minority contractors in local and state contractors' associations; and (5) in 1977, Congress made a determination that the effects of past discrimination had stifled minority participation in the construction industry nationally.[136]
> . . .

But, O'Connor says, "[n]one of these 'findings,' singly or together, provide the city of Richmond with a 'strong basis in evidence for its conclusion that remedial action was necessary.' "[137] Under strict scrutiny, stronger evidence, that specific individuals in Richmond have

---

be taken seriously.

There are, however, several available responses:

(1) The stigma in question is itself the result of prejudice; whites tend to believe that blacks can't possibly be "equally" qualified. Thus to bow to this kind of stigma is only to reinforce old patterns of discrimination.

(2) Governments can make clear that minorities "rewarded" under an affirmative action plan *are* equally qualified. And, as the number of minority professionals increase, and their contact with the public increases, it will become clear that they are, in fact, equally qualified.

(3) The danger of the stigma of special preference is, ultimately, less important than the overwhelming government interest in remedying the effects of past discrimination and increasing minority participation in American life.

[134] 109 S.Ct. at 723.
[135] *Ibid.*, quoting Wygant v. Board of Education, 476 U.S. 267, 275 (1986).
[136] 109 S.Ct. at 724.
[137] *Ibid.*, quoting *Wygant*, 476 U.S. at 277.

suffered from identifiable, discrete incidents of discrimination, is required. As in *Wards Cove*,[138] the Court demands better statistics and firmer evidence; the fact that "[t]here are roughly equal numbers of minorities and non-minorities in Richmond—yet minority-owned businesses receive *one seventy-fifth* the public contracting funds that other businesses receive,"[139] could be just an accident. Nor is a long history of discrimination in every aspect of public life sufficient evidence. Congress's findings of nationwide discrimination in the construction industry, cited in *Fullilove*, proves nothing about Richmond.[140]

Moreover, the city appears not to have considered the use "of race-neutral means to increase minority business participation in city contracting,"[141] and "the 30% quota cannot be said to be narrowly tailored to any goal, except perhaps outright racial balancing."[142] Thus the city has not demonstrated that this plan is absolutely necessary to remedy specific, identifiable discrimination.

In his dissent, Justice Marshall argues that Richmond's set-aside "is indistinguishable in all meaningful respects from—and in fact was patterned upon—the federal set-aside plan" upheld in *Fullilove*.[143] Congress's findings of fact there were "exhaustive," and "[t]he members of the Richmond City Council were well aware" of them, "a point the majority . . . elides."[144] The city council also heard ample testimony about the local construction industry, and "not a single person who testified before the City Council denied that discrimination in Richmond's construction industry had been widespread. . . ."[145] If "one views Richmond's local evidence of discrimination against the backdrop of system-

---

[138] See above, pp. 209–12.
[139] 109 S.Ct. at 747; emphasis in original.
[140] See *ibid*. at 726.
[141] *Ibid*. at 728.
[142] *Ibid*.
[143] *Ibid*. at 739.
[144] *Ibid*. at 742. On the question of congressional power versus state power to enforce the Fourteenth Amendment, Marshall finds that "our precedents have never suggested that" section 5 of the amendment "was meant to preempt or limit state police power to undertake race-conscious remedial measures." *Ibid*. at 755. On state police power, see Chapter 3.
[145] *Ibid*. at 743. Marshall quotes the former mayor of Richmond, who stated:

> I have been practicing law in this community since 1961, and I am familiar with the practices in the construction industry in this area, in the State, and around the nation. And I can say without equivocation, that the general conduct in the construction industry

atic nationwide racial discrimination which Congress so painstakingly identified in this very industry, this case is readily resolved."[146]

Marshall excoriates the majority's demand for absolute proof of harm to specific individuals. "[W]e have always regarded . . . factual inquiry as a practical one. . . . [T]he Court has eschewed rigid tests which require the provision of particular species of evidence, statistical or otherwise."[147] The Court's previous "unwillingness to . . . require specific types of proof in all circumstances reflects . . . an understanding that discrimination takes a myriad of 'ingenious and pervasive forms.' "[148]

Moreover, the evidence gathered and cited by the Richmond City Council was "strong," "firm," and "unquestionably legitimate."[149] The Court's "perfunctory dismissal of the testimony of Richmond's appointed and elected leaders is . . . deeply disturbing."[150] Further, Marshall "vehemently disagree[s] with the majority's dismissal of the congressional and Executive Branch findings noted in *Fullilove*. . . ."[151]

The opinion by Justice O'Connor

> concedes that Congress established nothing less than a "presumption" that minority contracting firms have been disad-

---

> in this area, and the State and around the nation, is one in which race discrimination and exclusion on the basis of race is widespread.
>
> I think the situation involved in the City of Richmond is the same. . . . I think . . . whether or not remedial action is required is not open to question.

Marshall also notes that a city manager, who "had oversight responsibility for city procurement matters, stated that he fully agreed with [the mayor's] analysis." *Ibid.* at 743, n.5.

[146] *Ibid.* at 743.

[147] *Ibid.* at 745.

[148] *Ibid.*, quoting University of California Regents v. Bakke, 438 U.S. 265, 387 (1978).

[149] 109 S.Ct. at 746.

[150] *Ibid.* at 747. Marshall says:

> Had the majority paused for a moment on the facts of the Richmond experience, it would have discovered that the city's leadership is deeply familiar with what racial discrimination is. The members of the Richmond City Council have spent long years witnessing multifarious acts of discrimination including, but not limited to, the deliberate diminution of black residents' voting rights, resistance to school desegregation, and publicly sanctioned housing discrimination. Numerous decisions of federal courts chronicle this disgraceful recent history. *Ibid.* at 748.

[151] *Ibid.* at 749.

vantaged by prior discrimination. . . . The majority, inexplicably, would forbid Richmond to "share" in this information, and permit only Congress to take note of these ample findings. . . . In thus requiring that Richmond's local evidence be severed from the context in which it was prepared, the majority would require cities seeking to eradicate the effects of past discrimination within their borders to reinvent the evidentiary wheel and engage in unnecessarily duplicative, costly, and time-consuming factfinding. No principle of federalism or of federal power, however, forbids a state or local government from drawing upon a nationally relevant historical record prepared by the Federal Government.[152]

On this question of fact finding, if nothing else, Marshall is surely correct. Is there any reason to doubt that patterns of racial discrimination discovered by Congress to exist nationwide would also exist *in Virginia*? Particularly when local officials testify that such discrimination does exist locally? The only conclusion is that the majority is determined to discredit the Richmond program, and make it virtually impossible to justify such a plan, no matter what lengths of absurdity it must travel to do so. Hence the use of strict scrutiny.

Marshall, however, argues that affirmative action plans should be subjected only to *intermediate* scrutiny, under which such a plan would be required to " 'serve *important* governmental objectives and must be *substantially related* to achievement of those objectives' in order to withstand constitutional scrutiny. . . ."[153] He finds the Richmond plan easily meets such a test. Richmond "has two powerful interests" in the plan.[154] First, there is "the city's interest in eradicating the effects of past racial discrimination. It is far too late in the day to doubt that remedying such discrimination is a compelling, let alone an important, interest."[155] Indeed, "[i]n *Fullilove*, six members of this Court deemed this interest sufficient. . . ."[156]

The city's second compelling interest "is the prospective one of preventing the city's own spending decisions from reinforcing and perpetuating the exclusionary effects of past discrimination. . . ."[157]

---

[152] *Ibid.*; citations omitted.
[153] *Ibid.* at 743, quoting University of California Regents v. Bakke, 438 U.S. at 359.
[154] 109 S.Ct. at 743.
[155] *Ibid.*
[156] *Ibid.*
[157] *Ibid.* at 744.

Court decisions "have often emphasized the danger of the government tacitly adopting, encouraging, or furthering racial discrimination even by its own routine operations."[158] Thus

> [t]he majority is wrong to trivialize the continuing impact of government acceptance or use of private institutions or structures once wrought by discrimination. When government channels all its contracting funds to a white-dominated community of established contractors whose racial homogeneity is the product of private discrimination, it does more than place its imprimatur on the practices which forged and which continue to define that community. It also provides a measurable boost to those economic entities that have thrived within it, while denying important economic benefits to those entities which, but for prior discrimination, might well be better qualified to receive valuable government contracts.[159]

In Marshall's view, "the interest in ensuring that the government does not reflect and reinforce prior private discrimination in dispensing public contracts is every bit as strong as the interest in eliminating private discrimination—an interest this Court has repeatedly deemed compelling. . . ."[160]

There is a realism here about government decision making, and about the economy, that is sorely lacking in Justice O'Connor's opinion. Even "neutral" government decisions may perpetuate a long and sorry history of discrimination. Economic institutions—labor unions, trade associations—do not automatically alter their composition when the government finally begins to distribute benefits in a neutral manner. Institutions persist, and affirmative steps may be the only way to overcome their inertia. Thus Justice O'Connor is being completely unrealistic when she dismisses the evidence that minority participation "in local contractors' associations was extremely low." Such evidence, she says,

> standing alone . . . is not probative of any discrimination in the local construction industry. There are numerous explanations for this dearth of minority participation, including past societal discrimination in education and economic opportunities as well as both black and white career and entrepreneurial

---

158 *Ibid.*
159 *Ibid.*
160 *Ibid.* at 744–45. Marshall here cites, among other cases, *Runyon*.

choices. Blacks may be disproportionately attracted to indus-
tries other than construction. . . .[161]

But why should such evidence "stand alone"? And what if the statistical disparity is as glaring as it is in Richmond? And what of her own admission that "past societal discrimination in education and economic opportunities" play a role? Despite all this, O'Connor would assume that the absence of minorities in local contractor's associations in Richmond could easily be a product of chance.

Having established that Richmond has compelling goals, Marshall proceeds to find Richmond's set-aside plan "substantially related to the interests it seeks to serve. . . ."[162] He notes that the plan was limited to five years, was not renewed, and contained a waiver provision.[163] Like the plan in *Fullilove*, "Richmond's has a minimal impact on innocent third parties. While the measure affects 30% of *public* contracting dollars, that translates to only 3% of overall Richmond area contracting. . . ."[164] Moreover, the city *had* previously explored the use of race-neutral measures—by outlawing discrimination by the city in awarding public contracts and discrimination by public contractors—to no effect.[165] And Marshall finds that the 30 percent figure is not random, but was "patterned directly on the *Fullilove* precedent."[166]

In sum, Marshall finds that the majority opinion "closes its eyes to . . . constitutional history and social reality."[167] Similarly, in a short, separate opinion, Justice Blackmun writes:

> I never thought that I would live to see the day when the city of Richmond, Virginia, the cradle of the Old Confederacy, sought on its own, within a narrow confine, to lessen the stark impact of persistent discrimination. But Richmond, to its great credit, acted. Yet this Court, the supposed bastion of equality,

[161] 109 S.Ct. at 726.
[162] *Ibid.* at 750.
[163] *Ibid.*
[164] *Ibid.*; emphasis in original.
[165] *Ibid.* at 751.
[166] *Ibid.* Marshall explains that
Congress's 10% figure fell "roughly halfway between the present percentage of minority contractors and the percentage of minority group members in the Nation." . . . The Richmond City Council's 30% figure similarly falls roughly halfway between the present percentage of Richmond-based minority contractors (almost zero) and the percentage of minorities in Richmond (50%). *Ibid.*; citations to *Fullilove* omitted.
[167] *Ibid.* at 755.

strikes down Richmond's efforts as though discrimination had never existed or was not demonstrated in this particular litigation. . . . History is irrefutable, even though one might sympathize with those who—though possibly innocent in themselves—benefit from the wrongs of past decades.[168]

VII.

History is, indeed, irrefutable, and, before *Croson*, was often considered essential to the definition of a suspect classification; racial minorities have always been taken as the paradigmatic example of a class "deserving" strict scrutiny. As the debate in *Croson* over whether to subject the affirmative action plan to strict scrutiny makes clear, much is at stake in this initial determination of which constitutional "test" to apply.

The Supreme Court has considered whether to extend the protections of strict scrutiny to a number of other groups; unfortunately, it has done so haphazardly and without much theoretical clarity. There is a widespread scholarly consensus that "the Supreme Court has been obscure about the reasons for stringent scrutiny of classifications based on some traits but not others. . . ."[169] Along with this obscurity has come some blatant wiggling; in some cases the Court has *said* it was applying the relaxed, rational relation test, but has in reality been applying a more stringent standard. The Court has also developed a third tier of "intermediate" scrutiny to handle some classifications it can't quite bring itself to consider "suspect," but regards as "semi-" suspect. To date, the Court has subjected classifications based on race, national origin, and alienage to strict scrutiny, although there has been a good deal of waffling on alienage;[170] it has subjected classifications based on gender and illegitimacy to intermediate scrutiny.[171]

In the cases dealing with these issues, two broad theoretical arguments emerge: an argument based on the general unfairness of basing legislation on certain traits, and an argument based on the political

---

[168] *Ibid.* at 757.

[169] Note, "Developments in the Law: The Family," *Harvard Law Review* 93 (April 1980): 1364. See also Judith A. Baer, *Equality Under the Constitution: Reclaiming the Fourteenth Amendment* (Ithaca: Cornell University Press, 1983), 28 and chapter 5; and Ely, *Democracy and Distrust*, 145–70.

[170] See below, note 210.

[171] "Developments in the Law: The Family," 1365.

powerlessness of the group involved.[172] The Court's first concern, for fairness, is "given content by analogy to discrimination against blacks, the original focus of the equal protection clause."[173] Thus, for example, the Court has on at least one occasion explicitly compared gender discrimination to racial discrimination.[174] Under this general heading, the Court has, on different occasions, pointed to "three properties a trait may possess that militate in favor of rigorous scrutiny. . . ."[175] The three traits are immutability, stigma, and general irrelevance to ability or merit.[176] That is, if the trait in question is something the individual cannot change, has no relationship to a "fair" question concerning ability or merit, and/or the possession of which leads the individual to be subjected to stigma, the Court has been more likely to consider the trait suspect.

The Court's second concern "derives from [its] sense of responsibility to protect politically handicapped groups from disadvantages imposed by the majoritarian political process."[177] In San Antonio v. Rodriguez,[178] a case in which the Court declines to invalidate the Texas system of school financing, the Court speaks of "the traditional indicia of suspectness": the classifications in *Rodriguez*—classifications between rich and poor or between property-rich and property-poor districts—were "not saddled with such disabilities, or subjected to such a history of purposeful unequal treatment, or relegated to such a position of political powerlessness as to command extraordinary protection from the majoritarian political process."[179]

All of these criteria have been applied by the Court willy-nilly; when it suits them, the justices talk of the immutability of a trait or whether it stigmatizes, and so forth. The existence of so many different criteria allows different justices (and commentators) an easy "out" when faced with a group they do not wish to protect; thus, it can be said that wealth is not a suspect classification because poverty is not immutable,[180] or that women are not a minority,[181] or that being a prisoner is not

---

[172] *Ibid.* See also Baer, *Equality Under the Constitution,* 120–22 and *passim.*
[173] "Developments in the Law: The Family," 1365.
[174] Frontiero v. Richardson, 411 U.S. 677, 685 (1973); see "Developments in the Law: The Family," 1365, n.89.
[175] "Developments in the Law: The Family," 1365.
[176] *Ibid.*
[177] *Ibid.*
[178] 411 U.S. 1 (1973).
[179] *Ibid.* at 28. See also Graham v. Richardson, 403 U.S. 365 (1971).
[180] See San Antonio v. Rodriguez, 411 U.S. at 18–28.
[181] See Ely, *Democracy and Distrust,* 164–70.

irrelevant to merit,[182] or that Hispanics are not politically powerless in certain places.[183]

All of the discussions of suspect classifications in these and other cases purport to derive from footnote four. But that footnote was hardly a complete theoretical discussion of the problem of minorities in American politics; it was, in fact, little more than a statement that a problem existed which the Court needed to address. Yet, in a very real sense, a great deal of modern doctrine derives from it.

It is thus worth pausing and asking what lies at the heart of footnote four. It presents, most fundamentally, a theory of legislative failure.[184] Under "normal" political circumstances, the Court assumes, different interests can protect themselves, and legislatures are competent to do the weighing and sifting and compromising necessary to the democratic process.[185] But, under some circumstances, legislatures may fail to represent at all, or may fail to represent fairly; thus all the Court's talk of "discrete and insular" minorities.

What the Court has not done, however, is pause and reflect on the different kinds of legislative failure, or their sources. Speaking very broadly, a legislature may fail for two different reasons. The failure may be a "mechanical" or a political one; that is, it may flow from "inadequate coalition-formation and incomplete electoral representation. . . ."[186] Thus the Amish in Wisconsin or Pennsylvania may be such a small group and so isolated from majoritarian politics that they may not be adequately represented in their respective state legislatures. About this kind of legislative failure the court has been relatively clear-headed.[187]

But there is a second reason legislatures may fail, about which the Court has been less than enlightened: the group in question may be viewed by the majority with prejudice. Footnote four speaks of "prejudice against discrete and insular minorities," yet the word *prejudice*

---

[182] See Rhodes v. Chapman, 452 U.S. 337 (1981), esp. at 348–49.

[183] See Casteneda v. Partida, 430 U.S. 482 (1977).

[184] See Laurence H. Tribe, *American Constitutional Law*, 2nd ed. (Mineola, N.Y.: Foundation Press, 1988), 1588, and Owen Fiss, "Foreward: The Forms of Justice," *Harvard Law Review* 93 (November 1979): 1–58.

[185] See Marshall's opinion in Dandridge v. Williams, 397 U.S. 471, 520 (1970).

[186] Tribe, *American Constitutional Law*, 1589. See also Ian Shapiro, "Three Fallacies Concerning Majorities, Minorities, and Democratic Politics," in John W. Chapman and Alan Wertheimer (eds.) *Nomos XXXII: Majorities and Minorities* (New York: New York University Press, 1990), 79–125, and the sources cited therein.

[187] See, e.g., Wisconsin v. Yoder, 406 U.S. 205 (1972).

often gets lost and the phrase "discrete and insular minorities" appears without it. A group may have its spokespersons and occasional legislative victories and still be the subject of prejudice; a group may even be a majority in the population (i.e., women) and yet still be the subject of prejudicial attitudes on the part of an overwhelmingly male legislature. As John Ely has commented, paying attention to the social psychology of prejudice "does supply the element that is missing in the usual rendition" of suspect classes, "[f]or whatever else it may or may not be, prejudice is a lens that distorts reality."[188] Prejudice can either be "direct," as it was when aimed at blacks before *Brown*, or it can be indirect, resulting in legislation that is based on stereotypes rather than on the relevant social facts; this is a possibility to which Justice Stevens is especially sensitive,[189] and is often at issue in cases alleging discrimination on the basis of gender.[190] Prejudice can "provide[] the 'majority of the whole' with that 'common motive to invade the rights of other citizens' that Madison believed improbable in a pluralistic society."[191] And there is good evidence that prejudice is extremely common;[192] "[t]hus generalizations to the effect, say, that whites in general are smarter or more industrious than blacks, men more stable than women, or native-born Americans more patriotic than Americans born elsewhere, are likely to go down pretty easily—and in fact we know they have—with groups whose demography is that of the typical American legislature."[193]

VIII.

Because it has lost sight of the relevance of prejudice and because of its general confusion over what is needed to make a classification "suspect," the Court has gotten itself into some fairly muddy waters. Thus, for example, in Cleburne v. Cleburne Living Center, a city

---

[188] Ely, *Democracy and Distrust*, 153.

[189] See his separate opinion in *Croson* and his dissent in Matthews v. Lucas, 427 U.S. 495 (1976).

[190] See the discussion of the *Feeney* case below, pp. 232–35.

[191] Frank Goodman, "DeFacto School Segregation: A Constitutional and Empirical Analysis," *California Law Review* 60 (March 1972): 315, as quoted in Ely, *Democracy and Distrust*, 153. Also see *Federalist* 10 in Alexander Hamilton, James Madison, and John Jay, *The Federalist Papers* (New York: New American Library, 1961), 77–84.

[192] See the discussion in Ely, *Democracy and Distrust*, 158, and sources cited therein.

[193] *Ibid.*, 159.

had denied a necessary permit to a group home for thirteen mentally retarded citizens.[194] The district court applied the minimum rationality standard and upheld the city. The Fifth Circuit Court of Appeals reversed, holding that mental retardation was a "quasi-suspect" classification triggering intermediate-level review; it then struck down the ordinance "because it did not substantially further any important governmental interests."[195]

The Supreme Court reversed, saying that mental retardation did not trigger heightened scrutiny. Mental retardation, the Court said, is not irrelevant to legislative decisions; mentally retarded individuals, who "have a reduced ability to cope with and function in the everyday world," are "different, immutably so, in relevant respects, and the States' interest in dealing with and providing for them is plainly a legitimate one."[196] The trait is not discrete; the mentally retarded "range from those whose disability is not immediately evident to those who must be constantly cared for."[197] The group is not politically powerless; legislation has recently been passed singling them out for special protection.[198] Moreover, labeling the mentally retarded "suspect" or "quasi-suspect" would be a dangerous precedent for the Court:

> if the large and amorphous class of the mentally retarded were deemed quasi-suspect . . . it would be difficult to find a principled way to distinguish a variety of other groups who have perhaps immutable disabilities setting them off from others, who cannot themselves mandate the desired legislative responses, and who can claim some degree of prejudice from at least part of the public at large. One need mention in this respect only the aging, the disabled, the mentally ill, and the infirm. We are reluctant to set out on that course. . . .[199]

So the mentally ill in *Cleburne* would seem to be out of luck, for, under the loose "rationality" standard, virtually any law, and certainly this law, would pass muster. But the Court fudges; it *says* it is applying the rational relation test, but it in fact applies a form of heightened scrutiny and overturns the ordinance as applied. It finds "irrelevant" the "differ-

---

[194] 473 U.S. 432 (1985).
[195] *Ibid.* at 438.
[196] *Ibid.* at 442.
[197] *Ibid.*
[198] *Ibid.* at 443–45.
[199] *Ibid.* at 445–46.

ence" between a group home for the mentally retarded and other multiple-living arrangements for which the city does not require a special-use permit, such as "boarding and lodging houses, fraternity or sorority houses, dormitories, apartment hotels. . . ."[200]

This judgment of irrelevance, as several justices point out,[201] is a far cry from the wide deference usually accorded legislative judgments under the rational relation test. "To be sure," Justice Marshall writes, "the Court does not label its .handiwork heightened scrutiny, and perhaps the method employed must hereafter be called 'second order' rational-basis review rather than 'heightened scrutiny.' "[202] But heightened scrutiny it surely is.[203]

The Court makes a similarly covert move in Plyler v. Doe,[204] invalidating a Texas law denying public education to the children of illegal immigrants. Although "[u]ndocumented aliens cannot be treated as a suspect class because their presence in this country in violation of federal law" is constitutionally relevant, "more is involved in [this] case. . . ."[205] The "more" that is involved is a subjective judgment that these children deserve some protection from an unfair Texas law. The law in question "imposes a lifetime hardship on a discrete class of children not accountable for their disabling status. The stigma of illiteracy will mark them for the rest of their lives."[206] The use of the words *discrete class* and *stigma* signals that the Court is trying to stuff a square peg into a round hole; that is, it is making a case for heightened scrutiny without actually declaring itself to be doing so. Thus "the discrimination contained in" the Texas statute "can hardly be considered rational unless it furthers some *substantial* goal of the state."[207] This is unlike any rationality review the Court has ever applied, and, as the dissenters charge, the Court majority, "by patching together bits and pieces . . . spins out a theory custom-tailored to the facts of these cases."[208]

---

[200] *Ibid.* at 447.
[201] See Justice Marshall's dissent, *ibid.* at 458.
[202] *Ibid.*
[203] *Ibid.* See also Tribe, *American Constitutional Law*, 1444.
[204] 457 U.S. 202 (1982).
[205] *Ibid.* at 223.
[206] *Ibid.*
[207] *Ibid.* at 224; emphasis added.
[208] *Ibid.* at 244. Relevant to the majority decision is not only the classification (the children of illegal immigrants) but also the interest at stake—education—which the Court regards with special care—when it chooses to. See Justice Brennan's opinion, *ibid.* at 221.

There can be no doubt that the mentally retarded of *Cleburne* and the undocumented children of *Plyler* are members of groups which are vulnerable to the legislative failure that footnote four is meant to address. It is also clear, however, that mental retardation and undocumented status are traits that are sometimes the legitimate subject of legislative decision making. As such, subjecting them to intermediate scrutiny—explicitly—would seem to be an appropriate and rational approach. The Court fears the beginning of a slippery slope from such an explicit declaration, in which numerous groups will press forward demanding heightened scrutiny. But sorting through such claims—honestly and explicitly—would be a far better tactic than the kind of mushy, covert scrutiny of cases like *Cleburne* and *Plyler*.[209] And sorting through such claims would at least recognize that, even when a trait is sometimes the subject of legitimate legislative concern, such a group may be socially vulnerable and have suffered a history of discriminatory treatment.[210]

[209] Tribe, *American Constitutional Law,* 1445.

[210] Similar reasoning—and honesty—would support treating aliens as a "semi-" suspect group. Although alienage is sometimes quite relevant to government decision making, and alienage is not a strictly immutable trait, it is nevertheless clear that aliens have been, and continue to be, subjected to widespread hostility and prejudice. See *ibid.,* 1545.

The Supreme Court's actual treatment of aliens has been confused in the extreme. In the early 1970s the Burger Court extended the full protections of strict scrutiny to aliens, ruling in Graham v. Richardson, 403 U.S. 365 (1971), that states could not deny welfare benefits to resident aliens, and in Sugarman v. Dougall, 413 U.S. 634 (1973), that states could not prevent them from gaining civil service jobs. Tribe, *American Constitutional Law,* 1547–48; Gerald Gunther, *Constitutional Law,* 11th ed. (Mineola, N.Y.: Foundation Press, 1985), 670–71. By the late 1970s, however, support for aliens had dwindled, and the Court began to sustain a number of alienage classifications. Tribe, *American Constitutional Law,* 1548–49; Gunther, *Constitutional Law,* 672. In Foley v. Connelie, 435 U.S. 291 (1978), a majority voted to sustain a New York law requiring that police officers be American citizens.

The Court had to struggle hard to reconcile its decision in *Foley* with precedents as recent as *Graham* and *Dougall*; it did so by claiming that strict scrutiny "was appropriate only where state action 'struck at the noncitizens' ability to exist in the community' by denying them important benefits or the right to engage in ordinary trades or professions." Tribe, *American Constitutional Law,* 1548–49, quoting *Foley,* 435 U.S. at 294–95. The Court quoted Justice Blackmun's opinion for the majority in *Dougall* to the effect that the state had the power "to preserve the basic conception of a political community," reasoning that Americans had a right to be policed by other Americans. Tribe, *American Constitutional Law,* 1549, quoting *Dougall,* 413 U.S. at 647. The Court then extended the reasoning of *Foley* to sustain a New York law banning aliens from employment as teachers in public schools. Ambach v.

IX.

There are two classifications that the Court ought to declare fully suspect and deserving of the full protection of strict scrutiny: gender and sexual orientation.

The Court came close to doing so on the question of gender in 1973 in Frontiero v. Richardson; four justices[211] voted to make gender a suspect class.[212] Three justices, however,[213] said that the issue would be resolved by the then-pending Equal Rights Amendment, and that the Court should not preempt that political process. In *Frontiero*, the issue was the right of a female member of the armed services to claim her spouse as a "dependent" for the purposes of obtaining increased quarters and medical benefits. The statutes in question allowed a man to claim his wife as an automatic dependent, but required a servicewoman to *prove* that her husband was "in fact dependent on her for over one-half of his support."[214] The government could only claim that the statutes served "administrative convenience," making the level of review a crucial question; under a rationality standard, "administrative convenience," would stand; under strict scrutiny, it would fall.

In his opinion arguing for strict scrutiny, Justice Brennan points out that gender is an immutable trait, "determined solely by the accident of birth"; thus discrimination on the basis of gender violates "the basic concept of our system that legal burdens should bear some relationship to individual responsibility. . . ."[215] Moreover, gender "frequently bears no relation to ability to perform or contribute to society."[216] There was "no doubt that our Nation has had a long and unfortunate history of sex discrimination," discrimination "rationalized by . . . 'romantic paternalism.' "[217] The position of women in the nineteenth

---

Norwick, 441 U.S. 68 (1979). Once again, this was a questionable move, as the Court in *Foley* had stressed the coercive power of police officers. Tribe, *American Constitutional Law*, 1549; see *Foley*, 435 U.S at 297–98.

As Gerald Gunther notes, the Court's "framework for scrutinizing alienage classifications represented a novel departure in equal protection doctrine: some alienage classifications continued to be subjected to strict scrutiny; but others, pertaining to 'governmental functions' (or 'political functions') were reviewed far more deferentially." Gunther, *Constitutional Law*, 670.

[211] Brennan, Douglas, White, and Marshall.
[212] 411 U.S. 677 (1973).
[213] Powell, Burger, and Blackmun.
[214] 411 U.S. at 678–79.
[215] *Ibid.* at 686, quoting Weber v. Aetna Casualty & Surety Co., 406 U.S. 164, 175 (1972).
[216] 411 U.S. at 686.
[217] *Ibid.* at 684.

century "was, in many respects, comparable to that of blacks under the pre–Civil War slave codes."[218] As a result, "our statute books gradually became laden with gross, stereotyped distinctions between the sexes. . . ."[219] Of course the situation "has improved markedly in recent decades," yet "it can hardly be doubted that, in part because of the high visibility of the sex characteristic, women still face pervasive, although at times more subtle, discrimination in our educational institutions, in the job market, and, perhaps most conspicuously, in the political arena."[220]

It is hard to argue with such logic and evidence. That discrimination against women may be subtle but is nevertheless pervasive has been documented thoroughly.[221] That discrimination against women is legislative discrimination against a demographic majority does not make it any less real. Yet, after the close call in *Frontiero*, and after the defeat of the ERA (which had been relevant to three justices in that case), the Court retreated, and has generally declared that gender deserves only intermediate scrutiny.[222] But the pervasiveness and covertness of discrimination against women is revealed in another case, *Massachusetts v. Feeney*,[223] which, on its face, has nothing to do with gender.

In *Feeney*, the Court was faced with a state program giving veterans an absolute lifetime preference for civil service positions. The female appellee had passed several competitive civil service exams for better jobs, but was each time ranked below male veterans who had achieved lower test scores.[224]

The Court decides that the statute's preference for veterans was not a "pretext" for gender discrimination. The majority points out that some women *are* veterans, and that many male non-veterans are harmed by the statute.[225] The Court admits that "[i]t would be disingenuous to say that the adverse consequences of this legislation for women were unintended, in the sense that they were not volitional or in the

[218] *Ibid.* at 685.
[219] *Ibid.*
[220] *Ibid.* at 685–86.
[221] Justice Brennan cites a number of sources, including Note, "Sex Discrimination and Equal Protection: Do We Need a Constitutional Amendment?," *Harvard Law Review* 84 (April 1971): 1499–1524; see also Note, "Developments in the Law—Equal Protection," *Harvard Law Review* 82 (March 1969): 1065–1192.
[222] The crucial case is Craig v. Boren, 429 U.S. 190 (1976).
[223] 442 U.S. 256 (1970).
[224] Brest and Levinson, *Processes of Constitutional Decisionmaking*, 614.
[225] 442 U.S. at 275.

sense that they were not foreseeable."[226] But the Court demands a showing of a "discriminatory purpose," and such a discriminatory purpose "implies more than intent as volition or intent as awareness of consequences. . . . It implies that the decisionmaker, in this case a state legislature, selected or reaffirmed a particular course of action at least in part 'because of' and not merely 'in spite of' its adverse effects upon an identifiable group."[227] In other words, the legislature would have to have *wanted* to hurt women, and not merely *known* that the statute in question would, in fact, hurt them.

Feeney is a difficult case, as the issue is the "disproportionate impact" of a gender-neutral statute. The case illustrates, above all, how important the level of review can be. Under rationality review the statute surely passes; helping veterans is a legitimate government goal, and the Massachusetts system a rational way of achieving such a goal. The plan might even survive intermediate scrutiny—the goal of helping veterans can be called "important" and the means chosen are, at least arguably, "substantially related" to that end. But the statute would not survive strict scrutiny, for, even if helping veterans were accepted as a "compelling" governmental goal, the means chosen—the absolute, lifetime preference—are not "necessary"; Massachusetts could have found a way of helping veterans that didn't so consistently hurt individuals such as Feeney.

Justice Marshall, in dissent, has no problem finding the Massachusetts scheme to be "purposeful gender-based discrimination."[228] A legislature may "seek[] to advantage one group," but this "does not, as a matter of logic or of common sense, exclude the possibility that it also intends to disadvantage another" group.[229] Legislative motive is difficult to ascertain, and thus "resort to inference based on objective factors is generally unavoidable. . . ."[230] Thus especially relevant are "the degree, inevitability, and foreseeability of any disproportionate impact" of a statute; the Court must also consider "the alternatives reasonably available."[231] Given the fact that "less than 2% of the women in Massachusetts are veterans," the plan "has rendered desirable civil service employment an almost exclusively male prerogative. . . ."[232] Moreover, "this consequence follows foreseeably, indeed inex-

---

[226] *Ibid.* at 278.
[227] *Ibid.* at 279.
[228] *Ibid.* at 281–82.
[229] *Ibid.* at 282.
[230] *Ibid.* at 283.
[231] *Ibid.*; citations omitted.
[232] *Ibid.*

orably, from the long history of policies severely limiting women's participation in the military."[233]

Because the impact of the statute is "so disproportionate" as well as foreseeable, "the burden should rest on the State to establish that sex-based considerations played no part in the choice of the particular legislative scheme."[234] Such a burden "was not sustained here," for "[t]he legislative history of the statute reflects the [state's] patent appreciation of the impact the preference would have on women, and an equally evident desire to mitigate the impact only with respect to certain traditionally female occupations."[235] Thus "[u]ntil 1971, the statute and implementing civil service regulations *exempted* from operation of the preference any job requisitions '*especially calling for women.*'"[236] The existence of this exemption means that

> for over 70 years, the [state] has maintained, as an integral part of its veterans' preference system, an exemption relegating female civil service applicants to occupations traditionally filled by women. Such a statutory scheme both reflects and perpetuates precisely the kind of archaic assumptions about women's roles which we have previously held invalid. . . . Particularly when viewed against the range of less discriminatory alternatives available to assist veterans, Massachusetts' choice of a formula that so severely restricts public employment opportunities for women cannot reasonably be thought gender-neutral.[237]

Marshall's logic here seems unassailable. The state knew it was hurting women, and took action (through the exemption) to keep on hurting

---

[233] *Ibid.*

[234] *Ibid.* at 284; citations omitted. Thus Marshall is not applying traditional strict scrutiny in so many words; he has long advocated a "sliding scale" of review that balances three factors: the character of the classification in question, the relative importance to the individuals in the class of the benefits or services in question, and the asserted state interests. See esp. his dissent in Dandridge v. Williams, 397 U.S. 471 (1970). One interpretation of Marshall's argument in these cases is that he is seeking to broaden the applicability of heightened scrutiny to classes that cannot be labeled fully "suspect" or to rights or benefits that cannot be labeled "fundamental," but nevertheless "deserve" heightened scrutiny. See Thomas E. Scanlon, "Equal Protection Beyond the Reign of Two-Tiered Hegemony" (unpublished M.A. thesis, University of California at San Diego, 1991).

[235] 442 U.S. at 284.

[236] *Ibid.* at 284–85; emphasis added.

[237] *Ibid.* at 285; citations omitted.

women. Other means of helping veterans could easily have been devised. Whether the Court will *require* the state to utilize such alternative methods depends entirely on what level of review is thought appropriate; that, in turn, depends not on the text of the Fourteenth Amendment but on how the Court interprets the social history and social facts concerning women as a class.

X.

Similarly, social history and social facts support the declaration of sexual orientation as a suspect class.[238] That argument is ably made by the Ninth Circuit Court of Appeals in Watkins v. U.S. Army.[239]

Perry Watkins had enlisted in the army at the age of nineteen; "[i]n filling out the Army's preinduction medical form, he candidly marked 'yes' in response to a question whether he had homosexual tendencies."[240] The army nevertheless accepted him; he served for fourteen years and was, "in the words of his commanding officer, 'one of our most respected and trusted soldiers. . . .' "[241] During his years as a soldier Watkins's homosexuality was "always common knowledge,"[242] and the army "has never claimed that his sexual orientation or behavior interfered in any way with military functions."[243] In 1981, however, new army regulations "mandated the disqualification of all homosexuals from the army without regard to the length or quality of their military service."[244] Watkins challenged his discharge.

Watkins's plight provides an excellent test case because he was discharged merely for *being* a homosexual; there was no real evidence in the record that he had ever engaged in homosexual *acts* with anyone.[245] What *was* clear from the record was that the army had all

---

[238] For the relevant facts, see p. 142.
[239] 837 F.2d 1428 (9th Cir. 1988).
[240] *Ibid.* at 1429.
[241] *Ibid.*
[242] *Ibid.*, citing the finding of the district court. Watkins v. U.S. Army, 551 F.Supp. 212, 216 (W.D. Wash. 1982).
[243] 837 F.2d at 1429.
[244] *Ibid.*
[245] The only evidence of homosexual behavior in the record was Watkins's admission to one army official that "he had been gay since the age of 13 and had engaged in unspecified homosexual acts with two other servicemen. Whether these acts involved sodomy or some other form of sexual conduct is not evident from the record." *Ibid.* The army "investigated Watkins in 1968 for *allegedly* committing sodomy, a criminal offense for a soldier," but "the investigation was dropped for lack of evidence." *Ibid.*; emphasis in original.

along known that Watkins was gay; he had performed as a female impersonator "in various reviews," always "with the permission of his commanding officer. . . ."[246] Thus Watkins's constitutional argument did not rely on a constitutionally protected right of privacy to commit homosexual acts, but rather on the charge that the army had "invidiously" discriminated against him in violation of equal protection principles. As the court notes, nothing in the Supreme Court opinion in Bowers v. Hardwick[247] "suggests that the state may penalize gays for their sexual *orientation.*" Moreover, the court says that "it cannot read *Hardwick* as standing for the proposition that government may outlaw sodomy only when committed by a disfavored class of persons," given that the Georgia statute upheld there was neutral with regard to gender.[248] The court concludes that "the driving force behind *Hardwick* is the [Supreme] Court's ongoing concern with the expansion of rights under substantive due process, not an unbounded antipathy toward a disfavored group."[249]

The court thus proceeds to decide whether homosexuals should be declared a suspect class. It says that "[t]he first factor the Supreme Court generally considers is whether the group at issue has suffered a history of purposeful discrimination,"[250] and finds it "indisputable" that homosexuals have been "the object of pernicious and sustained hostility."[251] Indeed, "[l]esbians and gays have been the object of some of the deepest prejudice and hatred in American society."[252] This conclusion is amply supported by the findings of social scientists; gay men and lesbians are usually found to be the most hated group in America.[253]

The "second factor" relevant to determining suspect classifications "is difficult to capsulize and may in fact represent a cluster of factors grouped around a central idea—whether the discrimination embodies

---

[246] *Ibid.* at 1430.
[247] 478 U.S. 186 (1986).
[248] 837 F.2d at 1439.
[249] *Ibid.* at 1440.
[250] *Ibid.* at 1444; citations omitted.
[251] *Ibid.* The court is here quoting Rowland v. Mad River Local School District, 470 U.S. 1009, 1014 (1985).
[252] 837 F.2d at 1444, quoting High Tech Gays v. Defense Industrial Security Clearance Office, 688 F.Supp. 1361 (N.D. Cal. 1987) (invalidating Defense Department practice of subjecting gay security clearance applicants to more exacting scrutiny than heterosexual applicants).
[253] Kenneth S. Sherrill, "Homosexuality and Civil Liberty" (unpublished paper delivered at American Political Science Association meeting, Atlanta, Ga., August 1989).

a gross unfairness that is sufficiently inconsistent with the ideals of equal protection to term it invidious."[254] On these grounds, "[s]exual orientation plainly has no relevance to a person's 'ability to perform or contribute to society.' "[255] "Indeed," in this particular case, "the Army *makes no claim* that homosexuality impairs a person's ability to perform military duties."[256] And, "as the Army itself concluded, there is not a scintilla of evidence that Watkins' avowed homosexuality 'had either a degrading effect upon unit performance, morale or discipline, or upon his own job performance.' "[257] Given that sexual orientation *is* unrelated to a person's "contribution to society," the court reasons "that classifications based on sexual orientation reflect prejudice and inaccurate stereotypes. . . ."[258]

The army responds that "the public opprobrium directed towards gays does not constitute prejudice in the pejorative sense of the word, but rather represents appropriate public disapproval of persons who engage in immoral behavior."[259] But this argument "rests on two false premises. First, the class burdened by the regulations is defined by the sexual *orientation* of its members, not by their sexual conduct. . . . To our knowledge, homosexual orientation itself has never been criminalized in this country." Further, "little of the homosexual *conduct* covered by the regulations is criminal."[260] The army's regulations govern "many forms of homosexual conduct other than sodomy such as kissing, handholding, caressing, and hand-genital contact. Yet, sodomy is the only consensual adult sexual conduct that Congress has criminalized. . . ."[261]

The court next considers the question of the "immutability" of homosexuality. It finds essential to the question of immutability, not that a trait can *never* change, but rather that "changing it would involve great difficulty, such as requiring a major physical change or a traumatic change of identity."[262] After all, "[p]eople can have operations to change their sex. Aliens can ordinarily become naturalized

---

[254] 837 F.2d at 1444.
[255] *Ibid.* at 1445, quoting *Frontiero,* 411 U.S. at 686.
[256] 837 F.2d at 1445; emphasis added.
[257] *Ibid.*
[258] *Ibid.*
[259] *Ibid.*
[260] *Ibid.*
[261] *Ibid.* Of course, a law outlawing consensual sodomy is open to challenge on privacy grounds; see pp. 134–40.
[262] *Ibid.* at 1446.

citizens. The status of illegitimate children can be changed. People can frequently hide their national origin. . . ."[263] Going further, the court "read[s] the case law in a . . . capacious manner," and concludes that " 'immutability' may describe those traits that are so central to a person's identity that it would be abhorrent for government to penalize a person for refusing to change them, regardless of how easy that change might be. . . ."[264] The court here has a valid point, which it drives home by commenting that "[r]acial discrimination . . . would not suddenly become constitutional if medical science developed an easy, cheap, and painless method of changing one's skin pigment."[265] On these terms, the court has "no trouble concluding that sexual orientation is immutable for the purpose of equal protection doctrine."[266] Even though "the causes of homosexuality are not fully understood, scientific research indicates that we have little control over our sexual orientation and that, once acquired, our sexual orientation is largely impervious to change. . . ."[267]

The last factor relevant to suspect classification analysis is the question of political powerlessness. Here, the court perceptively notes the connection between a suspect class and the majority's lack of empathy for certain traits. "The [Supreme] Court has held, for example, that old age does not define a discrete and insular group because 'it marks a stage that each of us will reach if we live out our normal span.' "[268] Such is not the case with homosexuality; "[b]y contrast, most of us are not likely to identify ourselves as homosexuals at any time in our lives. Thus, many of us, including many elected officials, are likely to have difficulty understanding or empathizing with homosexuals."[269] The court notes that "[m]ost people have little exposure to gays, both because they rarely encounter gays and because the gays they do encounter may feel compelled to conceal their sexual orientation."[270]

---

[263] *Ibid.*

[264] *Ibid.*

[265] *Ibid.* The court here cites Laurence H. Tribe, "The Puzzling Persistence of Process-Based Constitutional Theories," *Yale Law Journal* 89 (May 1980): 1073–74, n.52, and Note, "The Constitutional Status of Sexual Orientation: Homosexuality as a Suspect Classification," *Harvard Law Review* 98 (April 1985): 1303.

[266] 837 F.2d at 1446.

[267] *Ibid.*

[268] *Ibid.* at 1447, quoting Massachusetts Board of Retirement v. Murgia, 427 U.S. 307, 313–14 (1976).

[269] 837 F.2d at 1447.

[270] *Ibid.*

Moreover, "the social, economic, and political pressures to conceal one's homosexuality commonly deter many gays from openly advocating pro-homosexual legislation, thus intensifying their inability to make effective use of the political process. . . ."[271] And "[e]ven when gays overcome this prejudice enough to participate openly in politics, the general animus towards homosexuality may render this participation wholly ineffective. Elected officials sensitive to public prejudice may refuse to support legislation that even appears to condone homosexuality. . . ."[272] The court here is surely right, drawing an important link between widespread social prejudice and legislative failure: legislators may well be afraid of their prejudiced constituents.

For all of these reasons, the court declares homosexuals to be a suspect class, and proceeds to find the army's regulation unconstitutional under strict scrutiny. Conceding that "even under strict scrutiny, our review of military regulations must be more deferential than comparable review of laws governing civilians," it nevertheless finds the army guilty of "cater[ing] to private biases."[273] Equal protection "does not permit notions of majoritarian morality to serve as compelling justification for laws that discriminate against suspect classes."[274] To the army's worry that gay soldiers will hurt morale and increase tensions within military ranks, the court responds that "[t]hese concerns strike a familiar chord. For much of our history, the military's fear of racial tension kept black soldiers separated from whites. . . ."[275] The army's regulations are also "poorly tailored" to advance its interest in not having military discipline undermined "if emotional relationships developed between homosexuals of different military rank. . . ."[276] And military security cannot be breached if a soldier is open about his homosexuality.[277]

XI.

We are brought full circle by the lower court's recognition in *Watkins* that the majority's lack of empathy for homosexuals is highly

[271] *Ibid.*
[272] *Ibid.*
[273] *Ibid.* at 1448.
[274] *Ibid.* at 1450.
[275] *Ibid.* at 1449.
[276] *Ibid.* at 1451.
[277] *Ibid.* Watkins's case was reheard en banc; the full circuit avoided constitutional questions and held on more technical grounds ("equitable estoppel") that Watkins must be allowed to reenlist. Basically, the court held that the

relevant to the question of whether they constitute a suspect class. The Supreme Court's use of the rational relation test carries implicit within it the premise that there is sufficient empathy among different social groups to prevent any grave miscarriages of justice in the legislative process. In a case concerning the right to die, in which the majority of the Supreme Court refuses to upset the decision of the Missouri legislature, Justice Scalia writes in his concurrence that, in general, "[o]ur salvation" against "horrible" legislation "is the Equal Protection Clause, which requires the democratic majority to accept for themselves and their loved ones what they impose on you and me." Thus the Supreme Court "need not . . . inject itself into every field of human activity where irrationality and oppression may theoretically occur. . . ."[278]

But irrationality is not theoretical; prejudice exits. And oppression results. The experience of countless Americans—homosexuals, women—cannot be contradicted, and their experiences are not "theoretical." The members of a legislature may "accept for themselves and their loved ones" only those laws they have any reason to believe will actually touch them. Does the average legislator think he (or his loved ones) will be touched by a law regulating homosexual conduct, or the behavior of aliens? Will he be "touched" by laws governing the disabled? Does he know what it means to have a mentally retarded child? Can he even begin to understand what it is like to be a member of a community ravaged by AIDS? And even if, in these situations, he is enlightened enough and, somehow, empathic enough, can we expect him to stand up to the prejudices of his constituents?

To pose these questions is to answer them, and to reveal the fatuousness of Justice Scalia's reasoning. Democratic empathy guarantees only so much.

---

army could not refuse the reenlistment given its long-standing knowledge of Watkins's orientation. Watkins v. U.S. Army, 875 F.2d 699 (9th Cir. 1989). The Supreme Court let the decision stand.

[278] Cruzon v. Missouri, 496 U.S. __(1990).

CHAPTER 6

THE THRENODY OF LIBERALISM: LIBERTY AND COMMUNITY

I.

Each year, the city of Pawtucket, Rhode Island, erects a Christmas display in the center of its shopping district. For over forty years, the display has included, along with candy canes, reindeer, and Santa Claus, a crèche—a depiction of the Infant Jesus, Mary, and Joseph, angels, shepherds, and kings.[1] The crèche is owned and maintained by the city.

In 1984 the Supreme Court sustained the city's display of the crèche, ruling that it did not unconstitutionally "establish" the Christian religion. Rather, the Court said, the display celebrated the season in a constitutionally appropriate manner; the crèche refers to "our religious heritage." The display of the crèche, Chief Justice Burger wrote for the Court's five-member majority, "engenders a friendly community spirit of goodwill in keeping with the season."[2]

By invoking the magic word *community*, the Chief Justice touches upon one of the thorniest issues in contemporary academic debate. In fact, "community" has become a rallying cry, and the failure of a liberal society to foster a sense of community among its citizens has become the focus of voluminous commentary in both political theory and legal scholarship; the longing for community has arisen from so many voices it can be characterized as the threnody[3] of contemporary liberalism. Scholars in different fields and with different perspectives seem to share a weariness with the politics of interest and to yearn for the peace and quiet of fellowship and fraternity—the politics of love.

---

[1] Lynch v. Donnelly, 465 U.S. 668, 671 (1984).
[2] *Ibid.* at 685.
[3] In Greek drama, the song of lamentation or dirge.

The communitarian impulse arises from a variety of methodological and ideological perspectives, and it is striking that so many recent lines of analysis converge on this one central value. There are those, such as Alisdair MacIntyre,[4] for whom the call for community is part of a broad attack on liberal politics and liberal society, while there are those, such as Michael Sandel,[5] for whom the absence of community is part of a critique of liberal epistemology. Both of these scholars stand outside liberalism, as it were; the absence of community becomes a central prong of their attack. For other scholars, community is less central to the argument, although unmistakably present. Michael Walzer,[6] for example, discusses community from within the social democratic tradition, as part of a wide-ranging critique of liberal politics and society. Similarly, legal theorists and legal historians who take a critical view of liberal jurisprudence (for example, Laurence Tribe)[7] or legal institutions (for example, Jerold Auerbach)[8] similarly attach special importance to communitarian values.[9]

[4] Alisdair MacIntyre, *After Virtue* (Notre Dame, Ind.: Notre Dame Press, 1981).
[5] Michael Sandel, *Liberalism and the Limits of Justice* (Cambridge, Eng.: Cambridge University Press, 1982).
[6] Michael Walzer, *Spheres of Justice* (New York: Basic Books, 1983). In a more recent article Walzer has both criticized and praised various aspects of communitarianism; see "The Communitarian Critique of Liberalism," *Political Theory* 18 (February 1990): 6–23. In this article Walzer says that "liberalism is a self-subverting doctrine; for that reason, it really does require periodic communitarian correction." *Ibid.*, 15.
[7] Laurence H. Tribe, *American Constitutional Law*, 2nd ed. (Mineola, N.Y.: Foundation Press, 1988); "Structural Due Process," *Harvard Civil Rights–Civil Liberties Law Review* 10 (Spring 1975): 269–321; "Forward: Toward a Model of Roles in the Due Process of Life and Law," *Harvard Law Review* 87 (November 1973): 1–53.
[8] Jerold S. Auerbach, *Justice Without Law?* (New York: Oxford University Press, 1983).
[9] In choosing to discuss the work of these five scholars, I make no claim that they share anything more than a similar ideological preference for communitarian values, and that this preference informs at least some (if not many) of their specific arguments. Because I wish to critique this general ideological preference—this impulse toward community—I am, by necessity, ignoring many of the more specific and subtle arguments of each. Moreover, because I am discussing a general trend in recent thought, I will use the terms *the community, community,* and *strong community* more or less interchangeably, and will refer to "the communitarians," meaning those scholars who share the ideological impulse I am describing. I believe that this approach is warranted by the striking similarities on this question among otherwise dissimilar works, as well as by the failure of most of these scholars to define precisely what *they*

What is missing from all of these diverse approaches to community, however, is a consideration of concrete issues. Because they often do not look at such issues—at "hard cases"[10]—these critics of liberalism or liberal institutions spare themselves the painful task of examining the ways in which "community" may conflict with other values; hard cases are where the *dangers* of community become apparent.

In this light, examining community from the perspective of American constitutional theory is highly instructive. In fact, such a perspective yields a stark conclusion: that the longing for community is a chimera—romantic, naive, and in the end, illiberal and dangerous. Many recent discussions of community have been overly abstract, if not theoretically unsound, for they have misunderstood or ignored both the conditions under which a community can flourish and the methods by which a community must be fostered, as well as the costs or dangers of such conditions or methods.

If the theorists wishing to enhance community were to examine the current agenda in American constitutional law, they would see that many of this society's hardest questions take the form of constitutional arguments by groups of marginal persons (the disabled, aliens, and homosexuals, for example) who seek for their members some legal right. The issues raised by such groups cannot be resolved by invoking community sentiment, for these groups challenge too deeply the liberal understanding of *membership*. It is precisely *because* these groups are demanding more than the "community" or the polity wishes to grant them that these controversies exist in the first place. Thus, any "renewal" or strengthening of community sentiment will accomplish nothing for these groups; for them, the existence of any community is part of the problem, not part of the solution. The questions posed by today's constitutional agenda do not require the strengthening of the community's abstract values or fraternal ties; rather, the questions posed by today's constitutional agenda are messy and particular questions concerning who "belongs"—who is a full member of society—in the first place. If community is a territory, it is not so much its terrain that needs to be mapped and explored, but rather how the borders are policed, how the frontier is protected, to which we must attend. The problem of marginal groups poses only the latest form of the basic American constitutional question: how a nation can be formed and

---

mean by "community." Thus, if the terminology here is imprecise, this reflects the content of the works in question.

[10] The phrase is Ronald Dworkin's in *Taking Rights Seriously* (Cambridge, Mass.: Harvard University Press, 1977).

maintained out of diverse social units. This problem, of course, is as familiar to the authors of the *Federalist* as it is to us; the type of social group that must be integrated into the polity may have changed in two hundred years, but the political problem posed by them remains, in all essentials, the same.

Much more is at stake in the current debate over community than specific outcomes for particular marginal groups, however, for the communitarian impulse blurs or ignores the crucial distinction in liberal society—and in liberal theory—between the realms of the political and the civil.[11] Membership is a matter of social and psychological identification; citizenship is a formal political status. Only citizenship can be legislated; membership can be created and sustained only through a process that is both personal ("I choose to identify") and social—but not necessarily political. For some, citizenship may help create a sense of belonging; for others, it may have no significance at all. The communitarians are, in essence, suggesting that it ought to have significance for all. But alienation (the condition that, presumably, leads the communitarians to their enterprise) has many sources in the modern world; alienation from the political realm is only one of them. And alienation can be mitigated in many different ways; in a free society, politics must remain only one of the available mechanisms. Those who offer "community" as a solution to the problem of alienation in liberal society are (potentially, at least) bringing politics into the realm of the social and the personal; they are mixing public and private in an essentially Aristotelian, and antiliberal, manner.

Moreover, in wanting to provide more sense of belonging in liberal society, the communitarians[12] are ignoring a deeper flaw in the liberal understanding of citizenship and the definition of the "self" that lies at its base. Here, too, examining the constitutional issues involving "partial" members of the polity is instructive.

The most basic difficulty with the liberal understanding of "self" is not that it makes community difficult to achieve; rather, the difficulty lies elsewhere, in the manner in which liberalism limits the fundamental rights of *citizens* to fully mature, "deserving" *selves*. This equation of citizenship with mature selfhood is problematic for several reasons, the most basic of which is that classical liberalism's definition of the mature

[11] For a discussion of this point see Stephen T. Holmes, "The Permanent Structure of Anti-Liberal Thought," in Nancy L. Rosenblum (ed.), *Liberalism and the Moral Life* (Cambridge, Mass.: Harvard University Press, 1989), 227–53.

[12] See note 9 above.

self is too restrictive. Embedded in classical liberal theory and jurisprudence are assumptions that are, today, highly questionable—that most individuals possess a capacity to make rational and autonomous choices about their lives, and that those who are not fully competent to make such choices—or who make unacceptable choices—do not deserve full membership in the polity.[13] What an examination of the constitutional issues involving marginal persons reveals is that these assumptions are no longer sufficiently sophisticated for the controversies of the day. They are not subtle enough, or differentiated enough, to settle the cases concerning "partial" members of the polity that crowd the dockets of today's courts. Liberalism's definition of "choice" and "competence;" its decision rules for who "deserves" what, no longer serve us; they no longer help us decide hard cases. The problem of contemporary liberalism is not the absence of community, but rather the manner in which liberalism defines the mature, "deserving" self, and, by so doing, distributes the fundamental rights of citizens.[14]

Thus—to take only a few examples from recent controversies—complex theoretical questions of "selfhood" are involved in discussions of the rights of the physically disabled (how "competent" must a deaf student be before the state can be required to provide special interpretive facilities?),[15] of the institutionalized (does the state have an obligation to nurture a mental patient's minimal capacity for self-

[13] For a description and criticism of the liberal "model" of political participation, see Benjamin R. Barber, *Strong Democracy: Participatory Politics for a New Age* (Berkeley: University of California Press, 1984), Part I. For an application of this model of political participation to jurisprudential questions, see Rogers M. Smith, *Liberalism and American Constitutional Law* (Cambridge, Mass.: Harvard University Press, 1985); see also chapter 1, note 16. For a recent critique of the liberal model, see Martha Minnow, *Making All the Difference: Inclusion, Exclusion and American Law* (Ithaca, N.Y.: Cornell University Press, 1990).

[14] This argument—that the communitarians overlook the problematic nature of the liberal definition of rational capacity and choice—points toward a perspective in which both liberalism and communitarianism might be seen as sharing an inflated (and flawed) understanding of the "unity" of the self—although they define the essence of that self in different terms (liberalism defining it in terms of rational choice, communitarians in terms of social identity). From such a perspective, both liberal individualism and communitarianism might be viewed as complementary modes of social discipline, betraying, in both cases, the truly ambiguous and anarchic nature of the self. Such an argument has been made by those who draw upon the work of Foucault; see, for a discussion of Foucault in this light, William Connolly, "Discipline, Politics, and Ambiguity," *Political Theory* 11 (August 1983): 325–41.

[15] See Southeast Community College v. Davis, 442 U.S. 397 (1979).

care, and, if so, in what sort of setting?),[16] of homosexuals (is such a preference a rational "choice"? Since the best evidence is that it is not, can it be punished?),[17] and of aliens (can a state deny elementary education to the children of illegal migrant workers?).[18] All of these groups have been treated, socially and legally, as less than full members of the "community," all are demanding that their partial membership be expanded, that they be accepted as full and equal members and citizens. Liberalism's inability to fully accept or reject these groups—their consignment to a twilight zone of partial membership—is a result not merely of political indecision, but also of the inadequacy of the criteria by which such judgments are rendered.

Thus, the theoretical stakes are high if, as I will try to show, strong community and liberal constitutionalism are fundamentally incompatible. I will argue here that they are, that strong community can only be fostered through illiberal means. I will also argue that, even if such sentiment could be fostered, "community" would do little to answer many of the most pressing questions of the day. The cry for community is, to be sure, heartfelt; the language is often elegant and the sentiments noble. In the end, however, it is a cry for a medicine that cannot cure the pain, and that can produce a disastrous pathology of its own.

II.

Central to the argument of the communitarians is the theme of loss:[19] Liberal society has lost the ability to foster a sense of shared values among its members; citizens do not identify with the polity; it is no longer possible to speak of the public good, for the modern state is no more than the arena in which group competition goes forward. As MacIntyre says, modern man "is a citizen of nowhere, an internal exile wherever he lives. . . . [M]odern liberal political society can appear only as a collection of citizens of nowhere who have banded together for their common protection."[20] And, as Walzer writes, "there cannot

---

[16] See the discussion of *Pennhurst* and *Youngberg* in chapter 4, pp. 166–83.
[17] See pp. 142–43.
[18] See the discussion of *Plyler*, pp. 229–30.
[19] See, for example, Walzer, "Communitarian Critique," 12.
[20] MacIntyre, *After Virtue*, 147. Whether liberal society has ever produced the strong sense of community they favor is an empirical question these scholars do not tackle. A full exploration of this question is beyond the scope of this book; suffice it to say that historical evidence suggests that, in America at least, a strong community has never existed, except perhaps in localized form, before the calling of the constitutional convention in the late 1780s. See below, pp. 262–64.

be much doubt that we (in the United States) live in a society where individuals are relatively dissociated and separated from one another, or better, where they are continually separating from one another—continually in motion, often in solitary and apparently random motion. . . ." Such mobility, he says, has "an underside of sadness and discontent."[21]

Each of these scholars argues that a renewed sense of community is needed to reverse the direction of such characteristics, thereby making it possible for the liberal state to proceed with its most pressing task. The definition of the content of this task—and, hence, the characterization of the central dilemma of a liberal society—is different for each theorist, although there are some important similarities among them. For Walzer, the dilemma and the task are principally economic; he is concerned with achieving a just distribution of goods and services. For Sandel and MacIntyre, the dilemma is psychological; Sandel is concerned with the "limits" of the liberal state in the creation and maintenance of individual identity, and the failure of liberal society to educate modern man in the cultivation of the classical virtues. For Tribe, the task is more circumscribed: He wishes to find answers to pressing issues in constitutional theory, particularly those posed by vexing "new" property and "substantive" due process cases that pose fundamental questions of distribution and membership. For Auerbach, the task facing the legal order is to find means of dispute resolution that can serve as alternatives to litigation.

For political theorists, the current interest in a revival of community is, at least in part, a reaction to the publication and wide influence of Rawls's *A Theory of Justice*.[22] This reaction is most explicit in Sandel, who takes Rawls as a paradigmatically liberal theorist in the deontological tradition of Kant—that is, one for whom "society . . . is best arranged when . . . governed by principles that do not *themselves* presuppose any particular conception of the good. . . ."[23] Such principles, Sandel claims, "imply a certain theory of the person,"[24] and it is within this theory of the person, and the vision of community it necessarily entails, that Sandel finds the "limits" of justice.

The liberal self, Sandel charges, is radically "disembodied."[25] Essen-

---

[21] Walzer, "Communitarian Critique," 11–12.
[22] John Rawls, *A Theory of Justice* (Cambridge, Mass.: Belknap Press of Harvard University Press, 1971).
[23] Sandel, *Limits of Justice*, 1; emphasis in original.
[24] *Ibid.*, 10.
[25] *Ibid.*, 14.

tial to liberal personhood "is not the ends we choose but our capacity to choose them";[26] the liberal self is "an active, willing agent, distinguishable from [its] surroundings, capable of choice."[27] Such a self is "prior" to and separate from any connection to the polity or community, and it is this separateness—this individuality—that Sandel wishes, above all, to criticize:

> [T]he Rawlsian self . . . stand[s] always at a certain distance from the interests it has. One consequence of this distance is to put the self beyond the reach of experience, to make it invulnerable, to fix its identity once and for all. No commitment could grip me so deeply that I could not understand myself without it. No transformation of life purposes and plans could be so unsettling as to disrupt the contours of my identity. No project could be so essential that turning away from it would call into question the person I am. Given my independence from the values I have, I can always stand apart from them. . . .[28]

For Sandel, this liberalism presents a vision of personhood in which we lack commitments that can "grip" us and transformations that can "unsettle" us—in short, it is dull. And the political consequences of this vision of the self are enormous; for such a liberal self, politics can only be a matter of protecting one's interests rather than creating, or finding, one's identity. Because the essence—the core—of the liberal self is defined by its capacity to choose rather than by its substantive choices, it is not, in some very basic way, touched or changed by political experience.[29]

This vision of the individual and of society, for Sandel, is deeply flawed, both empirically ("we cannot coherently regard ourselves as the sort of beings [this] requires us to be")[30] and morally. Citizens whose identities cannot be altered by their political experience can be no more than "strangers, sometimes benevolent,"[31] and this "fails

---

[26] *Ibid.*, 19.
[27] *Ibid.*
[28] *Ibid.*, 62.
[29] For Rawlsian liberals, "community must find its virtue as one contender among others within the framework defined by justice. . . . The question then becomes whether individuals who happen to espouse communitarian aims can pursue them within a well-ordered society . . . not whether a well-ordered society is *itself* a community." *Ibid.*, 64; emphasis in original.
[30] *Ibid.*, 65.
[31] *Ibid.*, 183.

plausibly to account for certain indispensable aspects of our moral experience."[32] This vision of the self makes politics little more than trivial, according to Sandel; it contradicts the ways in which the political community (as well as other associations) do, in fact, influence who and what we are. If our political associations do not define us, Sandel says, we are not "ideally free and rational agent[s],"[33] as liberals would have it, but rather persons "wholly without character, without moral depth."[34] This liberal understanding of the self destroys political *allegiance*; contrary to the liberal view, we have, or should have,

> loyalties and convictions whose moral force consists partly in the fact that living by them is inseparable from understanding ourselves as the particular persons we are—as members of this family or community or nation or people, as bearers of this history, as sons and daughters of that revolution, as citizens of this republic.[35]

Thus, Sandel presents a highly sophisticated philosophical critique of Rawls that has, at its base, a romantic yearning for community—for its ability to grip us, engage us, transform us. But his yearning is highly abstract and nonspecific: How, precisely, should a community be essential to our identities? Is not personal identification with the political community sometimes irrational and dangerous? Although he concludes by telling us that "when politics goes well, we can know a good in common that we cannot know alone,"[36] Sandel never says what that "good" might consider of, or how such sentiments might be inculcated. And he never considers that the "good" we may know in common may, in fact, be evil.[37]

As Sandel wishes to foster community because doing so will allow politics to grip us, MacIntyre wishes to foster community because doing so will allow politics to improve us. For Sandel, the politics of community are the politics of moral identity; for MacIntyre, the politics of community are the politics of moral education.

MacIntyre's purpose is to trace the development of concepts of virtue in the Western political tradition; he laments the loss of the classical tradition best captured by Aristotle's definition of the *polis*.

---

[32] *Ibid.*, 179.
[33] *Ibid.*
[34] *Ibid.*
[35] *Ibid.*
[36] *Ibid.*, 183.
[37] See below, Section IV.

He mourns especially the loss of the understanding of the community and friendship that such a *polis* entails. The *polis* was bound by a "wide range of agreement . . . on goods and virtues."[38] Because we have lost the "moral unity" that makes this agreement and these affective ties possible, the polity as a whole can have no purpose: "[The] notion of the political community as a common project is alien to the modern liberal individualist world."[39] Modern man, for MacIntyre, suffers from a moral isolation and a moral narcissism: "To cut oneself off from shared activity in which one has initially to learn obediently as an apprentice learns, to isolate oneself from the communities which find their point and purpose in such activities, will be to debar oneself from finding any good outside of oneself. It will be to condemn oneself to . . . moral solipsism. . . ."[40] Modern man is fragmented, incomplete, isolated: "The bureaucratic manager, the consuming aesthete, the therapist, the protester and their numerous kindred occupy almost all the available culturally recognizable roles. . . ."[41] Politically, modern man has no standards, no basis for judgment: "[O]ur pluralist culture possesses no method of weighing, no rational criterion for deciding between claims based on legitimate entitlement against claims based on need."[42]

MacIntyre is sufficiently realistic to comprehend that the modern nation-state is not a viable site for the re-creation of the classical *polis*; it is in smaller subcommunities and subcultures that MacIntyre places his hope. What we need, MacIntyre tells us in his closing passage, "is the construction of *local* forms of community within which civility and the intellectual and moral life can be sustained through the new dark ages which are already upon us."[43] Indeed, some elements of the classical tradition he wishes to foster actually have survived in the modern world, especially "[w]ithin particular modern subcultures."[44] The classical understanding of virtue "survives . . . in the lives of certain communities whose historical ties with the past remain strong,"[45] particularly religious communities, groups "that inherit their moral tradition not only through their religion, but also from the structure of the peasant villages and households which their immediate ancestors in-

---

[38] MacIntyre, *After Virtue*, 146.
[39] *Ibid.*
[40] *Ibid.*, 240.
[41] *Ibid.*, 238–39.
[42] *Ibid.*, 229.
[43] *Ibid.*, 245; emphasis added.
[44] *Ibid.*, 210.
[45] *Ibid.*, 234.

habited on the margins of modern Europe."[46] In MacIntyre's work, then, the longing for community is explicit and central to the argument, and the purpose of community is clear. Only a community can educate modern man in the tradition of the virtues.

Like MacIntyre, Walzer admires small religious and ethnic communities; but as MacIntyre admires them for their capacity to educate, Walzer admires them for their ability to achieve a just distribution of goods. Walzer's purpose in *Spheres of Justice* is to describe general principles to govern distributions of basic goods. His first principle is that distributions of different categories of goods ought to be autonomous.[47] Political community is valued by Walzer because it is "the appropriate *setting* for this enterprise" of distribution.[48] This is so because "the political community is probably the closest we can come to a world of common meanings."[49] In a political community, "[l]anguage, history, and culture come together (come more closely together here than anywhere else) to produce a collective consciousness."[50] Although "[n]ational character . . . is obviously a myth," nevertheless, "the sharing of sensibilities and intuitions among the members of a historical community is a fact of life."[51]

Moreover, "[t]he community is itself a good—conceivably the most important good—that gets distributed."[52] Throughout his discussion of the various distributive spheres,[53] Walzer draws upon examples from historical communities, and it is here, in his choice of these examples, that we can see Walzer's admiration for religious, ethnic, and political subcultures. In his discussion of security and welfare Walzer describes classical Athenian and medieval Jewish communities; in his discussion of hard work he describes the Israeli kibbutz; in his discussion of free time he uses "the idea of the sabbath,"[54] in his discussion of the distribution of political offices he describes the Chinese examination system.[55] It is no accident that Walzer's examples

---

[46] *Ibid.*
[47] Thus, the distribution of money ought not unduly influence the distribution of leisure or prestige; the distribution of knowledge ought not unduly influence the distribution of security, and so on.
[48] Walzer, *Spheres of Justice*, 28; emphasis added.
[49] *Ibid.*, 28.
[50] *Ibid.*
[51] *Ibid.*
[52] *Ibid.*, 29.
[53] Walzer describes eleven spheres: security, welfare, money, commodities, office, hard work, free time, education, kinship, love, and divine grace.
[54] Walzer, *Spheres of Justice*, 192.
[55] *Ibid.*, 139.

are often drawn from premodern, small, isolated, and close-knit subcultures; only such groups can possibly provide the level of agreement
necessary to arrive at a consensual scheme of distribution. Community
is a key value for Walzer because of what must take place within its
boundaries. Like MacIntyre (although more implicitly), he seems to
recognize that the modern nation-state is too complex and heterogeneous to accomplish the tasks he defines as primary. But although both
MacIntyre and Walzer recognize this problem of modern complexity
and size, neither one of them allows it a leading place in his analysis;
neither do they allow it to alter their strong avowal of communitarian
values.

III.

Just as community has received renewed emphasis from political
theorists, it has become a prominent theme among legal theorists and
legal historians. The work of Laurence Tribe, for example, although
not addressing the same theoretical questions directly, nevertheless
unmistakably enshrines communitarian sentiment as the single underlying value of greatest importance.

Tribe comes closest to an explicit discussion of community in his
article "Structural Due Process,"[56] in which his purpose is to modify
the endless debate in American constitutional law over the subjectivity
of "substantive" due process. This he proposes to do by shifting emphasis away from a discussion of the content of a policy to "the structures
through which policies are both formed and applied. . . ."[57] Because
he believes that the legitimacy of a law is a function of "the gradual
evolution of shared values,"[58] Tribe holds that the Supreme Court's
most important role is "structuring a dialogue between the state and
those whose liberty its laws confine. . . ."[59] His concern for "dialogue"
and for what people believe about their laws leads him to a concern
for society's "moral consensus" on any given issue,[60] and the need
for courts both to respect that consensus and to contribute to its
development. Because he believes in "an evolutionary process of
growth in human awareness"[61]—that is, in progress—Tribe says that

[56] See note 7 above.
[57] Tribe, "Structural Due Process," 269; emphasis omitted.
[58] *Ibid.*, 301.
[59] *Ibid.*
[60] *Ibid.*, 309.
[61] *Ibid.*, 310.

courts of law can do much to contribute to what he calls his "fraternal conception."[62] What the law's "communal dimension"[63] requires, Tribe tells us, is that it deal as little as possible in stereotypes (in the language of the law, irrebutable presumptions) and as much as possible in the particular facts of every individual case. "[F]ixed rules" are not "intrinsically . . . fitting" as responses to "situations of moral flux," he writes: What is needed is "individual human confrontation."[64]

The link between this "confrontation" and community is clear: "One might, indeed, regard such confrontations between decisionmaker and disputants," Tribe writes, "as the *only* fitting response to any serious human controversy in a community worthy of the name."[65] Static, unchanging law is unacceptable to Tribe. In situations of moral flux, he tells us, fixed values are "inconsistent with any but an unacceptably atomistic, anomic, anticommunal conception of social life."[66] But Tribe here is collapsing an important distinction; he is equating the rigidity of fixed rules with the absence of community. Surely there must be *some* fixed rules even in a strong community. The impartiality of the law—the substitution of explicit and general rules for discrete decisions based upon the status or circumstances of particular individuals—is, after all, one of the greatest achievements of liberalism, and one of its principal methods of guaranteeing fairness. But this quality of fixedness has become, according to Tribe, an iron cage from which the law must escape. Although he concedes that his claim is somewhat "radical,"[67] Tribe nevertheless maintains that individualized treatment in these types of cases is necessary if we wish to achieve "a possible reconciliation of fraternal and formal conceptions of justice."[68]

What is relevant to the current discussion in this is the choice of normative values that lies at the base of what Tribe calls "the fraternal conception." Tribe concedes that he is presenting "teleologic visions."[69] He does not defend his choice, or present evidence to suggest that his choice is closer than any alternatives to the choices of the founding fathers, presumably because of what he considers to be the obvious and noncontroversial "values" he says are "psychological

[62] *Ibid.*
[63] *Ibid.*, 311.
[64] *Ibid.*
[65] *Ibid.*; emphasis in original.
[66] *Ibid.*
[67] *Ibid.*
[68] *Ibid.*
[69] *Ibid.*, 310.

landmarks" in the type of "individualized confrontation" he wishes to support. That these "values"—he lists them as "understanding, participation, reciprocal acknowledgment of humanity, catharsis, for example"[70]—are not all equally obvious, or noncontroversial, or desirable, is a possibility he does not seem to entertain. Tribe thus develops in his theory of "structural due process" a set of constitutional principles that he defends because of what he perceives to be their close connection to the underlying values of political community, but offers no justification for his choice of these values.

In a similar vein, Auerbach examines various historical examples of dispute-resolving mechanisms other than litigation because, he finds, "[l]itigation expresses a chilling, Hobbesian vision of human nature. It accentuates hostility, not trust. . . ." Litigation supports "competitive aggression" rather than "reciprocity and empathy"—values Auerbach finds nurtured only in the midst of a nonlitigious communal society.[71] Surveying the historical record of various political communities—Puritan Dedham, Massachusetts, in the seventeenth century; Jewish and Chinese immigrant cultures—Auerbach laments the fact that "law begins where community ends."[72] He writes that "[h]ow people dispute is, after all, a function of how . . . they relate" and says that "[i]n relationships that are intimate, caring, and mutual, disputants will behave quite differently from their counterparts who are strangers or competitors."[73] Auerbach decries the litigiousness of modern American society: "Armed with the sword of litigation," he writes, "Americans can wage ceaseless warfare against each other—and themselves— . . . [T]hey seldom contemplate their contribution to their own precarious isolation."[74] Auerbach finds that, despite this sad fact, there is a glimmer of hope: The "delegalization impulse"—that is, the desire to find alternatives to litigation—remains alive in American society:

> [D]ispute settlement preferences are not ultimate choices, but shifting commitments. Even in the most thoroughly legalized society there is likely to be a restless movement over time: between the strictures of the formal legal system and the lure of informal alternatives.[75]

[70] *Ibid.*, 311.
[71] Auerbach, *Justice Without Law?*, vii.
[72] *Ibid.*, 5.
[73] *Ibid.*, 7.
[74] *Ibid.*, 13.
[75] *Ibid.*, 7.

For our present purposes, the accuracy or completeness of Auerbach's historical survey of nonlitigious communities is less relevant than his fundamental conviction that communitarian values are always positive while legalistic values are always negative. Auerbach quotes approvingly the vividly worded conclusion of another legal historian, Grant Gilmore, that "[t]he better the society, the less law there will be. In Heaven there will be no law. . . . In Hell there will be nothing but law, and due process will be meticulously observed."[76] That law may serve positive functions, that "individual rights require an accessible legal system for their protection," is added by Auerbach only as the briefest of afterthoughts.[77]

Thus, at the base of Auerbach's work as well as Tribe's we see a fundamental commitment to the abstract idea of the political community—for Tribe, because only such a community can provide the "dialogue" among citizens necessary to preserve the long-run legitimacy of the state; for Auerbach, because only in a true political community can citizens hope to be free of the litigiousness that plagues contemporary American society. Like their counterparts among political theorists, Tribe and Auerbach lament the loss of the political and moral (and, in Walzer's case, economic) *corollaries* of a strong community.

IV.

But are these corollaries always and necessarily good things? What political and moral conditions are necessary for the creation of a community? And how can community be affected? Is community really compatible with a liberal political order?

It is striking that none of the scholars under discussion here presents a straightforward account of the conditions necessary for creating a community, or of the mechanisms needed to maintain one. Had they done so, they would have seen that two issues are vital to the creation of a community—questions of size and questions of social differentiation—and that two more factors are relevant to the maintenance of a community over time—moral education and homogeneity.

The problem of size is a fundamental one for the partisans of a strong community, as only MacIntyre discusses explicitly.[78] Yet even

[76] *Ibid.*, 13.
[77] *Ibid.*, 145.
[78] See, for example, the comments of Michael Taylor: "If a community is characterized by shared values and beliefs, direct and many-sided relations, and the practice of reciprocity, then it is clear that communities must be

MacIntyre tells us no more than that a way must be found to nurture *local* forms of community; he does not tell us (to take only the largest issues) what relation such local communities will have to the nation-state, or how conflicts between locality and nation will be solved, or how conflicts among these localized communities will be settled. Still, MacIntyre at least seems to recognize that modern man can do no more than imitate the ancients; even this faint note of realism is missing from the other works under consideration here.

This silence on the issue of size is striking, for one of the most conspicuous aspects of the place of community within the Western tradition is precisely that it often appears as a value of critical importance in the context of a small city-state—in the ancients, principally, and also in Rousseau.[79] It is because the theories of the ancients were so tied to the conditions of a tiny political unit that the collapse of the Greek states and the advent of the Roman Empire created a profound crisis—perhaps the most profound intellectual crisis—in the history of political thought. As Wolin, among others, has documented, "the loss of civic intimacy" after the political collapse of the Greek republics made necessary the contemplation of "political space."[80] With the advent of large-scale empire, "the attempt was repeatedly made to adjust the categories of political thought to the unprecedented situation where masses of men, scattered over great distances and differentiated by race and culture, had been gathered into a single society and governed by a single authority."[81] This "adjusting" of categories to accommodate "masses" of "scattered men" becomes a principal enterprise of political theory after the death of the city-state; it is striking how familiar the task sounds to modern ears. In a very real sense, both Stoic and later versions of natural law, as well as the universal Christian church—not to speak of American federalism or continental theories of the rights of man—are responses to this need for a theory defining membership after the Greek ideal of the citizen-participant is no longer a practical alternative. Yet to read the theories under consideration here, with their longing for the values that only a small community can provide, one would think that the *polis* could be recaptured merely by an act of intellectual daring. To enshrine community is to enshrine

relatively small and stable." *Community, Anarchy, and Liberty* (Cambridge, Eng.: Cambridge University Press, 1982), 32.

[79] See Sheldon S. Wolin, *Politics and Vision: Continuity and Innovation in Western Political Thought* (Boston: Little, Brown, 1960), 69–70.

[80] *Ibid.*, 71 and *passim.*

[81] *Ibid.*, 71.

an anachronism: The *polis* can perhaps serve as a metaphor for the modern polity; it cannot serve as its model.

Moreover, a community cannot be willed into existence; it must be created. And the creation of a community requires implementing sets of conditions that carry implications that are unattractive in the extreme; in their failure even to mention such conditions or their consequences the five scholars under consideration here are all equally at fault. For only individuals who share something can become, or remain, a true community, and whether that "something" is defined as a set of values or an ideology or a social position, either it must already exist—and thus the population in question must be, in some very basic way, homogeneous—or it must be created and maintained through a system of moral education. But both homogeneity and moral education can be politically dangerous in several ways: by encouraging the exclusion of outsiders; by encouraging indoctrination or irrationalism; by compromising privacy and autonomy. It is no accident, no failure of imagination, that causes liberalism to have no strong theory of community, for the conditions that would bring a community into existence, or maintain it over time, are precisely those conditions that liberalism is designed to avoid, or the absence of which create a void that only liberal politics can fill.

Of the two sets of conditions that can create and maintain a community—homogeneity and moral education—homogeneity is the most foreign, and the most dangerous, to a complex society. For only a modern society that ruthlessly engages in the practice of exclusion can be homogeneous. Exclusion can come in many forms: It can be literal or conceptual, self-selected or imposed, formal-legal or functional. And it can produce the most vivid and morally abhorrent politics imaginable: Racism can be a form of conceptual exclusion and genocide a form of literal exclusion.

Exclusion, however, need not be so dramatic. Religious or racial ghettos (whether imposed by the majority or chosen "freely" by members of the group) are perhaps the most visible form of exclusion. Walzer (who provides the most detailed account of membership and citizenship of the works under discussion here) tells us that a community must distribute membership before it distributes anything else—it must "constitute" itself.[82] But political history teaches us nothing if not that the avoidance of others—of strangers—is not always a pleasant experience for those who are excluded; they may be branded as heretics, or as genetically inferior, or as nonhuman barbarians, or

[82] See Walzer, *Spheres of Justice*, chapter 2, esp. 31.

any of the countless other categories that have been invented for the "nonmembers" of a community.

Moreover, the exclusion of nonmembers seems to be *necessary* for the maintenance of a viable political community, and not merely a possibility; "[l]ike clubs, countries have admissions committees,"[83] Walzer writes, and clearly (he seems to imply) no club worth its name has a completely open admissions policy. But if not completely "open," can an admissions policy be completely closed? Walzer tells us that "citizens *often* believe themselves morally bound to open the doors of their country—*not to anyone who wants to come in,* perhaps, but to a particular group of outsiders recognized as national or ethnic 'relatives.' "[84] A political community often (not always) feels bound to open its gates, and not to just anyone—for then, of course, it could no longer be a political community. (Thus, clubs may open their doors widely or just a crack, but, in either case, only for the right sort of fellow.)

But is there any political or moral principle that can *force* a community to open its doors, or to cease its practice of exclusion? What of a community rich in resources surrounded by a world of need—can such a community nevertheless be required to open its borders and share some of its wealth with strangers? Walzer answers "yes," for there is, he tells us, a moral requirement of collective "mutual aid."[85] A community may indeed have no choice but to take in needy strangers.[86] Thus, at first glance, the "need" of strangers seems to be a factor that severely limits the community's power to exclude. But this qualification is not as strong as it may first appear, for Walzer qualifies it in several important ways, thus retaining for the community much of its power of exclusion.

There is, first of all, the fact that the community can be required to share only that which is a surplus. Moreover, only very limited redistribution is required: "[T]here must be some limit, short (and probably considerably short) of simple equality, else communal wealth would be subject to indefinite drainage."[87] Finally, although (in some

---

[83] *Ibid.*, 40.
[84] *Ibid.*, 41; emphasis added.
[85] *Ibid.*, 33, 45–46, 65.
[86] See Walzer's discussion of White Australia, *ibid.* 46–48. Such admission of needy strangers, Walzer says, may not only be required morally (because of the principle of mutual aid) but may also be necessary simply to avoid violence, for needy men have a right to self-preservation, and thus may have the right to invade "available" space and "take" available resources. See *ibid.*, 45–46.
[87] *Ibid.*, 48.

circumstances) the community is morally bound to take in strangers, such admission, Walzer says, does not necessarily "entail *intimacy*."[88] Indeed, the community may legitimately decide to export some of its wealth precisely to avoid such "intimacy" with needy strangers. But Walzer is making an enormous qualification here, the full implications of which he does not consider. For it is precisely this civic "intimacy" that creates the moral bonds linking the members of a true community to one another in the first place.

Walzer's discussion of admission based on necessity points to a central proposition of his discussion, which must also be a major component of any strong theory of community—that the members of a community decide for *themselves* who is enough "like" them to merit inclusion in the (true, intimate) community. This, of course, mirrors our own understanding of political communities, and the freedom of association that lies at their base. Once admitted into the community, the needy must be granted citizenship, Walzer says; but is that sufficient to turn the needy into true members of the community? In one sense, Walzer's discussion is concerned merely with formal status—he recognizes only the categories "stranger" and "member," or "citizen" and "noncitizen." But his discussion of civic intimacy clearly suggests that formal citizenship is not enough—that the bonds between the members of a community rest upon their mutual recognition and sympathy. It is these psychological characteristics, rather than the formal status of citizenship, that creates the true community.

In fact, what we know about real political communities suggests that formal-legal citizenship is rarely enough to make an individual feel and act like a true member of the community, if for no other reason that the citizen may find him- or herself the victim of social discrimination of various kinds. And (as empirical research amply demonstrates)[89] social discrimination creates psychological conditions (such as apathy and alienation) that make its victims far less likely to exercise their political rights. Social discrimination is perhaps the best, and most readily available weapon of the community against those (like the needy they are reluctantly forced to accept in their midst)

---

[88] *Ibid.*, 45; emphasis added.

[89] See Lester W. Milbrath and M. L. Goel, *Political Participation: How and Why Do People Get Involved in Politics?*, 2nd ed. (Chicago: Rand McNally, 1977); Sidney Verba and Norman H. Nie, *Participation in America: Political Democracy and Social Equality* (New York: Harper & Row, 1972); Richard A. Brody, "The Puzzle of Political Participation in America," in Anthony King (ed.), *The New American Political System* (Washington, D.C.: American Enterprise Institute, 1978), 287–324.

whom they do not wish to treat as full members of the "intimate" community. This fact of life Walzer does not discuss, and only Walzer bothers to discuss citizenship at all.

Social discrimination and the resulting social class structure are not the only way in which the community can effectively exclude those whom it wishes to exclude; such exclusion can be accomplished through the political process itself. Walzer's principles, he says, require majoritarian democracy, and the simple logic of political democracy would require that a bare numerical majority of citizens consider each other enough "alike" to form a stable political coalition of some sort. Thus, the members of the political majority will probably form some kind of community, at least for political purposes. But does the logic of political democracy require anything more than this? Is there any set of empirical conditions or moral principles that requires the members of a dominant and stable majority coalition to treat the *losers* as true members of this political community? In fact, there are no such empirical conditions; on the contrary, the logic of stable majorities may well be continuing exclusion of minorities.[90] Small minority groups— whether racial, religious, ethnic, or social—may vote and enjoy all of the formal-legal privileges of citizenship, and yet still be functionally excluded from the life of the "true" political community. Walzer does not discuss apportionment, and this oversight is quite telling. His discussion of democratic politics places great emphasis upon the rights of speech and assembly, and the highly questionable premise that "[i]n democratic politics, all destinations are temporary"[91]—that is, all majority coalitions are shifting. "There are always new citizens for one thing," Walzer writes, "and old citizens are always entitled to reopen the argument—or join an argument from which they have previously abstained. . . ."[92]

This is far too simple; it ignores the fact that majority coalitions may be extraordinarily stable, and that a particular minority may be perpetually excluded. The history of racial apportionment in this country suggests quite convincingly that "one man, one vote" is often

[90] Such a conclusion is suggested by the literature on "minimum winning coalitions." See William H. Riker, *The Theory of Political Coalitions* (New Haven: Yale University Press, 1962), esp. chapter 7; Robert Axelrod, *Conflict of Interest: A Theory of Divergent Goals with Applications to Politics* (Chicago: Markham, 1970), chapter 8; and David R. Mayhew, *Congress: The Electoral Connection* (New Haven: Yale University Press, 1974), 111–15.
[91] Walzer, *Spheres of Justice*, 310.
[92] *Ibid.*

not enough, that only more complex methods of guaranteeing minority representation, policed by a highly active judicial system, can accomplish that goal.[93] And the extensive overlap between political parties on the one hand and ethnic or religious groups on the other, in virtually all Western polities, points to the same inescapable fact—social "losers" can become political losers, and political losers may be perpetually excluded from power. Thus, the facts of political life, like social stratification, can effectively exclude citizens from the community.

Exclusion, in its various forms, is the greatest danger of community,[94] but it is not the only one. Irrationalism is also a threat, for the members of a community must cohere around something—including some set of beliefs—and a common hatred or fear of the outsider or the "enemy" is just as likely as anything else to lie at the core of a community's ideology. Indeed, some hatred of racial, religious, or national groups can go far toward *creating* some semblance of community on a national scale, as the politics of the twentieth century amply demonstrates. It is tempting to speculate that such hatred is a far better impetus to community than more benign beliefs or emotions. What better way to create a community (a cynic might say) than to wage a holy war?

Community brings other dangers as well: Just as homogeneity is required to create a community, thereby raising the problems of social stratification and exclusion, a system of moral education will be required to maintain and strengthen the community over time, thus raising the specter of indoctrination and the compromise of autonomy. In classical thought, politics require *paideia*—the moral and cultural education of members of a community. Yet how is such education to take place if citizens enjoy complete autonomy in matters of belief?

---

[93] The literature on apportionment is vast. The basic Supreme Court cases Baker v. Carr, 369 U.S. 186 (1962), and Reynolds v. Sims, 377 U.S. 533 (1964); see also Avery v. Midland County, 390 U.S. 474 (1968). For a discussion, see Martin Shapiro, *Law and Politics in the Supreme Court: New Approaches to Political Jurisprudence* (New York: Free Press, 1964), 174–252.

[94] Of course, any liberal state has methods of exclusion as well. But I would argue that such forms of liberal exclusion are less dangerous than those possible in the world imagined by the communitarians, if for no other reason than that liberal constitutional regimes provide avenues of access and redress to those who are the targets of exclusion. In this light, it is interesting to examine the Supreme Court's opinions in "new" property cases, such as Goldberg v. Kelly, 397 U.S. 254 (1970), concerning whether a state must provide a hearing to those it claims are illegally receiving welfare payments. The Court concludes that it must.

And without such education, how is a strong community to survive? It thus may be impossible to reconcile community with the First Amendment, a fact seemingly lost on the defenders of community.[95]

V.

If the scholars under consideration here can be faulted for failing to consider the conditions necessary for the creation or maintenance of community, they can also be faulted for failing to consider the place of community in the American past. It is true that community has been a part of the American ideology from its earliest days—in Puritan thought, certainly (as Auerbach documents), as well as in the thought of the founding fathers. There is, certainly, a strain of communitarian sentiment in the writings of a number of early American thinkers, particularly Jefferson.[96]

Yet, the implementation of the constitutional system represents a sharp dividing line in American political thought, and the true lesson of the American Constitution is that community could not be sustained. In a very real sense, the movement to revoke the Articles of Confedera-

---

[95] In an exceedingly brief passage, Auerbach points to this danger, which, he says, is inherent in any system in which the presence of community sentiment makes possible informal forms of dispute resolution, as among the American Puritans:

> The tenacious indwelling sense of common purpose that turned communities away from litigation to alternatives like mediation and arbitration is likely to fascinate but ultimately distress modern Americans. It is not easy to empathize with our communitarian forbears. They were too involved in each other's lives to satisfy our craving for privacy and solitude. They were mutually supportive, but also intrusive and suspicious; they were cooperative, but also coercive. The strength of a unified community, after all, implies the ability to compel adherence to its norms, at the expense of contrary individual preferences. The choice of non-legal alternatives to adjudication never was a decision to replace power with love, or coercion with cajoling. It was the application of power to serve the common interest at the expense of competing individual claims. It was, therefore, the exercise of power by the community on its own behalf. *Justice Without Law?*, 15–16.

Yet Auerbach goes on to wax eloquent about the appeal of a strong community as if such dangers did not exist. And he is the only one to pause long enough to note that this aspect of community may, indeed, have a darker side.

[96] For an excellent discussion of Jefferson, see Wilson Carey McWilliams, *The Idea of Fraternity in America* (Berkeley: University of California Press, 1973), 200–223.

tion and replace them with the Constitution became inevitable only when the Federalists realized the "community" and the politics it fostered were no longer possible on a national scale; the split between Federalists and Anti-Federalists was a split between those who wished to design institutions to fill the void left by the death of community and those who still believed community to be a viable means of political organization.

The Federalists, of course, were preoccupied with the size of the new republic and the need to design institutions to neutralize the effects of faction. This preoccupation grew out of their reading of history as well as their understanding of their own predicament; both history and experience taught them that a republic could flourish only in a small, homogeneous community, and that faction was the evil that resulted from heterogeneity. Gordon Wood has meticulously documented the Federalists' slow and painful realization, during the years preceding the calling of the constitutional convention, that America was *not* homogeneous; that political majorities in the states could act unwisely and selfishly.[97] Factions were inevitable, given that "[t]he latent causes of faction are . . . sown in the nature of man."[98] Moreover, history demonstrated that "[r]eligion and exhortation" were "ineffective in restraining the rash and overbearing majorities of small republics."[99]

Thus, the Federalists had no choice but to control the effects, rather than the causes, of factions, and it was to achieve this purpose that the Constitution was written. It was the absence of community that made complex constitutional mechanics necessary; the relation between the people and their representatives had to be more indirect, "[s]ince experience in America had demonstrated that no republic could be made small enough to contain a homogeneous interest that the people could express through the voice of the majority. . . ."[100] America was not homogenous; Americans could not be sufficiently molded by religion and moral education; America was no community but a collection of small communities, each pursuing its own interest. Based upon these premises, the Federalists designed a system that would thwart any direct relation between factions and government.

It was not the defenders of the Constitution but the Anti-Federalists

[97] Gordon S. Wood, *The Creation of the American Republic, 1776–1787* (New York: W. W. Norton, 1972), esp. Part 4.
[98] *Federalist* 10 in Alexander Hamilton, James Madison, and John Jay, *The Federalist Papers* (New York: New American Library, 1961), 79.
[99] Wood, *Creation of the American Republic*, 504.
[100] *Ibid.*

who, in their arguments opposed to the Constitution, demonstrated a continuing commitment to the communitarian ideal, as Herbert Storing has documented extensively.[101] The Anti-Federalists hoped to maintain a small republic, because only a small republic could "enjoy a voluntary attachment of the people to the government and a voluntary obedience to the laws," because only a small republic had a capacity to ensure a strict "responsibility of the government to the people";[102] and especially because only a small and homogeneous republic could hope to cultivate civic virtue, "a devotion to fellow citizens and to country so deeply instilled as to be almost as automatic and powerful as the natural devotion to self-interest."[103] In short, only a small republic could *be* a community. In their concern for civic education, in their concern for "the maintenance of religious conviction as a support of republic government,"[104] the Anti-Federalists' critique of the Constitution was a critique based upon a commitment to community.

As we know, the Anti-Federalists lost their ideological battle; America became a large republic in which "community" could not flourish on a national scale, where the best that could be achieved was to insulate the national government from the stresses of politics so that wise men would be allowed to seek the national interest. America as we know it began with the death of community. All of those factors that led the Federalists to conclude that it could not be brought back to life—size, complexity, heterogeneity—have only intensified over the course of two centuries, making its rebirth even less likely now as then. Like the values enshrined in the classical *polis*, the communitarian strain in American thought, always somewhat faint, is an anachronism.

VI.

Even if community were not a dangerous and anachronistic ideal, could it still be effective? If a way were found to circumvent the problems of size and complexity, irrationalism and indoctrination, could community serve to integrate marginal groups into American society? This question is one test against which community must be measured, for if a community cannot integrate groups of marginal

---

[101] See Herbert Storing, *What the Anti-Federalists Were For* (Chicago: University of Chicago Press, 1981).
[102] *Ibid.*, 16.
[103] *Ibid.*, 20.
[104] *Ibid.*, 22.

persons—if minority groups are left out of the American community—
it is a value of little relevance to the politics of the age.

From the point of view of practical politics, the "decision" to "include" a previously excluded group could only come about in one of
two ways. Either the community itself would reconsider the basis of
its exclusion, and decide that it has been in error (or that the situation
of the group had changed dramatically), or the community would be
told, in effect, that it has no choice—that it must admit the group
because its act of exclusion is based on invalid grounds. The first
alternative—spontaneous generosity—will not often take place in the
real world, so long as the community retains for itself the power
to choose its own members; under these conditions, the most likely
"decision" of the community will be to continue its previous act of
exclusion. Indeed, the exclusion may be so taken for granted, so much
a part of the community's image of itself, that even the notion of
consciously reconsidering its own composition may itself be an unacceptably radical idea; one thinks particularly in this connection of
communities that exclude racial groups, from the antebellum South to
South Africa during much of its history.

The second alternative is to take a community by force, as it were:
to impose a new set of legal or moral definitions of itself from "outside." Such a function can, of course, be served by a constitutional
court. Some would say that this is one of the principal functions of the
Court in a democratic society such as the United States: to articulate
various aspects of the American creed in such a way as to make acts
of inclusion more likely than acts of exclusion for minority groups.[105]
Indeed, one senses that this definition of the Court's role lies behind
the liberal jurisprudential theories that have dominated American legal
commentary in the decades following Brown v. Board of Education.[106]

Yet we ought to pause and reflect upon what we are doing when we
assign the American Supreme Court the heavy burden of policing the
community's acts of exclusion; we ought to consider whether the
Court can do more than guarantee formal-legal equality—for the Court
would have to do far more if it were truly to "expand" the community.
Can the Supreme Court, with the stroke of a pen, change the American
majority's sense of itself? Can such an institution really alter the moral
decision a given community has evolved concerning any particular

---

[105] Such an argument is implicit in Martin Shapiro's early analysis of the
nature of judicial review; see Freedom of Speech: The Supreme Court and
Judicial Review (Englewood Cliffs, N.J.: Prentice-Hall, 1966), 32–37.
[106] 347 U.S. 483 (1954).

trait—homosexuality, for example? The Court can say that, as a matter of law, this or that group must be guaranteed this or that right—the disabled must be granted equal educational environments, or the children of aliens must be educated, for example. But—and this is crucial—can such a Court decision change the way Americans *feel* about the disabled or aliens?

In the very long run, perhaps the answer is a partial "yes"; a legal victory may *commence* the process of moral reevaluation that would be necessary for such a change of attitude to take place. But such a long run (decades? generations?) may be cold comfort to the currently discriminated-against members of a minority group. If nothing else, this is one lesson of America's thirty-year effort to deal with race as a constitutional issue. The Court can, without question, guarantee formal equality in various settings, from schools to metropolitan fire departments. The Court can tackle various issues, from apportionment to affirmative action. The Court can touch a moral chord, spark a political debate, suggest possible answers to difficult questions. But a court cannot force human beings to change their definition of their own community if they do not wish to—for what is implicated in this definition of their community is their understanding of their own selves. This is perhaps why busing is a problem seemingly without a legal solution, for it lies in that twilight area in which legal equality and a community's sense of itself merge and intermingle. A court can order school districts to bus pupils from here to there, but it cannot eradicate the social attitudes that constitute racism. This, of course, does not necessarily mean that the Court should refuse to bus; but it does mean that we ought to soberly assess the extent to which a community (as opposed to a polity, or a city) can be altered by law. Just as the borders of small nations can be altered or erased from the map while the "nation" remains alive and unchanged among its people, communities can be expanded or contracted by court order but remain, at their base, unchanged.

In truth, there is no "community" in America, there are only sub-communities. And we must remember that it is not the imposition of ideas, whatever their source, but rather a slow and painful process of *social learning* that can alter a subcommunity's sense of itself and makes possible the *psychological* inclusion of previously excluded groups. The members of any particular community will believe that the disabled, or the mentally deficient, or homosexuals, are morally acceptable and enough "like" themselves to merit inclusion only if they are exposed to such persons and find them, over time, acceptable. The empirical literature that documents this proposition is vast,[107] yet its lesson is lost to many. A conclusion that a social group is acceptable, however relentless the logic or firm the scientific evidence upon which it is based, is only the beginning of that group's struggle for inclusion.

The point here is not that law can do nothing for these groups, but rather that it can only do so much. Groups that are perpetually excluded or short-changed by the political process can, and do, turn to law, but this fact should give pause and not encouragement to those who offer strong community as the antidote to the coldness of the liberal state. For law cannot force a community to admit those it has excluded except in the most limited and formal sorts of ways. The counsel of community is thus, for many, the counsel of resignation and struggle within the pluralist arena, and particularly within the legal system.

But before the partisans of community criticize such limited and "formal" inclusion—before they condemn the "procedural republic"[108]—we should pause and consider just what it is we lose if we jettison such limited and "procedural" or legal goals and replace them with a stronger national community. Quite apart from the tangible benefits to individuals that procedural justice provides, participation by antagonistic groups in a political and legal system that all regard as fair can bring mutual respect; such mutual respect *can* be the first step toward mutual recognition, understanding, and empathy. This is no small benefit; indeed, the mutual respect brought about by common participation in the political process may be as close as we can come to the fraternal ties sought by the communitarians. And it may be as close as we should *want* to come in a liberal, tolerant regime, one respectful of the rights of minorities. Moreover, the liberty that protects the political process itself—rights of association, speech, and privacy— also protect the process by which individuals form subcommunities, where the values of fraternity and solidarity are more easily and consistently met.[109] This, too, is no small consolation. Indeed, in the modern world, the intimacy and fraternity of such subcommunities—and the freedom to choose one's affiliations—must be respected and nurtured

---

[107] For a thorough discussion of this literature and a defense of the social learning hypothesis, see Herbert McCloskey and Alida Brill, *Dimensions of Tolerance: What Americans Believe About Civil Liberties* (New York: Russell Sage, 1983), chapter 6.

[108] Michael Sandel, "The Procedural Republic and the Unencumbered Self," *Political Theory* 12 (February 1984), 81–96.

[109] See MacIntyre's comments concerning subcommunities, quoted above.

above all. Such freedom and diversity can only be threatened when community is sought as part of a national agenda.[110]

VI.

We began this chapter with the display of a Christmas crèche in Pawtucket, Rhode Island. In sustaining the crèche, the Chief Justice of the United States invoked the values of the "community." But the Chief Justice was wrong; the display of the crèche may have invoked the values of the majority of the citizens of Pawtucket, but not of the whole community. There are Jews in Pawtucket, and atheists, and even a few Moslems. The display of the Infant Jesus did not sit well with them, and they, too, are a part of the "community." There *is* no community of spirit in Pawtucket, but rather a large Christian majority and several small minorities. The only "community" that truly exists—and includes everyone—is the political entity of the city itself.

The federal district court that first considered the Pawtucket case ruled that the crèche violated the establishment clause of the First Amendment; the city, that court ruled, was trying "to endorse and promulgate religious beliefs. . . ." The district court ruled that the erection of the crèche had "the real and substantial effect of affiliating the City with the Christian beliefs that the crèche represents. . . ." Lastly, the district court ruled, the display of the crèche fostered the kind of political divisiveness over a question of religion that the establishment clause was meant to prevent.[111]

---

[110] On this point, see the comments of John Rawls, *Theory of Justice*, 442; emphasis added:

> [A]s citizens we are to reject the standard of perfection as a political principle, and for the purposes of justice avoid any assessment of the relative values of one another's way of life. . . . Thus what is necessary is that there should be for each person *at least one* community of shared interests to which he belongs and where he finds his endeavors confirmed by his associates. And for the most part this assurance is sufficient whenever in public life citizens respect one another's ends and adjudicate their political claims in ways that also support their self-esteem. . . . This democracy in judging each other's aims is the foundation of self-respect in a well-ordered society.

See also the comments of Walzer on the importance of voluntary associations in "Communitarian Critique," and the important argument of Will Kymlicka, "Liberal Individualism and Liberal Neutrality," *Ethics* 99 (July 1989): 883–905.

[111] 465 U.S. at 672.

The district court is exactly on the mark. Political argument over questions of religion is precisely the kind of evil the founders hoped to prevent with the establishment clause.[112] When a majority acts on behalf of the whole "community," we must be especially vigilant of the sensibilities—and rights—of minorities. To do any less is to ignore the most basic commitment of the American Constitution. Even if the number of citizens in Pawtucket offended by the crèche is exceedingly small, the Constitution still protects them. Of that, at least, we should be sure; of that, at least, we can be proud.

[112] See p. 46.

INDEX

INDEX OF CASES